definition - identity

nothing ess
definition

self and group.

myself ~~self~~ ourself

birth - m/f - physical

toddler - pink
blue

"socialized"

George Herbert Mead
self in relation to others

I - temperment

me ⟺ social

adolescent - puberty
body in conflict w/ "identity"
intellectuals - rebel
[ppl. try to fit in - problem is
you
↳ knowledge and discussion - "salons"
support group.

Separated until recently - public
awareness - not alone - community discussions
to effect change - large #'s,
tragedy. economic, lobby for laws,
lawsuits

Self-Made Men

Identity and Embodiment among Transsexual Men

HENRY RUBIN

VANDERBILT UNIVERSITY PRESS

© 2003 Vanderbilt University Press
All rights reserved
First Edition 2003

This book is printed on acid-free paper.
Manufactured in the United States of America

Library of Congress Cataloging-in-Publication Data

Rubin, Henry, 1966-
Self made men : identity, embodiment, and recognition
among transsexual men / Henry Rubin.
    p. cm.
    Includes bibliographical references and index.
    ISBN 0-8265-1434-0 (cloth : alk. paper)
    ISBN 0-8265-1435-9 (pbk. : alk. paper)
    1. Female-to-male transsexuals. 2. Female-to-male
transsexuals—Identity.   I. Title.
HQ77.9 .R83 2003
305.9'066—dc21

                        2002155487

Dedicated with love to my mother and father

Contents

Acknowledgments

This book has taken many shapes on its way to this, the final version. Though I alone am responsible for this version, I thank the countless eyes that read each successive draft, in part or in whole, and gave me priceless feedback and endless encouragement. It is to them that I owe what intelligibility I have achieved. Without them, I never would have completed this project. I am especially indebted to circle of Brandeis Ph.D.s who had the wisdom to form writing groups and the kindness to include me in them. Cameron Macdonald, PJ McGann, Joan Alway, Faith Ferguson, Jean Elson, Monisha das Gupta, Amy Agigian, Betsy Hayes, Janet Kahn, and Sadhana Berys have nurtured my writing and aided me in all my endeavors. The faculty at Brandeis, especially Peter Conrad, Gila Hayim, Maury Stein, and Karen Hansen also supplied advice and encouragement well after I finished the dissertation that was the basis for this book. I am immensely grateful to my students and colleagues in the Committee on Degrees in Social Studies at Harvard University, in spite of the fact that they often ate up my precious writing time. My involvement in the culture of Social Studies raised the intellectual and spiritual stakes of this project and of the foundations of my thought.

To document the thesis of chapter one, I was lucky enough to have access to the Countway Medical Library at Harvard University. This collection's rare books and extensive journal holdings made it possible to do this research on endocrinology and surgery in the nineteenth and twentieth centuries in my own backyard. Christian

Hamburger's article on the 465 letters he received after Christine Jorgensen's case was publicized was among the treasures at Harvard. Dr. Michael Dillon's book *Self* (1946) was made available thanks to Susan Stryker's generosity. In order to document the thesis of chapter two, I made extensive use of three archives with primary documents collected from old gay life both before and after 1970. I worked at the Lesbian Herstory Archives in Brooklyn, the Gay and Lesbian Historical Society in San Francisco, and the Schlesinger Library at Radcliffe College. The first two provided the best material on old gay life, including documents from *Vice Versa*, the first known lesbian magazine in the U.S., from as early as 1948. They also had the most useful material on the lesbian view of the conflicts as feminism met lesbianism. I used the archives at Harvard to get a perspective on the heterosexual women who revived feminism in the 1970s. The Gay and Lesbian Historical Society had a strong collection of the back issues of *The Lesbian Tide*, which provided the basis for a comparison between the East and West coasts of the country.

My gratitude goes to the many transsexual men in Boston, New York, and San Francisco who were willing to share their life stories with me. These interviews are the backbone of the book. Wherever I met you and whatever you told me, I hope I have brought something of your experiences to the public or to one transsexual man who needed to hear that he was not alone.

Thanks to Doug Mitchell at the University of Chicago Press for helping me hone my critical sensibilities and my understanding of the state of the field of Queer Studies. I am grateful to my editor, Michael Ames, who understood this project from the start and was willing to give it a second chance.

True colleagues are hard to find, but I have the good fortune to have several. Thanks to all of you who informed the book with your insights and supported me with your friendship: Lynne Layton, Shelly Tenenbaum, Dan Chambliss, Mitchell Stevens, Dennis Gilbert, Paula Rust, Dana Luciano, Sharon Hays, Clare Hemmings, Jay Prosser, Vivianne Namaste, Carolyn Dinshaw, Susan Stryker, Vernon Rosario, David Halperin, Dean Kotula, Jason Cromwell, and Ben Singer. I give special recognition to Dr. Judith Vichniac at Harvard/Radcliffe whose irreplaceable advice has guided me for a decade.

I also acknowledge the handful of friends who have been with me during the writing of this book: Anne Murdock, Barbara Brousal, Mark Hood, Beth Apfelbaum, Samanta Sassi, and Russell Fernald. The years on Bay State Avenue provided nourishment of all kinds necessary for long blocks of writing. The extended clan of Penlands was supportive even before I married into it. Thanks, Daniel, for last-minute editing and moving during crunch time. Love and gratitude to my family, Michael, Lauren, Brent, Veronica, Nancy, Mark, and Tobi, who will be pleased to see this book completed after learning not to ask when it would be finished. And finally, no single intellectual, moral, or physical presence took more care to see that I had whatever I needed to finish this book than my love, my wife Liz.

Self-Made Men

Introduction

■ Standing on the podium in her Oscar-night gown, with wispy hair and a slight figure, Hilary Swank was hardly recognizable. Seconds before, she had been a young woman with a bit part past and an attractive husband, Chad Lowe, who carried more name recognition than the nominee herself. Now, as the winner of the Oscar for best actress in 2000, she was a different person entirely: a Hollywood up-and-comer, the next big thing. She had beaten out stiff competition, which included the starlet of the hour, the overwhelmingly pregnant wife of Warren Beatty, Annette Bening. Bening had been nominated for her performance in the picture that later took the Oscar for best feature film of the year, *American Beauty.*

Swank's performance in *Boys Don't Cry* had netted her the Oscar and made her, if not a household name, then the most recognizable new face in Hollywood. Her huge eyes and wide-mouthed grin were camera-ready features. The incredible irony in Swank's meteoric rise from unknown starving actor to instantly recognizable Hollywood star is that the role for which she won the best actress Oscar was that of a young *man.* Swank had played Brandon Teena in the true story of his life and violent death in small-town America. On Oscar night, Swank as a woman was unrecognizable to most of her audience because the character she had played was male. In a profession where status depends on being recognizable, Swank had taken on a role that practically guaranteed her continued obscurity, in a film that had seemed doomed to a marginal "art house" existence. Yet she received the highest acting honor for that year.

Doubling the irony was the fact that Brandon Teena was born with a female body and raised as a girl named "Teena Brandon." Brandon Teena was a female-to-male transsexual (FTM), who longed to live life as a man, despite the female body he wore like a costume. While some might have chosen to exploit the fact that Swank, a woman, was playing a "woman" who was "playing" the role of a man, Swank resisted this temptation. In her own characterization of her part in *Boys Don't Cry*, Swank emphasized Brandon Teena's struggle to have his true self acknowledged. Rather than viewing him as a woman who was playing at being a man, Swank saw Brandon's story as the search for self-recognition and the recognition of others.

The making of *Boys Don't Cry* was, as Swank herself attested in her acceptance speech on Oscar night, a remarkable achievement: "To think that this movie wouldn't have been made three and a half years ago, and we made it now for under two million dollars." Swank's astonishment parallels my own; *Boys Don't Cry* is only one of several movies about FTMs. The three and a half years between Brandon Teena's death and the movie radically changed the status of this previously invisible group of people. As they have only recently come to the attention of the general public, there is still much misinformation and misunderstanding about FTMs. Sometimes confused with lesbian women or transvestites,[1] they are often invisible counterparts to their sister male-to-female transsexuals (MTFs). Drawing attention to the public emergence of FTMs and correcting the misconceptions about FTMs are the most basic goals of this book.

One of the biggest misunderstandings of FTM transsexual lives is that they conform to traditional notions of gender. It is certainly true that many (though not all) FTMs wish to blend into the "normal" world around them, to avoid sensationalism, and to have private relationships with others away from public scrutiny. The desire for the ordinary was emphasized in the marketing campaign for *Boys Don't Cry*. Swank and the producers pitched the movie as a universal story that everyone could identify with rather than encouraging the sensationalism that usually attends the stories of transsexuals in the media. Swank's portrayal of Brandon Teena evoked sympathy and understanding from non-transsexuals. Judging from public response to the movie, the desire to be oneself and to lead an ordinary, untroubled life would seem to be universal.

Ordinary lives, unmarked by suspicion and hostilities, should not be confused with gender conformity. As she spoke from the award platform that night, Swank made a brief statement, not quite political, but certainly more pointed than most acceptance speeches, regarding her character and the courage his life demanded. She proclaimed this film to be an important one and Brandon Teena's life to be "an inspiration to us all. His legacy lives on through our movie to remind us to always be ourselves, to follow our hearts, to not conform. I pray for the day when we not only accept our differences, but we actually celebrate our diversity." Swank's comments and the story of *Boys Don't Cry* point out that men like Brandon Teena, in order to be themselves, must take unusual risks that put them in great danger.

The voices of the men that I interviewed for this book confirmed the risks of not conforming. My interview subjects were twenty-two transsexual men, like Brandon Teena, in search of recognition for their true selves. In this search, they required a willingness to flout social conventions about gender, embodiment, and nature. Because of their potentially dangerous identities, many of these men prefer to be invisible. Although there has been, in recent years, a growing group consciousness among transsexuals, many of these subjects remain happily anonymous and want only to be recognized as the men they feel that they have always been. They resent the insinuation that they are gender conformists and do not generally want to draw attention to themselves. The tension between the ordinary and the unconventional structures every element of their lives.

Though there are many competing accounts of Brandon Teena's life and death, none of which are definitive because of his murder, Swank portrayed him as a female-bodied person who always identified as a male and who simply wanted to love and live as an ordinary man. This interpretation of Brandon Teena's life is much like the way that I interpret the lives of the twenty-two men whose stories I analyze in the pages of this book. I believe that my interview participants' courage to live ordinary yet unconventional lives should be the thing to take from their stories, and that their diversity should be celebrated. Swank's closing exhortation—to always be oneself and not conform—is what this book is all about.

Fieldwork

The ethnographic material for this book was generated through in-depth life interviews and fieldwork observations in San Francisco, Boston, and New York. These urban centers provide the anonymity, medical expertise, and community support systems that make it relatively easy to transition and that make FTMs easy to find. Though there are differences between the cultures of the East and West Coast FTM communities, they share these common elements. These FTMs may be different from FTMs in rural, inland areas that lack anonymity, medical specialists, or community support.[2]

My subjects were drawn from the community institutions that provide support for these urban FTMs. During the development of the proposal for my project, I sent out contact letters to FTM support/informational groups, therapists, newsletters, and prominent figures in the developing community. I also attended the march on Washington, D.C., for gay, lesbian, and bisexual civil rights in 1992, which had a special series of meetings designed to mobilize transsexual leadership and grassroots transsexual activism.

In June 1994, I arrived in San Francisco for a three-month intensive field trip, which was followed up in January 1995 with a much briefer stay. I used a "call for interviews" flyer to solicit participation. Six of the eleven interviews from that summer were respondents to this flyer or from FTM support group meetings. The others were friends of this original group or friends of my contacts in the queer community. I met them through socializing in the bars, the cafés, and the sex clubs that make up the queer culture in San Francisco. Most of the people I spoke to knew me from meetings or through a trusted friend or acquaintance. A second set of interviews was culled from Boston. I met these five men through community groups and networks similar to those in San Francisco. All but one of the FTMs in the first and second set of interviews reported having a lesbian career. A third set of interviews solicited FTMs who had not had a lesbian career. I found these six men in New York and Boston by means of the internet and the friendship networks within both communities.

My guiding principle was to provide the FTMs with as much control as possible in the interview process. Usually they took me all the way through their interview without my having to refer to the various categories of the interview guide I had prepared, simply by discussing their life history with me. When an area of the interview guide, usually sexuality, was not touched on spontaneously, then I would again provide a broad initial question designed to open the inquiry without directing it. I usually opened our interviews with this sort of introduction:

> So it's a conversation. If any of the questions I ask seem to you illegitimate or irresponsible or not getting to the point of the matter, you certainly should feel free to reframe them or ignore them or critique them.
> Texas: Oh, I will.

The interviews lasted between one and three hours, with most ending after about two hours. Usually they were conducted at the interviewee's home, but several were at my apartment in San Francisco or Cambridge. All were taped on a micro-cassette recorder and transcribed into texts.

A total of twenty-six interviews were conducted, but two men withdrew their agreement to be included in the final project. Two of the interviews were follow-ups with two of the San Franciscans in January 1995. In all, twenty-two men are represented here. Several of the FTMs in this research chose to use their real names instead of pseudonyms. Occasionally, this can be confusing, such as when I quote from interviews with two different "Matthews." Though both of them are gay FTMs, East Coast Matthew and West Coast Matt are two different personalities entirely. The choice to use their real names indicates that some FTMs are now choosing to be more public about their histories and their transitions.

One of the interviewees, Mark, was specifically chosen because of the paradox of his identification:

> Well I said that I identify as a dyke. And as a gay leather top man who
> happens to be into girls. Which is a bit of a twist and a bit of a tweak.
> But also in terms of gender stuff, I identify as ninety percent male and
> ninety percent female. So, I don't see that as a paradox.

I included Mark because I felt s/he would make a powerful contrast
case to the others in my study. The interview with Mark reverses the
trend of including one FTM in recent collections of essays and performance art shows about butch lesbians (e.g., Burana, Roxxie, and Due
1994). In each case, an "other" is included to mark off space, to delin-
eate identity. Mark maintains a lesbian career with a twist—he says he
is a gay leather man who likes to dominate women.

These twenty-two transmen varied from working-class to upper-
class, with most claiming a middle-class status. Two came from the
upper classes, seven claimed a working-class background, and nine said
they were middle-class. Three reported a change from working-class to
middle-class family status during their youth. One reported going down
from upper middle-class to working-class due to familial ostracism.
The FTMs were remarkably savvy about the difficulties of fixing their
present class status with any certainty. Several noted that "class" might
rest on cultural values more than on income. Others noted that education did not always correlate with income. Many simply told me their
occupation, their incomes, their education, and the education of their
parents and said, "You figure it out." One FTM was particularly
thoughtful about the ways his family "passed" as upper middle class in
much the same way that he now "passes" as a man. In occupation, the
FTMs included a bartender, an executive, a healer, a writer, graduate
students, a technician, a librarian, a leather craftsman, a police officer,
a salesman, a psychologist/lawyer, office workers, artists, and a film-
maker.

The guys are mostly white with European heritage. At least a quarter
note that they are of mixed descent, ethnic hybrids. More than one
note that they are Jewish and not white. In these cases, the men are
trying to say something about their heritage, but also to demonstrate
their difference from dominant, white masculinity. Several of the others resist the label "white" and report that they checked the "other" box
on forms. Two of the men have Native American backgrounds. An-

other identifies strongly with his Gypsy heritage. Finally, one man is tri-ethnic. By claiming these minority identities, these FTMs resist the status of white, heterosexual men.

The participants represent a range of religious affiliations: Jewish, Catholic, Protestant, Unitarian, and Buddhist. Most report that they are no longer practicing the rituals and ceremonies associated with their respective religions, though they do not correlate this with their transsexualism. One man converted from Protestant to Catholic after substantial research on the differences between these spiritual frameworks. Several of the men suggest that they are not religious, but that they incorporate spiritual practices of one kind or another. They tell me that their transitions require a spiritual kind of consciousness that they have not gotten in either everyday life or in organized religion.

The research participants range in age from twenty-three to forty-nine years old at the time of their interview. As a general rule, none of the men look their age, most looking between five and ten years younger than their birth ages. There are nine men in their twenties. Seven men are in their thirties and the remaining six are in their forties.

Thirteen men describe lesbian careers which preceded their FTM identification. Seven men say they never identified as a lesbian. Of those who had lesbian careers, six men claim that they are sexually attracted to women. They categorize themselves as heterosexual men or as queer-identified heterosexual men. Four of these ex-lesbians also switched their object choice over the course of transition and now identify as gay men. One now identifies as bisexual. A twelfth man who prefers women would not discount the possibility of having gay sex with another FTM. Finally, one man abstains from sex for the most part, though he thinks of himself as heterosexually oriented. Of the seven who do not have a lesbian career, two are homosexual (male sexual object choice) and three are heterosexual (female sexual object choice). Two are bisexual. One of the heterosexual men switched his object choice over the course of transition, from male partners before transition to female partners after transition.

All but three of the research participants were on testosterone at the time of our interview. Many of the guys mark the start of hormones as the beginning of their transitions. Using this marker, the most "cooked" participant had transitioned ten years prior to our interview while Texas, Matt, and Jake had just begun their new lives. Twelve of the men had clocked three years or less on hormones. Six of the men had taken testosterone for four years or more.

Almost all of the men have had or plan to have chest reconstruction surgery. A few are small enough that such surgery is unnecessary. They plan a hard-core gym routine in lieu of surgery. Francis is not planning to modify his body with surgery because of his pacifist belief that he was born in a female body to avoid being drafted into the armed services. Nine of the men have already pursued chest reconstruction surgery at the time of the interview and at least three more have had the procedure since that time. Several report that financial concerns are dictating the timing of this most wanted surgery. At least four of the men have had a hysterectomy and four others are planning for it. As for surgeries to construct a phallus, only two of the men have had any of the available procedures. Six plan on some kind of procedure. Two have specific plans for a metoidioplasty, which "frees" the enlarged clitoris. Most of the men say that they are disappointed with the status of phallus construction and are waiting for improved craftsmanship before taking this step.

My early criterion for interview participation was that the subjects had to be aware that they had a gender identity that did not match their bodies. What they wanted to do with that knowledge was not my concern. All of the interviewees for the project fit this criterion. I was surprised, therefore, when given a sharp rebuke and a piece of advice from one of the participating interviewees. He argued that I should emphasize and make an effort to include more FTMs who had taken hormones. For him, this was true transsexualism. All others were somehow less authentic from this man's point of view. He emphatically told me that I should interview FTMs who were on hormones in order to get a true picture of who and what FTMs were. Intimidated by his status in the community and wanting to get the truth about transsexualism, I followed his advice for the remainder of my fieldwork in San Francisco and on the East Coast.

I have discovered that the opinion of the FTM who gave me this advice reflects a hierarchy within these communities. Despite all the contrary advice to carefully consider one's options and take time to make the right decision, community standards stress that hormones make the man. This fact makes me acutely aware that my historical argument does not resonate with the FTMs I interviewed. They resent any hint of a familial resemblance between themselves and lesbians. A few posit a continuum between butches and FTMs, but most of those that spent any time in the lesbian community report that they had "detoured" or "hid out" there. Those who had never passed through the lesbian community resent the presumption that they are lesbians. Two FTMs dropped out of the study because they disagree with the ideological direction they believe my work is taking. The historical thesis provokes a wave of disidentification from the FTMs. The resistance to the historical thesis is an interesting social fact. Resisting any identification between transsexual men and butches is part of the formation of identity. The history and the resistance to it account for the hostilities between lesbians and transsexuals and the commonalities found in their personal histories. It explains the later emergence of the gay FTM as a "deviation" from the normative notion of the FTM experience. It also explains the sudden surge in the numbers of FTMs in the 1970s as well as reasons they might locate their problems in their bodies.

Ultimately, the rough spots in the research produce the most interesting questions. How can sociology account for bodies and biology as they are lived by our research subjects? Why is it that most people are methodological individualists when it comes to making sense of their personal lives? Should we, as sociologists, charge our research subjects with a lack of sociological imagination? What other means of explanation do research subjects deploy to make sense of their lives? Can sociology recognize and analyze these explanatory systems without recourse to the notion of false consciousness?

My reflections on all of this have led me to ask some troubling questions about the epistemological underpinnings of new research strategies. Supposedly, by including the research participants, the sociologist is sharing the responsibility for producing the knowledge that informs us on the research topic. However, it dawns on me that no matter how much control the researched had in the interview setting and throughout the write-up process, it is still my internal sieve that distinguishes the trivial from the salient.

In her account of her ethnographic practices, *Social Science and the Self: Personal Essays on an Art Form,* Susan Krieger reflects on her authorship of *The Mirror Dance: Identity in a Women's Community,* her well-known study of a lesbian community of which she was a part.

> I was, at one point, overwhelmed by the voices of all the women in that community. They were all telling me what to do, and they were each telling me something different. It took a long time—longer than I expected—to find, in myself, a voice by which I could speak back to them (Krieger 1991, 183).

> People who read my book say, "But that is you saying it is not true. It is you claiming to know what is true in an objective sense." However, that is not what I am saying. I am saying that I also have only what I hear people say. Given that, I am trying to figure out, Why does it make sense to say the things they do? That is why I separate my models in the beginning, to really just be me in that part, and distinguish it from them (Krieger 1991, 231).

Ultimately, this is what I am doing. Both the historical model and the reconstructed, analyzed versions of the transsexual interviews are mine. The knowledge put forth here about female-to-male transsexualism is my own. I imagine it may be useful to other transsexuals, to sociologists, or to anybody with stakes in the sex and gender matrix. That is not the condition of its production. This responsibility rests only with me.

What Matters

When we ask what is the matter with someone, we are often in search of a diagnosis and a cure. If, alternatively, we ask what matters *to* someone, we are asking after their taste of the world—how it looks to them, what is salient and what irrelevant. The former pathologizes, while the latter inquires. I asked twenty-two FTMs what matters to them and they told me that their bodies mattered. Their bodies, they explained, had betrayed them. As their bodies underwent adolescence, they were no longer recognizable to others (or even sometimes to themselves) as boys or men. In an unparalleled act of treachery, they had lost their androgynous, prepubescent bodies. After the treacheries of puberty, most of my participants experienced an extraordinary sense of discomfort with their bodies. They longed to restore the link between their bodies and their core identities in order to be recognizable again.

The experience of body dysphoria points to one of the most significant findings of this book—that bodies are a crucial element in personal identity formation and perception. Bodies are far more important to (gender) identity than are other factors, such as behaviors, personal styles, and sexual preferences. As gender identity has become increasingly detached from particular behaviors or preferences, bodies have become the main way of determining gender. Other researchers claim that bodies, specifically genitalia, are not important to the process of gender attribution.[3] My findings support the claim that bodies, especially secondary sex characteristics, facilitate intra- and inter-subjective recognition of a core (gendered) self. Bodies matter for subjects who are routinely misrecognized by others and whose bodies cause them great emotional and physical discomfort. One would do well to remember this when theorizing about the body. To get our heads around "the body," we must come to terms with the experiences that subjects have of their bodies. Simply stated, *subjectivity matters*.

The idea of an essential self is not currently a popular one, but I believe that FTM reports of the perception of a core self are sociologically significant. As I have suggested elsewhere (Rubin 1998), the reasons for being suspicious of a notion such as core identity should be historically situated and understood as a counter-reaction to philosophical and sociological theories that take the transcendental subject and his or her experience to be the only meaningful source of knowledge. In today's climate, however, I am in favor of tipping the epistemological seesaw in the other direction, toward experience, to counterbalance what I believe is an undue emphasis on structural constraint and the discursive constitution of the subject.

Since the idea of a core self is so often criticized, we must account for the contrary experience of an internal and unchanging identity. Experience is one source of knowledge about bodies and identities that we can (or should) still trust, even or especially in times of suspicion toward essentialist identities. We must ask ourselves what it means that individuals feel like they have a "true self," even if we accept the idea that (gender) identities are fictionalized constructs of our collective imagination. We should be wary of simple attempts to dismiss all experience as false consciousness. Perhaps because transsexuals are already considered suspicious subjects, I insist on taking their experiential reports of a core identity seriously. Since transsexuals have been regarded as monstrous, crazy, or less than human, it is doubly important to make their experiences matter.

Experience must not, however, be taken as the *only* measure of a body or the subject that inhabits it. When considering the body and subjectivity we must also notice that *history matters*. Society puts some limits on the infinite ways a subject can make sense of his or her life experiences. It provides categories like male and female, man and woman, transsexual, homosexual, and intersexual. Society's categories and the relationships between them change over time, often in response to the attempts of individuals to fit themselves within such categories. Categories of identity are cultural abstractions that are never exactly met by any single person or any sum of individual life experiences; identity categories are always inadequate when individuals try them on.

This gap between culturally abstracted categories and lived experiences puts into motion a dialectic of identity. The dialectic of identity is the perpetual motion that occurs when individuals rely upon historically variable categories in their search for intersubjective recognition. All experiences must be situated within the flow of history. Although experience should not be discounted as a valid source of knowledge, it should also not be taken uncritically and without reflection on the historical terms and conditions that make such experience meaningful to the subject and to others. The FTMs in this study use historically specific categories and relationships between categories to make sense of their experiences. To understand the horizon of cultural meanings within which these FTM subjects make their experiences intelligible, it is necessary to provide a history of these meaningful categories.

Depth of Subject/Death of Subject

> The source [of morality] we have to connect with is deep in us. This is
> part of the massive subjective turn of modern culture, a new form of
> inwardness, in which we come to think of ourselves as beings with
> inner depths (Taylor 1991, 26).

> The thing about inwardly derived, personal, original identity is that it
> does not enjoy this recognition a priori. It has to win it through ex-
> change and it can fail. What has come about with the modern age is
> not the need for recognition but the conditions in which this can fail. . . .
> In pre-modern times, people didn't speak of "identity" and "recogni-
> tion," not because people didn't have (what we call) identities or
> because these didn't depend on recognition but rather because
> these were then too unproblematic to be thematized as such (Taylor
> 1991, 48).

Everyone has an internal identity. This interior is not just filled with
organs and bones, but is also filled by something we might call a soul
or self. There are many terms for this idea of internal identity, including "hermeneutic subject" and "core identity." What all of them refer
to is the sense of an internalized subjectivity that is sealed off from
other subjects by virtue of being contained within the body. A philosophical term for this internal identity is "deep subject." In some of its
extreme formulations, the deep subject appears to be an ahistorical
and culturally universal phenomenon. In its more narrowly circumscribed form, the deep subject exists as a particular cultural form with
a history.

The notion of the deep subject has sustained several blows in contemporary debates. Perhaps the strongest critiques have come from
feminist and Foucauldian theorists. These critiques can be grouped
under the rubric of the "death of the subject." Whether this death is
bemoaned or celebrated, the claim is consistently made that the deep
subject is a fiction of our combined cultural imaginations. However,
for FTMs, depth—not death—is the principle that governs subjectivity. Based on its importance in the narratives of these research participants, we cannot dismiss or minimize the continuing sociological im-

portance of the deep subject. We must theorize its significance to the people and communities we research.

Charles Taylor's account of the philosophical roots and social consequences of the deep subject puts at our disposal two related terms: "authenticity" and "recognition." These terms are useful both in the specific task of understanding transsexual subjectivity and in the more general project of theorizing identity. The culture of authenticity depends upon the idea that moral authority no longer derives from any outside source, be it king, country, or god. Authenticity also infuses modern human nature with individualism. Taylor sees the culture of authenticity in two main forms: an atomistic, post-modern form and a more communal form balanced by intersubjective recognition. Taylor agrees with the critics who see that the present culture of authenticity has a tendency to slide into relativistic and anomic radical freedom where every individual pursues his or her own authenticity at the expense of cultural integration. This atomistic authenticity results in conflict and in a nihilistic culture where anything goes in the search to find oneself. When taken as the only form, this version of authenticity is rightfully criticized for its moral relativism and alienated isolationism.

Taylor suggests that there is another form that would allow for maximal individual freedom without sacrificing social integration. This form of authenticity depends upon intersubjective recognition. Identities, he says, are always formed in dialog with and against "significant others" (Mead 1934). Recognition is the intersubjective principle that guarantees social integration and shared moral principles, as well as individual authenticity.

To illustrate the concept of intersubjective recognition in terms that sociologists and psychologists may be more familiar with, Jessica Benjamin's ideas may be of some use. In *The Bonds of Love,* Benjamin writes:

> Recognition is the essential response, the constant companion of assertion. The subject declares, "I am, I do" and then waits for the response "You are, you have done." Recognition is, thus, reflexive; it includes not only the other's confirming response, but also how we find ourselves in that response (Benjamin 1988, 21).

Recognition is a function of two relationships: a relationship of distinction and a relationship of integration. On the one hand, there must be two bounded entities, a "self" and an "other," for recognition to occur. On the other hand, the insistence on mutuality is a defining feature of recognition. If one seeks recognition, one must be willing to grant recognition to others. Therefore, recognition is a relationship of reciprocity between two distinct, authentic individuals.

Identities are formed in dialog with significant others. Though neither Taylor nor Benjamin addresses this, it is consistent with their thinking to argue that one of the most significant others is the self. The ability of the self to recognize itself is a significant and necessary achievement that must precede intersubjective recognition. However, to fall back on intra-subjectivity alone is to revert to what Taylor has called the radically individualistic culture of authenticity. A self needs others to recognize its authenticity.

As we shall see, authenticity is a leading principle behind an FTM's life. FTM lives are a search for recognition of the innermost self. What FTMs realize is that their innermost selves are authentically male. Once they make this realization, they modify their bodies to express this authentic identity. This modification process is not simply a "do-your-own-thing" version of radical freedom or an individual nihilism that denies all cultural norms regarding gender, embodiment, and identity. Rather, FTM body modification is a situated, contextual project of authenticity based on the principles and demands of recognition in modern society. Without body modification, most FTMs are subject to misrecognition both by others and by themselves. As Taylor suggests, misrecognition—the refusal of recognition by others—is a form of oppression.

By mobilizing the cultural connection between identity and embodiment, FTM men address the misrecognition of their authentic selves. This "authenticated" self provides the moral foundation for securing the democratic rights and obligations these men deserve.

Sex, Gender, and Other Terms

Sociology, feminism, and Queer Studies have each made gender or transsexuals into a proper object of its domain at one time or another. Each field contributes something to the methods and questions of this book. Sociological work on transsexuals includes one of the most famous and foundational essays of ethnomethodology. Harold Garfinkel's "Passing and the Managed Achievement of Sex Status in an 'Intersexed' Person (part I)" points out the *social construction of gender.* Based on interviews with a male-to-female transsexual named Agnes, Garfinkel concludes that *gender is something we do rather than something we are.* For ethnomethodologists, the study of transsexuals provides an unveiled look at the everyday work required to present oneself as gendered. According to Garfinkel, this is *universal* work, which all members of a culture perform, though only "deviants" can illustrate the immense effort required to make gender seem "natural." The social constructionism that informs this early work on transsexualism remains a prominent feature of the fields within which I situate myself. Without it, one would be hard-pressed to discuss the work that is necessary for FTM transsexuals to put themselves together as recognizably gendered men. Yet the universalism behind the claim that gender is socially constructed is problematic.

Another sociologist, Robert Bogdan, taped hundreds of hours of interviews with the woman pseudononymously called Jane Fry in order to illustrate the achievement of gender by a transsexual woman. *Being Different: The Autobiography of Jane Fry* (1974) consists of Jane Fry's own words about being a transsexual woman. Her subjectivity is more fully represented in this work than Agnes's was in Garfinkel's. Jane Fry emphasizes the experience of *being different,* which Bodgan identifies as a central characteristic of a transsexual life. Fry and Bogdan's minoritizing view is in sharp contrast with Garfinkel and the ethnomethodologists, who place their emphasis on the universalism of doing gender.

Feminist work on transsexuals, like that of Susan Kessler and Wendy McKenna (1978), continues to build on sociological insight into the social construction of gender. Kessler and McKenna's study of MTFs and FTMs is one of the few early studies of transsexuals to include

FTMs. Kessler and McKenna do not notice much difference between FTMs and MTFs, and emphasize, like Garfinkel, that gender is universal work. Kessler and McKenna overlook some important issues. They do not concern themselves with the differences between MTF and FTM identities or with the differences between transsexuals and non-transsexuals.

Janice Raymond's 1979 polemic, *The Transsexual Empire,* argues that medical practitioners who are involved in "sex changes" are violating the integrity of the whole person. In addition to misrecognizing transsexual authenticity, this account also fails to take into consideration the subjectivity of transsexual men. Raymond tries to elucidate the motives of transsexual men using the notion of false consciousness. She believes that transsexual men are the dupes of patriarchal culture and of their male doctors.

As different as they are from one another, each of these two feminist studies of transsexuals fails to give sufficient credence to transsexual subjectivity. Nonetheless, feminist political work and scholarship on gender since the 1970s have been deeply committed to taking *female* subjectivity into account. In order to correct for gender-blindness and to provide a sense of a woman's experience of the world, feminists have started their analyses with the lived experiences of women. This focus on experience and the differences between men and women has been incredibly productive for feminist scholarship.

More recently, in feminist analyses of gender, some scholars note that subjectivity and experience tend, nowadays, to outweigh all other factors. This leads some feminists, like Joan W. Scott, to *historicize* the categories of experience that gendered people use to make sense of themselves (Scott 1988, 1993). The balance between experience and history is hard to strike. Emphasis on history and social construction in the study of gender (and transsexuals) is a crucial counterweight to experience, but should not supplant experience.

Studies of transsexuals, like Bernice Hausman's (1995), tend to emphasize history over experience. Since Foucault's 1980 work on sexuality, Queer Studies incorporates a historical component into work on gender and transsexualism. Some of this work fails, like some early ethnomethodology, to take subjectivity into account. Due to the lack of attention to the subjective experiences of being a transsexual, these studies ignore the crises and troubles that befall transsexual men and women. Other queer ethnographic work of butch lesbians and transgendered people (Newton 1993, 1972; G. Rubin 1992; Davis and Kennedy 1993) do a better job of balancing history and subjectivity.

In most scholarship, FTMs are subsumed under the general study of transsexualism. It is only quite recently that FTMs have been considered apart from MTFs. Holly Devor's 1997 sociological account of FTMs is the first of its kind. James Green, then head of FTM International, said in his keynote address to the First All-FTM Conference of the Americas, in August 1995, that most people assume transsexualism is about "men in dresses." Now, female-to-male transsexualism is emerging as a distinct phenomenon, not reducible to a mirror image of male-to-female transsexualism. It is important to try to understand FTMs on their own terms.

This book relies on Gayle Rubin's essay "The Traffic in Women," which separates "sex" and "gender" into two categories.[4] Rubin defines the sex/gender system as "the set of arrangements by which society transforms biological sexuality into products of human activity" (G. Rubin 1975, 159). Her definition is criticized for its failure to question the assumption that our anatomical bodies are divided by nature into two exclusive categories. Intersexed individuals and transsexuals reflect a more complex notion of "sex" than Rubin laid out. Judith Butler is the most outspoken proponent of the idea that "sex" is just as mediated through culture as "gender":

> If the immutable character of sex is contested, perhaps this construct called "sex" is as culturally constructed as gender; indeed, perhaps it was always already gender, with the consequence that the distinction between sex and gender turns out to be no distinction at all. It would make no sense, then, to define gender as the cultural interpretation of sex (Butler 1990, 7).

The social organization of bodies into "sex" is a significant theoretical insight, but the move to collapse sex and gender ignores the defining tensions of transsexual narratives. In a scheme where sex and gender are equated, there is no room for individuals who experience an existential rift between their gender (identity and role) and their sex (bodies).

In this book, "gender" refers to socially mediated expectations about an individual's role. Society divides these roles into two inflexible categories: man and woman. This strict social division is usually grounded in naturalistic assumptions that women are anatomically female and men are anatomically male. Similarly, "sex" refers to an interlocking set of social expectations that bodies are divided and regulated into two discrete categories, male and female, which are hegemonically defined by the presence or absence of a penis and by secondary sex characteristics.

The terms "female" and "male" always describe sexed bodies. The term "female-bodied" suggests that not all those with female bodies are women. Female-to-male transsexuals begin as female-bodied, though they are not women. The terms "woman" and "man" refer to gender roles and identities. The term "female-to-male transsexual" refers to an individual who is in transition or who has made the transition from one sexed body to another. "Transgender" is an innovative concept that many transsexuals, transvestites, cross-dressers, passing women, butch lesbians, and nellie gay men (feminine or effeminate male homosexuals) are claiming as their own. It is often used as an umbrella term to build political bridges and alliances. Gender-inverted individuals who are not modifying their bodies surgically or otherwise sometimes use it to describe themselves. The FTMs in this study have all undergone or are undergoing bodily modification.

The term "transsexual man" is commonly misunderstood; it refers to a female-to-male transsexual who is living as a man. Transsexual men are often contrasted with "genetic men." This term privileges the "natural" process of birth and genetic make-up and denies legitimacy to other ways of becoming a man. The transsexual community has created the term "non-transsexual man" in order to undercut the privilege associated with being born male-bodied.

In contrast to sex, the term "sexuality" refers to sexual desire. Social categories of sexuality are most often delineated according to sexual object-choice.[6] A person is homosexual if he or she has a sexual desire for someone of the same gender. A person is heterosexual if he or she has a desire for someone of another gender. Female-to-male transsexuals are homosexual if they desire men, heterosexual if they desire women, and bisexual if they desire women and men. Chapters one and two use terms associated with female homosexuality. A female homosexual is called "lesbian" or occasionally "dyke." A female homosexual with "gender inversion" is called a "butch lesbian," "butch dyke," or simply "butch." The phrase "gender inversion" refers across historical periods to the experience of a gendered identity/role, which is at odds with one's sexed body. Gender inversion manifests itself at different periods of history in different cultural forms.[6]

The category of "intersexuality" has a complex history; this history sometimes overlaps with the history of transsexuals. "Intersexual" refers to a body that is ambivalently sexed. Physicians have created several typologies of intersexuality, each with their own diagnostic criteria and their own treatments. More and more, intersexuals are challenging medical typologies and advocating for self-determination, especially over surgical modification. In the historical period described in chapter one, intersexual bodies were classified according to the condition of their gonads and their genitalia.

Transsexuals also have their difficulties with medical typologies. Doctors designate a patient according to his or her sexed body at birth. In medical terminology, a "female transsexual" is an FTM and a "male transsexual" is an MTF. This is exactly the opposite of the ways these terms are used in this book. This leads to special confusion when talking about sexuality. For example, in medical parlance, an FTM is "homosexual" if he has sexual desires for women. Endocrinologists developed sexed terminology to refer to hormones as well. Testosterone had been considered a male hormone, while estrogen had been considered a female hormone. When it was discovered that "normal" men and women have both hormones, endocrinologists designated these hormones as either "hetero-sexual" or "homo-sexual," depending on the body they were in. Accordingly, estrogen is the "homo-sexual" hormone for female bodies and testosterone is the "hetero-sexual" hormone.

FTMs begin as female-bodied individuals. They change their sex using a variety of methods. These methods include injections of test-osterone and surgical procedures. FTMs group their surgeries by regions of the body, into "top" surgeries and "bottom" surgeries. "Top" surgery removes breast tissue by means of liposuction or double mastectomy and chest reconstruction including nipple grafts. "Bottom" surgeries include phalloplasty, genitoplasty, and/or hysterectomy. Not every FTM has the same surgical procedures: some do not undergo surgery at all. FTM transitions have no linear progression, and their goal is nothing other than living as a man. For those who would like more information on FTM practices and procedures Lou Sullivan's *Information for the Female to Male Cross Dresser and Transsexual* is a good resource.

Methods: Genealogy and Phenomenology

This project is informed by two methods: genealogy and phenom-enology. The genealogical method informs the first two chapters and the phenomenological method structures the next two chapters. The former emphasizes the discursive constraints on human knowledge and action. The latter privileges lived experience and embodied agents capable of knowledge and action. These different approaches balance each other.

Some reflections on the strengths and weaknesses of each method follow. The genealogical accounts in chapters one and two confirm and challenge the accounts of FTM experiences. Phenomenology as a method expands our vocabulary for talking about transsexual bodies and subjectivity. Using both of these methods together generates findings that either one of these methods, used alone, would not.

Strengths and Limits of Genealogy

The first impulse behind this research is to trace the genealogy of a new species of man, a new identity: female-to-male transsexual. This history describes the rise of endocrinology and plastic surgery. Nascent FTMs who wanted hormones and surgeries had both to distinguish themselves from other female-bodied inverts and to establish their similarity to intersexuals by locating their dis-ease in their bodies. Together, chapters one and two argue that though the feelings of being gender-inverted are timeless or transhistorical, the phenomenon known as female-to-male transsexualism has only recently emerged as a separate and distinct identity enacted through particular technologies of the self.

Genealogy foregrounds the discursive constraints and freedoms of any given historical period. It illuminates the historicity of the categories that individuals use to make sense of their lives—how they are generated and how they are altered. Genealogy shows the movement of historical categories. It captures the ways in which subjects and subjectivity are made recognizable within the available categories of the moment. Genealogy gets past the methodological individualism that gives total authority to the experiences of the subject.

Foucault's genealogies replace the positivist goals of the history of "origins" with a search for "lines of descent" and "emergences." For Foucault, descent is

> the ancient affiliation to a group, sustained by the bonds of blood, tradition, or social class. [It] permits the discovery, under the unique aspect of a trait or a concept, of the myriad events through which—thanks to which, against which—they were formed (Foucault 1984a, 80–81).

By descent, Foucault means the lines of familial relations between the subjects of history and the progeny of these relations. He calls his method "genealogy" because its goal is to trace these familial relations in much the same way and for the same purposes that one traces one's family tree. Foucault suggests that these lines of descent leave traces of their emergence.

> Emergence is always produced through a particular stage of forces. The analysis of *Entstenhung* must delineate this interaction, the struggle these forces wage against each other or against adverse circumstances, and the attempt to avoid degeneration and regain strength by dividing these forces against themselves. No one is responsible for an emergence; no one can glory in it, since it always occurs in the interstice (Foucault 1984a, 83–85).

The emergence of new social forms is not neat and tidy. New social formations only come about through struggle and in response to adverse conditions.

Though genealogical accounts of subject positions have explanatory power, genealogies also have some limits. The most glaring limit is its tendency to deny the significance of subjectivity and lived experience. Foucault writes, "One has to dispense with the constituent subject, to get rid of the subject itself, that's to say, to arrive at an analysis which can account for the constitution of the subject within a historical framework" (Foucault 1984b, 59). Genealogy's structuralist underpinnings can only comprehend subjectivity as a product of forces. Genealogy cannot do justice to the experience of interiority or to the experience of being embodied. It tends to undermine the authority of individuals and contributes to their marginalization.

Genealogy's inability to theorize interiority, and the ways that it undermines the authority of subjects, is apparent in my fieldwork. Most of the participants hold the positivist belief that transsexual men have always existed throughout history. FTMs resist the genealogical accounts that historicize gender inversion or insinuate any family likeness between FTMs and other female-bodies. The genealogies discussed in chapters one and two provoke deep hostility. These accounts do not resonate with their own experiences of "essential difference" from female homosexuals. Even among the men who had lesbian careers, few of them frame their transitions historically.

One of the research participants, James, frames his life history in a fashion typical to the participants in this study. His responses both challenge and confirm the historical account of FTM emergence:

> When I was in my early twenties, in the 70s, I think there was a period . . . there were butches who were involved in very butch-femme relationships that were patterned after "Leave it to Beaver." Well, actually they were sort of more patterned after the Honeymooners. They were very working-class, go to work every day in a factory. Sometimes they would even refer to the butch with male pronouns and stuff like that. Those people got driven out by politics, by feminist politics. I think a lot of it had to do with the fact that they so emulated male roles and that their partners even called them "he."

This part of James's narrative confirms the genealogy of FTM identity. James says he knew working-class butches who were male-identified. He does think that these male-identified butches became outcasts of the community. He even discusses how he was treated as the lesbian-feminist revolution took hold.

> I always got tons of pressure from women around me for being too male. I was excluded from women-only events. It was a joke.
> Henry: You were excluded from women-only events?
> James: Yeah! By my friends. Y'know, "Oh you can't come, you're really a boy." . . . They didn't want me around sometimes. . . . My group of friends would be hanging around saying, "Oh I'd like to go to that," and I'd say, "I don't know if I want to go to that," and they'd say "Well, that's all right, you're really a boy anyway and this is for women only." So I never really felt that bad about . . . I didn't want to go to those things anyway.

The woman-identified model of lesbianism had become hegemonic and it left him outside the boundaries of this community.[7]

However, James challenges the genealogical account of FTMs that insinuates any family resemblance between himself and (butch) lesbians. For him, there is an essential difference, a transhistorical difference, between FTMs and female homosexuals.

> *No.* I knew butches. I mean a lot of people would identify me as a butch because I was very androgynous and seemed very male. I was androgynous in appearance and male in spirit. A lot of people would classify me as butch. But there were a lot of older women in particular who I would identify as butch and even women my own age who I would classify as butch, *they were much more butch than me. But I was much more male than they were.*

James draws an essential distinction between being butch and being male. In his worldview, these are distinct identities. James situates himself clearly with respect to maleness by disidentifying from butches.

While James has a socio-cultural account that approximates the genealogies in chapters one and two, he relies more on an essentialist understanding of the categories of "butch" and "transsexual" to explain his own life. James says he is transsexual because he has an essential male-identity, not because of any external border war or the development of a logic of treatment for female-bodied inverts. He knows the difference between an FTM and a lesbian because of the different ways they feel about their bodies. Where butches manage to stay in their bodies, FTMs cannot.

It is hard for genealogy to grasp these essential identities and differences. Foucault writes:

> If the genealogist refuses to extend his faith in metaphysics, if he listens to history, he finds that there is "something altogether different" behind things: not a timeless and essential secret, but *the secret that they have no essence, or that their essence was fabricated in a piecemeal fashion from alien forms* (Foucault 1984a, 78; emphasis added).

Genealogy also has a hard time grasping the claim that bodies tell the truth about people. Where the genealogies in chapters one and two are structuralist, these transsexuals' explanations go deep into their flesh.

This strong essentialist counter-narrative from my respondents requires the thick description of phenomenology. The findings presented in chapters three, four, and five are based on the phenomenological method summarized below.

Phenomenology as Method

"I am the absolute source, my existence does not stem from my antecedents, from my physical and social environment; instead it moves out towards them and sustains them" (Merleau-Ponty 1962, ix). This first precept of the phenomenological method returns agency to transsexuals and authority to their narratives. It justifies turning to the self-reports of transsexual subjects as counter-discursive knowledge. However, we no longer accept this claim uncritically; Merleau-Ponty's absolutism can be upheld only by hegemonically situated theorists who have dominant positions in society. It may be possible for discursive analysis to correct for the absolutism of Sartre and Merleau-Ponty. In that case, phenomenology returns legitimacy to the knowledge generated by the experiencing *I*.

Phenomenology considers bodies as the ultimate point of view. In as much as knowledge is constituted by a point of view and by perception, phenomenology recognizes the epistemological significance of bodies, the lived experience of the *I*, and of the world. This *I* confronts the world as a series of *essences* that are contingent upon an embodied location. Phenomenology recognizes that bodies are the ultimate point of view on the world. Bodies are never static or reified. Phenomenology replaces the more naive notions of fixed essences and identities that are familiar to us with a version of essences and identities that are always unfolding. This method has the power to theorize the significance of the body, to grasp the function of essences, to acknowledge agency, and to describe and validate all life projects as equally worthy of inquiry.

Sartre's Three Levels of Bodily Ontology

In his existential sociology, Sartre emphasizes the body as our means of existence in the world. More than this, the body as we experience it is the way that the world comes into being for us. The body as it is inhabited, as it exists for oneself, is the point of reference by which the whole world unfolds. Sitting here, at my keyboard in my study, the world unfolds first as a computer screen and hands, then a desk. In the periphery is the stack of books on phenomenology and then off in the corner of my vision is the window with the cool breeze and the bright light of a sunny day and my neighbor's yard. Beyond that are Cambridge proper, Boston, and the seaside. The world is always my world.

Sartre recognizes that "the body" is fundamentally fragmented. The levels of bodily ontology are radically distinct and permanently irreconcilable. The first level of bodily ontology is the body-for-itself: the body as the point of view, as it is lived for the *I* that inhabits it. This body is an *absolute* point of view. It is a point of view from which one can never get out. It is "the point of view on which I can no longer take a point of view" (Sartre 1956, 329). As such, the body-for-itself can never be known as an object of knowledge like other objects. This body is lived, not known.

This body-for-itself is constituted both by necessity and by contingency. It exists so that the world exists for me. This body also exists according to particulars, this body is sexed, muscular, and dark. *That* I am is the necessary body. *What* I am is the contingent body.

> My birth . . . my race . . . my class . . . my nationality . . . my physiological structure . . . my character . . . my past, all this in so far as I surpass it in the synthetic unity of my being-in-the-world is my body as the necessary condition of the existence of a world and as the contingent realization of this condition (Sartre 1956, 328).

The second level of bodily ontology is the body-for-others. This is the body as object, the body that is touched, as one might touch a peach. It is an instrument for others. This is the body as flesh, as corporeal reality. "What for the Other is his *taste of himself* becomes for me the Other's flesh" (Sartre 1956, 343). The third level of bodily ontology is the alienated body, when the *I* is coerced into taking the viewpoint of the other on its own body. For Sartre, relentless alienation becomes indistinguishable from psychoses. The "alienated man," Sartre claims,

> is vividly and constantly conscious of his body not as it is for him but as it is for the Other. This constant uneasiness, which is the apprehension of my body's alienation as irremediable, can determine psychoses . . . these are nothing but the horrified metaphysical apprehension of the existence of my body for the Others (Sartre 1956, 353).

Sartre leaves the issue of psychoses at this point, but Merleau-Ponty helps to explicate in phenomenological terms what this set of perceptions might mean, stripped of their pathological associations.

Merleau-Ponty: Body Image and Anosognosia

Part of Merleau-Ponty's phenomenology focuses on phantom limbs and a condition known as "anosognosia." A phantom limb is the persistent perception of an absent limb. Due to accidental circumstances (war injuries, industrial accidents, etc.), a person's limb is severed, yet many of these injured persons report that they continue to experience the presence of the missing limb. This condition and anosognosia, its opposite, perplex physiologists and psychologists alike.

Anosognosia (alternatively called "agnosia") is typically defined as the failure to recognize a part of one's own body, usually a limb or extremity: "anosognosia is the *absence* of a fragment of representation which ought to be given, since the corresponding limb is there" (Merleau-Ponty 1962, 80). According to the psychologists, anosognosia "becomes a bit of forgetfulness, a negative judgment or a failure to perceive" (Merleau-Ponty 1962, 80). Merleau-Ponty notes that each of these positions on anosognosia and phantom limbs pathologizes the sufferer. His critique of both interpretations is also a reconceptualization of Sartre's notion of psychoses:

> [W]e are imprisoned in the categories of the objective world, in which there is no middle term between presence and absence. In reality the anosognosic is not simply ignorant of the existence of his paralyzed limb: he can evade his deficiency only because he knows where he risks encountering it (Merleau-Ponty 1962, 80).

In order to get at the twin phenomena of phantom limbs and anosognosia, Merleau-Ponty articulates the concept of "body image." He defines body image in a variety of ways, as (1) a map or a means of knowing the location and relation of one's body parts, (2) a "compendium of our bodily experience, capable of giving a commentary and meaning to the internal impressions and the impression of possessing a body at any moment," and (3) a form, "a total awareness of my posture in the intersensory world" (Merleau-Ponty 1962, 98–100). The body image is more than a map of the corporeal body as it is, but a psychical representation of the body as it is for the subject. The body image need not correspond directly with the physical body. It is no more and no less than one's body consciousness as it is of use to the *I* in its life work.

For Merleau-Ponty, the notion of a "body image" explains agnosia and phantom limbs. The body image represents a self who refuses the body's limitations or disfigurements and resists the forces that seek to dissuade them from their life projects. These selves are resilient and willful, though "the refusal of mutilation in the case of the phantom limb or the refusal of disablement in anosognosia are not deliberate decisions, and do not take place at the level of positing consciousness"

(Merleau-Ponty 1962, 81). They do not consciously call into being a body image that, through the addition or subtraction of psychical parts, mobilizes their will. However, they do use that body image to live in the world. The body image, often configured differently than the corporeal body, enables a continued engagement between the subject and the world.

Transsexualism and Phenomenology

Phenomenology makes sense of transsexualism by accommodating the transsexual awareness that one's body significantly shapes one's experience of the world. It assumes the necessity of being a body, but as Sartre recognizes, bodily existence is contingent. A transsexual must inhabit a body. The question that phenomenology allows us to address is, which one?

Phenomenology's split levels of bodily ontology provide a particularly apt system for describing the transsexual experience. Transsexual men have a body consciousness, a body image, that is at odds with their second-level bodies, their physical bodies. They are, in Sartrean terms, alienated bodies. Sartre's definition of psychosis as the "horrified metaphysical apprehension of the existence of my body for the Others" (Sartre 1956, 353) sounds like nothing other than a transsexual's painful realization that his flesh, his body-for-others is female, and not what he sees in his body image. However, "psychosis" is loaded language when it comes to describing the experience of being a transsexual. While Sartre's theory of conflict between the two bodies is helpful in understanding the phenomenological content of transsexual identifications, we can turn to Merleau-Ponty to undermine its potential pathologization.

In Merleau-Ponty's terms, transsexuals are agnosic and they perceive phantom limbs. They "fail" to recognize parts of their body as their own. For transsexual men, this includes the insistent ignorance of breasts and female genitalia or the fantasization of a penis and scrotum. Transsexual men know that they have female bodies. They are not psychotic. They merely ignore the features of their bodies that do not conform to their body image. Agnosic transsexuals resist the binary terms of sickness and health, absence and presence, and real and unreal. This willful ignorance/knowledge is the assertion of the *I* committed to remaining active in the world and to working on a life project.

Phenomenology is a framework capable of comprehending transsexual life projects. Phenomenology returns agency to transsexuals as subjects and authority to their narratives. It recognizes the agency of embodied subjects who mobilize around their body image to sustain their life projects and justifies a turn to the self-reports of transsexual subjects as a place to find counter-discursive knowledge. At this stage of trans scholarship, where trans subjectivity is so often delegitimized, this is no small commitment. In light of the tendency to define and judge transsexual lives by non-transsexual standards, it seems particularly prudent to incorporate a method that not only legitimates subjectively informed knowledge, but also recognizes the significance of bodies for the lived experience of the *I*.

By welding phenomenology and genealogy together, it is possible to formulate a more complex picture of the emergence of FTM identity. Discursive genealogy can historicize phenomenological accounts, while phenomenology can insert embodied agents into genealogical accounts. Phenomenology and genealogy are complementary, not contradictory, methods. Foucault's work makes it impossible to ignore that subjects and knowledge are discursively constituted. At the same time, genealogy is a limited approach for the study of subjectivity. With a combined approach, we can make sense of both the historical horizon of possible identities *and* how subjects inhabit the positions that genealogies trace.

The combined method fulfills a sociological injunction issued by C. Wright Mills to write at the intersection of history and biography.

> We have come to know that every individual lives, from one generation to the next, in some society; that *he lives out a biography, and that he lives it out within some historical sequence.* The sociological imagination enables us to grasp history and biography and the relations between the two within society (Mills 1959, 5–6; emphasis added).

Mills encourages a sociological approach that melds history and biography. He points out the methodological individualism that character-izes most men's sense of themselves as unconstructed. For him, history overcomes this individualism.

> Seldom aware of the intricate connection between the patterns of their own lives and the course of world history, ordinary men do not usually know what this connection means for the kinds of men they are becoming and for the kinds of history-making in which they might take part. They do not possess the quality of mind essential to grasp the interplay of man and society, of biography and history, of self and world (Mills 1959, 4).

Genealogy also rectifies the methodological individualism that many of these FTMs share with ordinary men. Still, Mills cautiously emphasizes the limited agency of historically situated subjects: "By the fact of his living *he contributes however minutely, to the shaping of this society and to the course of its history,* even as he is made by society and by its historical push and shove" (Mills 1959, 5–6; emphasis added). Interviews with these FTMs provide an account of these subjective experiences and point to the sites of agency that even Mills acknowledges as part of every historical condition.

Though the accounts of lived experience tend to occlude history, these FTMs have their own explanations for the transsexual struggle for identity. The experiences of FTMs become sociological data and generate another level of analysis that can complement the genealogies of the FTM subject. They provide another framework for coming to terms with the difference between butches and transsexuals and help us understand what motivates some people to modify their bodies with testosterone and surgeries. Placing these phenomenological findings next to the genealogies in chapters one and two clarifies how FTM subjects construct meaning within a historically specific set of categories and conditions.

Chapter 1

The Logic of Treatment

■ The category of "transsexual" is a relatively recent achievement of culture and not a transhistorical phenomenon. Harry Benjamin, long considered the father of modern transsexualism, writes

> The phenomenon of gender-role disorientation, that is . . . anatomic females feeling themselves to be men and wanting to change sex has existed in rare individuals since time immemorial and was, in more modern days, occasionally described by psychologists as "total sex-inversion," or with similar designations. *Its clinical picture, however was never seen as a definite, recognizable entity,* rare in the general population, fascinating for the science of sexology, and impressive in its often tragic consequences for the individual (Benjamin 1969, 1; emphasis added).

As Benjamin suggests, until quite recently, the clinical picture of transsexuals had gone unrecognized or had been subsumed within other categories, such as "sex-inversion." Sexuality (sexual instinct with a particular object choice) had not been distinguished from gender (one's psychosocial outlook), which were both neatly tied to one's sex (anatomy, morphology, and physiology). Disorders of any one of these always implied a totally disordered system called "sex-inversion." Benjamin's modification of this diagnosis with the adjective "total" implies that, from his perspective in 1969, these disorders could now present themselves as *partially* disordered systems of sexuality, gender, sex, or any combination thereof.

Benjamin's claims are unusual for a medical practitioner because he does not abide by the positivism that traditionally guides medical histories. Benjamin acknowledges that transsexuals did not exist until a medical diagnosis and a logic of treatment took shape. Prior to these developments, there may have been individuals who felt that their bodies did not represent their gendered subjectivity, but these were not transsexuals. A history of the emergence of female-to-male transsexualism can be told as the medicalization of inversion and the making available of medical techniques appropriated from both the emerging science of endocrinology and the surgical treatment of war veterans.

This chapter is a Foucauldian genealogy of these techniques and of the systems of thought about gender, sex, and sexuality that such techniques generated and within which they are embedded. A positivist history of transsexuals would assume that they have existed throughout time, and would return to the historical record to locate transsexuals who had previously been misidentified as lesbians, passing women, or some other misnomer. Genealogy suggests instead that positivist moments of "misidentification" are not merely due to poor science or clumsy history, but rather to the historic variability of the categories that organize our understanding of bodies and identities. Where a positivist assumes that better science or more nuanced history could accurately identify and distinguish between categories of sexuality or gender, a genealogist refuses the assumption that individuals exist apart from the historically changing categories that make them.

Genealogy of Female-Bodied Inversion

The substance of Foucault's work included a genealogy of the emergence of the homosexual man as a new species of man (Foucault 1980, 43). Although Foucault did not pursue a genealogy of female-bodied inversion, this task has been picked up by historians of gay and lesbian social formations, like George Chauncey Jr., who use genealogy as a method for documenting the emergence of "deviant" female-bodied categories of identity. Chauncey has developed a genealogical account of the emergence of female homosexuality from the late nineteenth century through the first third of the twentieth century. In his article "From Sexual Inversion to Homosexuality: The Changing Medical Conception of Female 'Deviance,'" Chauncey points out that late nineteenth-century medical models assumed that gender inversion, in forms such as cross-dressing, smoking, or dislike for needlework, was the necessary criterion for female-bodied "deviance." Loving another woman was considered *secondary* to the more salient gender inversion. By the 1920s, Chauncey argues, this had changed so that anyone who desired someone of the same sex was considered "homosexual."

> "Sexual inversion" referred to a broad range of cross-gender behavior (in which males behaved like women and vice-versa) of which homosexual desire was only a logical but indistinct aspect, while "homosexuality" focused on the narrower issue of sexual object choice. The differentiation of homosexual desire from cross-gender behavior at the turn of the century reflects a major reconceptualization of the nature of human sexuality, its relation to gender, and its role in one's social definition (Chauncey 1989a, 88).

At the end of his article, Chauncey suggests that the process of separating gender from sexuality is far from a *fait accompli* and is, in fact, a project that continues. The goal of these first two chapters is to continue the genealogy of female-bodied "deviance." The chapters focus on the emergence of the category "female-to-male transsexual" as a distinct socio-cultural subject position, separate from, yet still dependent upon, female homosexuality.

Pre-History of Experimental Endocrinology

> Our salvation, the preservation of our youth and activity and of the harmonious equilibrium of all our functions can only be ensured if we can find the means to come to the help of the noble cells of our organs. Therein lies the most logical solution of the tormenting problem of our downfall, of our old age. . . . Nature . . . has provided us with a wonderful source of energy. . . . Such is indeed the role of the genital glands. . . . These glands elaborate the elements of future life, which

are destined to fecundate the ovule in order to give birth to a new being and to transmit to the species the creative energy, held by the individual. At the same time, however, they secrete a liquid which, passing direct into the blood, carries to all the tissues the stimulus and the energy necessary to the individual himself. In this we are able to observe a marvelous manifestation of the design of creation. In a single organ Nature has united the source of the life of the individual and that of the species. This is confirmed by the fact that the emasculated male loses both powers at the same time (Voronoff 1928, 44).

From one perspective, the birth of endocrinology was a reincarnation of the search for the fountain of youth and everlasting life. Endocrinology promised to isolate the physiology of life in the ductless glands and their "internal secretions." This search led first to the isolation of sex glands as the source of virility and fertility in men. Then sex hormones were discovered. These new discoveries were each seen, in turn, as the determining factor of body morphology, anatomy, and psychosexual outlook in men and women. This triad of vitality, virility, and fertility propelled endocrinology into the study of pathological conditions and gave shape to the scientific paradigm from which female-to-male transsexualism would emerge.

Thomas Kuhn, a historian of science, explains how a new scientific paradigm functions. He writes that a scientific paradigm "define[s] the legitimate problems and methods of a research field for succeeding generations of practitioners." A useful paradigm breaks new ground and is "sufficiently unprecedented to attract an enduring group of adherents away from competing modes of scientific activity. Simultaneously, it is sufficiently open-ended to leave all sorts of problems for the redefined group of practitioners to resolve" (Kuhn 1970, 10). The endocrinological paradigm that developed in the nineteenth and twentieth centuries was built on three essential tenets: (1) The normal functioning of sex glands and sex hormones affects anatomy and secondary sexual characteristics; (2) all humans have a hermaphroditic bedrock; and (3) hermaphroditic deviations are natural, treatable conditions. These tenets emerged from decades of endocrinological experiments.

The late eighteenth century witnessed endocrinology's first experiments. John Hunter established a "remote sympathy" between the sex glands of animals and their sexual characteristics through experiments on pigeons, cocks, hens, pigs, and cows. This "remote sympathy" was a causal relationship between the gonads and traits that were not visibly connected, such as plumage color, size of male organ, lactation, and fertility. Hunter demonstrated this relationship by removing and transplanting the male and female gonads. In his *History of Endocrinology*, Victor Cornelius Medvei suggests the importance of Hunter's early work to endocrinology:

> It should be made clear at this point that Hunter's transplant experiments of the spurs in fowl and of the testes in cocks . . . were intended to study the 'vital principle,' assumed to be responsible for the union of the graft with the host, and for the survival and growth of the graft. This 'vital principle' was supposed to work independently of the nervous system and humoral mechanisms acting as integrating factors in the body. These experiments were, therefore, not carried out with any underlying endocrine speculations . . . they happened to fit—subconsciously, as it were—into the endocrine framework of a later era (Medvei 1982, 196).

Hunter's own words suggest contained only a passing reference to the sexual significance of his experiments. "Here is the testicle of a cock, separated from that animal and put through a wound made for that purpose, into the belly of a hen, which mode of turning hens into cocks is much such an improvement for its utility as that of Dean Swift when he proposed to obtain a breed of sheep without wool" (Hunter, in Medvei 1982, 197). Hunter did not see much use-value resulting from this experiment. He could hardly have anticipated that individuals in the twentieth century would draw upon his work to enact a female-to-male sex change, but transsexual sex changes are built upon the early endocrine experiment whose original purpose was to isolate a "vital principle."

Hunter speculated on the effects of the gonads on sexual power and on the direction of that sexual instinct. He believed the gonads, the testes in particular, were responsible for the sex drive but its direction was independent of the gonads. These brief comments set the stage for twentieth century debates on hormone treatments.

In 1849, A. A. Berthold, a German experimental endocrinologist, made the link that Hunter had noted between the gonads and the sex characteristics of animals explicit. While Hunter had wanted to know whether gonads could be transplanted and what vital force lay within them, Berthold was interested in the effects of transplants on sexual nature. Berthold experimented with the castration of cocks and found that castration caused the comb to atrophy. He hoped to reverse the effects of castration with transplantation. Experiments like Berthold's were pursued in the later decades of the nineteenth century and in a form of treatment in the early twentieth century called "organotherapy." As a result of his experiments, Berthold speculated that the sympathy between the gonads and the sexual characteristics might rely on an intermediary source running through the blood stream, but it was only later that hormones were found to be that missing link. In the meantime, organotherapy was all the rage.

Organotherapy: A Use-Value for Internal Secretions

Organotherapy was the use of sexual glands or glandular tissue as a therapeutic means of restoring what the patient lost in aging.[1] The claim to have found the vital principle and to be able to treat the weak and infirm by means of it was received with both skepticism and enthusiasm. The skeptics thought the results were due to autosuggestion, while enthusiasts believed the rejuvenating effects were genuine. From the organotherapeutic experiments of Charles Brown-Séquard in the 1890s to the work of Serge Voronoff in the 1920s, organotherapy was as closely followed by medical journals and the popular press as was the cloning of sheep in the 1990s. The discovery of hormones led to the dismissal of organotherapy as quackery and nonsense.

Brown-Séquard and Voronoff both challenged a basic law of nature: bodies always exhaust their resources. They sought an effective means of countering the aging process. Although men (and women, though they were of a lesser interest to these practitioners) had always aged and eventually died, they thought that organotherapy could force this law to succumb to human control.

From the period of my observations among the eunuchs in Egypt, which revealed to me the importance of the internal secretion of the interstitial glands, I was haunted by the idea that it might be possible to gain control over this wonder potential force, and *utilize it for our needs, when as we advance in age, its natural source begins to show signs of exhaustion* (Voronoff 1928, 63; emphasis added).

Voronoff and the others established organotherapy as the means of overcoming the law of exhaustion. Organotherapists viewed science as an unproblematic means of surpassing nature. Voronoff compared endocrinology to the science that allowed humans to "fly" higher than birds, and "swim" to the depths of the sea by submarine. These beliefs accelerated the race for individual immortality and the survival of the species.

Endocrinology had found a use-value for its knowledge about internal organs and hormones. Voronoff and the organotherapists also believed that ovarian tissue held a woman's vital principle and suggested that she also be treated with gonad transplants or extracts. They observed that a woman's vitality decreased with the onset of menopause and argued that she would benefit from ovarian treatments.

Voronoff began his research and treatment using monkey glands. In 1919, Voronoff's harvesting of glands from the bodies of monkeys literalized the French colonization of the Algerian body politic. Like his colonialist stance toward Algerians, Voronoff thought monkeys were "almost human," standing on the evolutionary scale below Western, white men. They seemed like perfect subjects for the experimental trials of organotherapy. However, transplanting monkey glands into humans, even for the purpose of rejuvenation, proved too threatening. The scientific community and the public, concerned about inter-species mixings, produced such an outcry that Voronoff abandoned his Algerian monkeys. However, it took more time for the French to grow uncomfortable with their harvest of the Algerian body politic.

Voronoff turned to public perceptions of Egypt to justify his research and organotherapeutic treatments. The Egyptian "other" was a deathly danger to Western achievements. The fate of the Egyptian eunuch, who had lost all vitality, was to be avoided at all costs. In Voronoff's eyes, Egypt served as the outline of the pathology that could befall aging Westerners. Voronoff's Egypt is one where he "was constantly in touch with eunuchs, and . . . present at the [early] deathbed of several of them" (Voronoff 1928, 58). The organotherapeutic logic of treatment was based on aversion to a figure that represented the antithesis of the West's ideal man. In their eagerness to avoid the fate of eunuchs, who were essentially feminized men, Westerners were willing to use glandular therapy to revitalize themselves, bolster their masculinity, and increase their fertility.[2]

Nationalism also plays its part in the logic of organotherapy. Brown-Séquard, a Frenchman, and Eugene Steinach, an Austrian, each had patriotic stakes in the rejuvenation of their men. Brown-Séquard was actually born in England, but became a naturalized citizen of France. The social construction of national identity informed Brown-Séquard's scientific beliefs about overcoming the natural limits of life. If national identity and national membership were a social matter, and not conferred automatically by birth, then other "natural" phenomena, such as life and death, could also be a matter of culture. If national identity was really a modifiable social phenomenon, then it seemed possible to manipulate other things, such as gender and sex. Steinach's nationalist agenda was determined by his location in Austria. His work on rejuvenation in the interwar period was consistent with themes of German regeneration. Hitler was not supportive of his later work, however, and the German occupation of Austria made Steinach an exile in Switzerland.

Steinach, Voronoff, and Brown-Séquard each mobilized nationalist themes and fears of the East to increase the appeal of organotherapy. To fight against popular and medical fears of inter-species mixing, Voronoff marshaled white fears of the East and nationalist dreams of revitalization to promote his elixir of life. The transplanting of monkey glands to human bodies seemed scandalous, but the call to revitalize oneself was successful because of a fear of Egyptian eunuchs. Where Hunter, Berthold, and the early organotherapists who used animal transplants failed to overcome popular opinion, the use of nationalist ideals allowed later scientists to continue their work in organotherapy.

Synthesizing Hormones, Mapping the
Normal Hermaphroditic Bedrock

The shift from organotherapies to hormonal therapies began in 1905. Early genetic theory had posited the gene as the determining factor of sex, but biochemical endocrinology claimed that hormones were the supplementary agents that finished the task of becoming a sex. One of endocrinology's main projects in the 1920s and 1930s was the isolation of sex hormones. Along with its goal of mapping the normal hormonal constitution, endocrinology produced synthetic hormones that could be used with greater success in treatments for sexual "dysfunction."

The isolation and classification of natural estrogens proceeded at a more rapid pace than did testosterone. Animal urine, especially from pregnant mares, became a source for estrogenic products, while testosterone was more expensive, time-consuming, and complicated to collect. Twenty-five thousand liters of male urine generated a mere fifty milligrams of testosterone in 1931. In the 1930s, endocrinology began collecting testosterone from the urine of captive populations—soldiers or prisoners—for male hormone treatments, but until then, testosterone was not available in the same quantities as estrogens. Nelly Oudshoorn documents the difficulties of obtaining enough specimens to produce any marketable treatments of male sex hormones:

> The first standardized preparation of male sex hormones was not put on the market by Organon until 1931; five years after the equivalent drug for women. . . . Technical problems further delayed the actual marketing of the first standardized male sex hormone preparation. The major problem was how to produce a highly purified hormone preparation free from other substances of similar solubility, and in particular free of female sex hormones (Oudshoorn 1994, 98).

Oudshoorn claims that the emerging field of gynecology was already medicalizing women's bodies. Men's bodies were not subject to regular examination in the same way. This sped up the isolation of estrogens and provided a use-value for female sex hormones.

These asymmetries delayed the investigation into the nature or function of testosterone and its utilization as a treatment. Without the

possibility of testosterone treatment, nascent FTMs remained unrecognizable as transsexual subjects. Although the synthetic production
of testosterone was achieved in 1936, slightly earlier than estrogens,[3]
natural estrogenic preparations were obtained earlier and with greater
technical ease than testosterone. The slower process of isolating and
categorizing "male" hormones explains a delay in the use of testosterone as a treatment for FTMs. It also explains the slower historical emergence of an FTM identity.

During the zigzag process of isolating and synthesizing hormones,
endocrinologists were also at work mapping the normal hormonal state
of men and women. Endocrinology surprised itself by discovering the
presence of "male" hormones in normal females in 1931 and "female"
hormones in normal males in 1934 (Oudshoorn 1994, 25–26). These
discoveries created the possibility of sex change treatments.

These results challenged the dualistic model of sex, which dictated
that men be treated exclusively with "male" hormones and women be
treated only with "female" hormones. Oudshoorn's study of endocrinology details the decline of the dualistic model and the rise of a new
endocrinological paradigm.

> In the 1920s, there emerged a lively dispute in the scientific commu-
> nity about the dualistic assumption that sex hormones are strictly sex-
> specific in origin and function. A growing number of publications ap-
> peared contradicting the pre-scientific idea of a sexual duality located
> in the gonads and underlying the concept of the sexual specificity of
> sex hormones (Oudshoorn 1994, 24).

The dualistic model of sexed bodies assumed that men and women
were two completely distinct types of human beings whose bodies were
homologous. This dualism assumed that androgens were exclusively
male and estrogens were exclusively female.

The discovery of hormones discredited the dualistic model of sex
that viewed male and female as exclusive categories. It challenged the
notion that there was any ascertainable site of male and female essences. Instead, these chemical agents were free-flowing and hard to
pin down. The isolation of hormones indicated that men and women
have both "male" and "female" hormones.

By the 1930s, endocrinology had replaced the dualistic model with a hermaphroditic model. According to this model, all people have a hermaphroditic bedrock of hormones. Men and women each have both kinds of hormones. In the normal condition, there is a proper balance of male and female hormones and the anatomical manifestations of sex are unambiguously male or female.

> Instead of locating the essence of femininity or masculinity in specific organs, as the anatomists had done, sex endocrinologists introduced a quantitative theory of sex and the body. The idea that each sex could be characterized by its own sex hormone was transformed into the idea of relative sexual specificity (Oudshoorn 1994, 38).

The pathologies that the endocrinologists now categorized were deviations of degrees.

> The model suggested that, chemically speaking, all organisms are both male and female. . . . In this model, an anatomical male could possess feminine characteristics controlled by female sex hormones, while an anatomical female could have masculine characteristics regulated by male sex hormones (Oudshoorn 1994, 39).

Normal men and women were latently hermaphroditic, while the ill and the treatable were manifestly hermaphroditic.

Textbooks demonstrate the adoption of this new model at the clinical level. In a chapter called "Sex Glands" from the 1924 book *Organotherapy in General Practice*, there are several mentions of the basic principle of the new model of sex—latent hermaphroditism.

> Biedl assumes that there is always present a *hermaphroditic groundwork*. . . . "It is only by the assumption of a *hermaphroditic primitive genital trace,* together with the dependence of the somatic and psychic sex characteristics upon the *internal secretory activity of the genital glands,* that we can explain those cases in which complete alteration of single sex characteristics, or even of the entire sexual character, takes place during the life of the individual" (G.W. Carnick Co. 1924, 136; emphasis added).

The experimental endocrinologist Arthur Biedl, quoted in this passage, identifies a latent hermaphroditic bedrock and the role of hormones as key factors in human development. The notion of a hermaphroditic bedrock gained strength throughout the 1930s, becoming the basis for a new logic of treatment for sexual pathologies in the 1940s and 1950s.

The assumption that all bodies were a combination of male and female hormones provided an epistemological space for nascent transsexuals to lay claim to sex change technologies. In the older, dualistic model of sex, paradoxical treatments (male sex hormones in female bodies) were contra-indicated because of fears about cross-sex contamination. The new hermaphroditic model had no way to block paradoxical treatments because both men and women were already in possession of estrogens and androgens. With the discovery of "paradoxical hormones" in all men and women, a way opened up for transsexuals to appropriate hormones to transform their bodies.

Cures for Inversion:
A New Use-Value for Internal Secretions

From the 1930s through the 1950s, endocrinology treated inverts with hormones. Though there was a general consensus that inverts could benefit from hormones, clinicians and experimenters disagreed about which hormones were appropriate for particular bodies. Which hormones would cure inversion?

The treatment protocol constructed in the 1940s and 1950s is one of the cleaving knives that cut up the category of "inversion." Physicians started their treatment by deciding if a case was acquired or innate. If it was acquired, it was possible to treat the condition with homo-sexual hormones. The term "homo-sexual hormones"—estrogens for females and testosterone for males—relies on the old dualistic paradigm according to which only men have testosterone and only women have estrogens. Like organotherapy, homo-sexual hormones were designed to balance a patient's sexual accounts.

If a case of inversion was considered innate, it was deemed resistant to homo-sexual hormone treatments. Innate homosexual inverts

could be treated with hetero-sexual hormones—testosterone for females and estrogens for males. The use of hetero-sexual hormones came
from the newly discovered paradoxical finding that female bodies had
"male" hormones and male bodies had "female" hormones. The purpose of treatments of hetero-sexual hormones was to hormonally castrate inverts and prevent them from acting out their pathological natures. The use of estrogens in cases of innate male inversion was justified
by locating an innate, incurable illness in their bodies. By anchoring
inversion in the body, male-bodied inverts began to qualify for heterosexual hormones (estrogen). Hetero-sexual hormone treatments for
female-bodied inverts, however, was still contra-indicated by a particularly gendered and sexualized logic of treatment. This resulted in
an asymmetry in the treatment of male- and female-bodied inverts.

Many inverts were treated against their will. This practice is a black
stain on the history of endocrinology. These same events are significant to the history of transsexualism because they mark some of the
first uses of hetero-sexual hormones to alter the character or the body
of inverts. These events have two historical trajectories; one is homosexual and the other is transsexual. The homosexual history is about
unwanted treatments and the removal of the homosexual diagnosis
from the *Diagnostic and Statistical Manual* of the American Psychological Association in 1974. Without a doubt, the end of unwanted
treatments is a success story. The transsexual history is a record of the
logic that paved the way for desired treatments. This history is also a
success story, but its end is the creation, rather than the removal, of a
diagnosis. With this diagnostic category, transsexuals became recognizable and treatments were made available.

Endocrinologists held the belief that inversion was as much a disorder of sex and gender as it was a disease of sexuality. Such disorders
were all wrapped into one ball of wax. This belief system is summarized with hindsight by historian of science Dr. Heino F.L. Meyer-
Bahlburg in 1984:

> The general rationale underlying these studies [in the 1940s and 1950s]
> was derived from the well-known relationships of testosterone and
> other androgens to masculine body characteristics and in animals, to
> certain aspects of masculine behavior, as well as from the analogous

relationships of estrogens to feminine somatic and behavioral characteristics. Accordingly, the expectation was that male homosexuals
would show a deficiency of testosterone and/or other androgens,
and/or an excess of estrogens whereas female homosexuals would
show the reverse. Other endocrine disorders were thought to be
possibly associated with the sex hormone abnormalities as cause or
consequence (Meyer-Bahlburg 1984, 376).[4]

This account shows the belief that inversion was a deficiency of hormones that a dose of homo-sexual hormones would cure. The earliest
studies exhibit the hope that homo-sexual hormones would correct
the direction of the inverts' desires as well as their gender presentation.
C. A. Wright was one of the early advocates for treating male homosexual inverts with testosterone and female inverts with estrogen.

> The sex attraction of the true congenital homosexual is based on an
> endocrine imbalance. . . . In as much as the gonadotropic factor gov-
> erns development and the normal functioning of the sex glands, it
> seems indicated to use [testosterone] in the treatment of these cases
> in the male. It is probable that the addition of estrin . . . is indicated in
> women (Wright 1938, 449–52).

Out of the twelve cases reported by Wright in his original study, nine
showed an improvement in hormone levels, a return to heterosexual
behavior, and a concomitant reform of their psychosocial outlook. Four
case reports on male inverts from Dr. Louis A. Lurie of Cincinnati,
Ohio in 1944 were typical of the period. Lurie's discussion divides
homosexual inverts into two categories, innate and acquired, the endocrine factor was crucial in the former type. Treatments with testosterone were virilizing in such cases. Only one of the four boys in this
series was "overtly" homosexual; he had had homosexual experiences.
Lurie noted with confidence that the other three were latent homosexuals. The boys' gender inversion was being treated as much as their
sexual "disorder."

> In general, the physical examination was negative. . . . The endocrine
> picture was very suggestive. The boy was of average height but 15
> pounds overweight. The fat distribution was principally of the mons-

mammary-girdle type. There was no hair on the face. . . . The genitalia were small. It was noted that C. was very effeminate. He talked in a high-pitched girlish voice and walked with a mincing gait. His face was round and his cheeks were rosy. He was extremely neat about his person and always looked clean and well dressed. He did not engage in any rough play with the other boys. He was very easygoing and very seldom asserted himself. . . . He had a huge appetite and drank a great deal of water between meals. He always asked for milk. He appeared extremely phlegmatic and very sleepy. He yawned constantly. . . . He preferred being by himself. . . . He appeared to daydream a great deal (Lurie 1944, 181).

Lurie found no genital irregularities, but he read this boy's body as hormonally deficient. His appetite and yawning were symptomatic of his testosterone deficiency and indicated the necessity for revitalization. He, like the other boys in Lurie's study, was "successfully" treated with homo-sexual hormones—testosterone. His body changed, as it would have anyway in the case of this thirteen-year-old adolescent, and he joined the armed forces.

These early accounts were countered by Glass and Johnson's "Limitations and Complications of Organotherapy in Male Homosexuality."

Insofar as homosexuality is concerned organotherapy failed to influence the psychosexual behavior in eight of the subjects but seemed to benefit the other three. . . . Among the eight who failed to respond favorably, [five] complained of an actual intensification of the homosexual drive so that further treatment was withheld or abandoned by them (Glass and Johnson 1944, 541–42).

The endocrinologists were disappointed that the treatments exacerbated their patients' homosexuality. It became apparent to them that testosterone could affect the power but not the direction of the sex drive.

Heller and Maddock point out the other treatment options available in 1947: "Diametrically opposed to this type of therapy is the use of castration in over 100 cases of sexual perversion and homosexuality reported by Sand and Okkels (1938) who note that the results have been gratifying in all but one case" (Heller and Maddock 1947, 420). This review of the literature in 1947 concludes:

> The *power* of the human sex drive is largely dependent on *physiological factors*, i.e. proportional to the amount of circulating androgen (or estrogen in the female). On the other hand, the *direction* of the human sex drive seems to be largely dependent upon *psychological* factors, which are conditioned by the early environment and sexual experiences of the individual. It would seem to follow that vigorous androgenic treatment would tend to increase the power of the sex drive in both the normal and homosexual male without influencing the direction of the sex drive in either case. Similarly, castration will markedly diminish, but not abolish, the power of the sex drive, and the diminished drive in the case of normals will continue in the direction of heterosexuality, whereas the small drive remaining in the homosexual will continue in the direction of homosexuality (Heller and Maddock 1947, 422).

In 1947, physicians decided that male inverts could not be "cured" of their homosexual inversion, but they could be rendered *sexually inactive*. Libido reduction, through estrogen treatments, was the next best thing to a true change of sexual object choice.

The clinical literature of this period ignores female inverts, in part because medicine assumed that females were the mirror of the male inverts. It was also clear that estrogen was an ineffectual treatment for females with sexual direction disorders and testosterone treatments were contra-indicated due to their virilizing effects. The association of testosterone with virility justified homo-sexual hormone treatments for male inverts with deficient masculine desires or gender presentation. This same equation of virility and testosterone foreclosed testosterone treatments for nascent FTMs.

In the 1940s, female inversion was considered medically untreatable. Their condition did not respond to estrogen. Testosterone was not yet available to female inverts because of the belief that it would virilize them and increase their libido. Male inverts might be treated with testosterone, to virilize them, or estrogens, to castrate them.

This asymmetry of treatment options delayed the recognizability of female inverts qua FTM transsexuals.

Becoming Treatable: Two Types of Inversion

Without a treatable physical abnormality, the care of female inverts would pass into the domain of the psychologists. Dr. Michael Dillon's 1946 book, *Self: Ethics and Endocrinology*, was an attempt to make a case for the hormonal treatment of female inverts. Dillon had changed his sex from female to male in the 1940s, first his birth certificate and then his body. Though he does not mention his own sex change, the argument in *Self* might represent the logic he used to convince his physicians to do what he wanted. His text positions people like himself as a special kind of invert.

Dillon starts off by suggesting that there are several grades of sex, from male to female, and intersexuals of all kinds in between: "[T]hese intersexes . . . have the primary characteristics of male or female, i.e. the gonads, the ovary or testis; but they display also the secondary characteristics of the other, including the temperament. This state is known as homosexuality" (59). Dillon tries to establish inverts as homosexuals who need treatment like intersexuals.

Dillon then outlines a typology of the different types of these "homosexuals." He starts with a standard distinction between permanent and transient homosexuality. Adolescent exploration is the transient type, whereas other types are not bound by either time or geography. Both male and female homosexuals exist. The rest of his article explores the female types.

Dillon's next distinction is between permanent homosexuals whose disorder stems from endocrine imbalances and those whose disorder is psychological in nature. In order to determine which homosexuals belong within the domain of endocrinology, Dillon separates mannish inverts, whose disorders are acquired or deliberate, from masculine inverts, whose disorders are innate.

> It is not a new distinction but it is one that is all too frequently overlooked. The difference is that of the deliberate adoption and imitation of the habits, interests and dress of the other sex . . . and of the natu-

ral acquisition of them as the result of the innate possession of the mental outlook and temperament of the other sex (44).

Dillon notes that psychologists do not make a distinction between mannish and masculine inverts and he believes this to be a flaw in their typologies.

> Yet, there is a clear distinction. Where the one imitates and acquires, the other seems to develop naturally along the lines of the other sex. Invariably, [the latter] cry "I have always felt as if I were a man." In these instances the body may approximate in essentials to one sex . . . but the personality is wholly peculiar to the opposite one (51).

Dillon then claims that Radclyffe Hall's 1929 novel, *The Well of Loneliness,* portrays a girl of the innate masculine type.[5]

Dillon closes by arguing for medical treatments for masculine female homosexuals. Psychologists are of no use to this type, he says, as some hidden physical condition must dictate their nature. Until this factor can be discovered, these special inverts should be treated with testosterone. Dillon argues, "Surely where the mind cannot be made to fit the body, the body should be made to fit, approximately, at any rate to the mind" (53). With a discussion of the moral blamelessness of homosexuals, Dillon makes a final recommendation that these victims should be given care free of charge.

Dillon clearly believes that there are similar features among female types—what they were, what they did, and what their bodies were like. By parsing the categories of homosexuals, he *repositions* one type of female invert as the cousin of intersexuals. Although the people he refers to as "masculine inverts" are like other homosexuals, they are more like intersexuals, and are deserving of testosterone treatments. This repositioning was necessary because of a lack of treatment protocols that could justify testosterone injections for female inverts in the 1930s and 1940s. Dillon asserts that those of his type are more like intersexuals so that they can remain in the hands of the endocrinologists.[6]

More Like Hermaphrodites:
Treatment for Bodily Disorders

In his chapter, "Hermaphrodism," Dillon makes the second move that repositions masculine inverts closer to intersexuals and provides the dominant logic of treatment for the group soon to be known as female-to-male transsexuals. As in his previous chapter on homosexuals, Dillon makes no explicit mention of his own transsexualism. He is still on a course that approaches, but does not directly name the condition. This he leaves for Cauldwell in 1949. In lieu of a name and a diagnosis, Dillon draws on types of intersexual conditions to develop a logic of treatment for others like him.

Intersexuals were usually classified as either true or pseudo-hermaphrodites: "[T]rue hermaphrodism does not depend upon the shape or existence of the external organs, it is the presence of both ovary and testis in the abdomen that makes for it" (59). Dillon emphasizes that hermaphrodites do not necessarily have external, visible anomalies. By establishing this fact, he could suggest that doctors should treat people like himself despite their apparently normal bodies. Intersexual pathologies were hidden in the abdomen and undetectable to the naked eye. Scientific progress would eventually be able to find the physiological basis for inversion, but for now, abnormalities like his were hidden.

Dillon moves from the "hidden pathology" analogy to examples of intersexed individuals who have incompletely formed or entirely absent penises. This condition, known as hypospadias, is seen as legitimating medical intervention. Usually, he notes, these individuals are mistaken for girls at birth and reared as girls until puberty when male secondary sexual characteristics emerge. Of all the intersexed conditions, the hypospadic comes closest to the phallic lack of FTMs.

> There is, in addition, sometimes complete lack of a penis altogether, and this and the undescended testicles cause the parents to suppose that their child is a girl. As such, therefore, he is brought up—with disastrous results when the error is discovered a puberty, for at that time the voice may break, the muscles develop and the skeletal growth assumes adult male proportions. Sometimes, however, *the changes*

are not so evident that the individual may live for some years under the delusion he is a female unless his instincts gain the upper hand (61; emphasis added).

Lack of a penis or a small penis due to a gonad failure is treatable, and, Dillon argues, should be treated, but only in the cases where the individual's psychosexual outlook does not correspond to the sex assigned at birth.

> Certain patients who have realized that they were not the same, physically, as other girls, have been horrified to discover that in reality they were men, undeveloped males. Some such cases on record refused treatment, preferring to go on living as women, and, being without external genitalia, they are outside the scope of the law and have a perfect right to do as they wish (62).

These women are hypospadic pseudo-hermaphrodites with feminine psychosexual outlooks. In such cases, Dillon claims it would be inappropriate to intervene. However, if the hypospadic individual has a masculine psychosexual outlook, Dillon argues that it is in their best interest to be treated.

Though Dillon does not mention the types of treatment he has in mind, he refuses to call this treatment a "sex change" because the term causes sensational media coverage. He also says that it does an injustice to the psychosexual outlook of the patient. Dillon emphasizes that, since the body is unremarkably female, claims to manhood may seem outlandish to others. Because they view these patients as women, others can make sense of the desired treatment only as a "change" of sex.

> [I]t is not surprising that his statements are met with some incredulity. . . . They may never have been given real cause before to doubt his sex was female, why should they alter their view now? Far easier to assume that, by pure perversity, he has wanted to "change his sex" and that by some curious means he has managed to accomplish a pseudo-alteration (63).

Despite the assumptions made by others, these individuals have only changed their bodies to conform to their psychosexual outlook. They have not changed their sex. "Sex confirmation" may be a better term for what Dillon has in mind, though he does not use this phrase.

The remainder of Dillon's chapter on intersexuals is devoted to the role of genetics in inversion. Dillon hoped to pinpoint the cause of inversion at a deeper, microscopic level of the body in order to strengthen the proposed kinship between intersexuals and inverts of the innate/masculine type. "There is no reason to suppose that sex variations of character are less able to be [genetically] transmitted than those of the body" (71).

Dillon's logic of treatment for intersexuals and some inverts rests upon two principle assumptions about embodiment and subjectivity. The first of these is in line with traditional medicine, but the second seems counter-intuitive. First, a body shall not be treated unless there is an obvious and identifiable physiological or anatomical pathology. Failure to find such an anomaly precludes treatment or engenders a more penetrating search for bodily errors.

Second, the mind, not the body, should indicate the appropriate type of treatment. The correct course of treatment depends on the patient's psychosexual outlook. This unusual diagnostic protocol continues to be a point of conflict among physicians.[7]

Psychological Treatment of FTM Transsexuals

The logic of treatment put forth by Dillon was reflected in the scattered case studies in the medical literature in the 1950s (Cauldwell 1949; Hamburger 1953; Benjamin 1954), but his efforts were ultimately only partially successful. The treatment of female-bodied inverts was remanded to the psychologists who favored psychoanalysis or aversion therapy.

It is possible to trace the consolidation of the logic of treatment by examining the reasons psychologists employed to reject medical treatment. The psychologists viewed nascent FTMs as a type of female homosexual with internalized homophobia. They disregarded their patients' claims of intersexuality. According to psychologists in the 1950s and 1960s, such patients had a mind problem, not a body problem. Each of these case reports summarizes the physical condition of the patient and concludes that there are no observable anatomical anomalies and therefore no justification for hormone treatments. Throughout the cases, there is evidence that these patients tried to establish their similarity to intersexuals and their difference from female homosexuals. The case reports demonstrate that FTMs magnified these differences and grew insistent on their similarities to intersexuals. As medical treatments became less available, their claims of difference from homosexuals and similarity to intersexuals grew stronger.

In 1956, Bowmen and Engle reported on a case of a man and a wife, each of whom were "transvestic." "Transvestism" was the preferred term of psychologists who categorized transsexuals as an extreme type of cross-dressing homosexual. They focused on social presentation, especially clothes, and sexual object choice, rather than on bodies, in order to assert their control over these patients. They conclude, "according to psychological explanations, transvestitism is the result of intense castration fears, as are homosexuality, exhibitionism, and fetishism" (Bowmen and Engle 1956, 587). They conceded that no psychological treatments have proven successful. However, Bowmen and Engle counsel psychological intervention over medical treatment because the latter "does not really solve the problem" (Bowmen and Engle 1956, 587) and can be the cause of legal mayhem.

A 1959 report on fifty cases (thirteen FTMs and thirty-seven MTFs) emphasizes the "homosexual" desires of these patients and dismisses the notion that transvestites and transsexuals had physiological anomalies like intersexed patients.

> There was no evidence of genital dysplasia or male anatomical conformation. . . . With one notable exception the female patients were homosexually oriented. These 12 women [sic] had experienced homosexual attachments, and the wish to take the male role in sexual intimacy with a Lesbian partner was the predominant and expressed reason advanced by those who wished for trans-sexualization" (Randell 1959, 1450).

The one exception was an FTM in a partnership with an MTF. In an effort to bolster his theory that transsexuals are a type of homosexual, Randell goes on to cite a 1955 study that "failed to discover abnormal gonadal status in transvestite patients. . . . [Worden and Marsh] believe that such patients are in conflict over strong, but unacceptable sexual urges and feel threatened by all sexual activity whether hetero-, homo-, or masturbatory" (Randell 1959, 1451). Of his thirteen FTM cases, and the entire series of fifty, Randell asserts, "no convincing evidence of anatomical intersexuality was found" (Randell 1959, 1451).

Until the 1980s, "true" female-bodied transsexuals had feminine women as their preferred sexual object choice. Psychologists argued that female-bodied gender inverts with sexual desires for men were, by definition, not true transvestites.

> Heterosexual [sic] individuals with transvestitism are generally psychopaths who want to attract attention. That variety is not considered genuine transvestitism. . . . Consequently, sexuality among genuine transvestites is mostly homosexual along the conventional lines. Accepting Dukor's theory that genuine transvestitism is the final consequence . . . of a female, active type of homosexuality it will hardly be possible to include the absence of desire for homosexual contacts in the characteristics of true transvestitism since from their own point of view their sexual contacts with individuals of the same somatic sex are heterosexual (Hertz and Westman 1961, 291).

Psychologists recommended psychotherapy for inverts with homosexual desires and transvestic presentation. They believed that medical intervention was contra-indicated.

Within these same reports are scattered references to how the FTM patients viewed their situations. Almost all of the reports make references, in belittling tones, to the patient's claim to have a physiological disturbance, or to be intersexed. Throughout these reports, psychologists choose to use the female pronouns to emphasize their belief that the FTMs really were women. Bowmen and Engle make this comment about the "wife" in the case of the transgendered couple: "His wife took a man's name, dressed as a man, and worked outside the home as a man. She had for some time taken testosterone and felt that a lump in her groin was a testicle" (Bowmen and Engle 1956, 587). This report, with its use of the female pronoun, demonstrates the mocking tones of the psychologists. It also shows how FTMs actively constructed their situation in terms that would be most likely to secure medical treatments. By claiming to have a testicle, this patient could locate his condition in his body and indicate that his true sex was male. These two claims made medical treatment more likely.

Likewise, a case report from 1961 describes the case of a twenty-five-year-old who claimed "she had had no menstruation for 13 months. She pointed out that her appearance had gradually assumed more masculine features. Her voice had become deeper, her breasts smaller, her musculature had developed, her feet and hands had grown. She had observed a weak growth of beard and she had started shaving" (Hertz et al. 1961, 289). This report echoes Dillon's description of the hypospadic hermaphrodite who, having been brought up as female, goes through a surprise male puberty with all the attendant physical changes.

The FTMs also asserted that they were not homosexuals. Hertz writes, "She stated that she had a distinct feeling that in some way she was a man. In consequence of this idea she did not consider the above-mentioned woman [the patient's partner] a homosexual person, nor did she admit that she herself was homosexual. 'A homosexual woman would be repugnant to me'" (Hertz et al. 1961, 290). These refusals to be categorized as homosexual or to have his partner categorized as a lesbian are counter-discourses that these FTMs marshaled against the psychological discourses that foreclosed medical treatments. In another report, a psychologist called in to ascertain the sanity of an FTM accused of a crime writes, "she has been continually harassed throughout her life by 'everybody, ' and labeled a 'freak,' 'homo,' or 'hermaphrodite.' A.C. always thought these derogations were unjust. She considered herself to have always been masculine and knew that her wife felt about her and accepted her as such" (Redmount 1953, 95).

Similar reports indicated that it was not at all unusual for FTMs to present themselves as intersexed, and that some even took additional steps to secure this representation of themselves by gaining access to and self-administering hormones. One psychologist reports, "The rationale she offered was that she was a pseudo-hermaphrodite. She was noncommittal about a prior bilateral mastectomy, though admitted having taken male hormones over a period of time" (McCully

1963, 437). This patient "admitted" to taking hormones, an act which was obviously a crime to the psychologist. This psychologist is well aware that the patient's claims to being hermaphroditic would legitimate the desired course of treatment and suggests that these claims are made for that very purpose: "Putting herself across as an hermaphrodite would achieve one of her ends, an operation. She grudgingly accepted that she had some physical female anatomy, giving that much lip service to reality since it furthered her goals. She herself believed that she had functioning male sexual organs" (McCully 1963, 437). On the one hand, this psychologist believes that the patient had deliberately presented his case in a way that would guarantee the desired surgery. On the other hand, the psychologist summarizes the patient's belief system as delusional.

This choice, between viewing the patient's claims as delusional or strategic, is found in many of the accounts, but nowhere as starkly as in the aforementioned report on an FTM criminally accused by his mother-in-law of fraudulent financial affairs. Dr. Robert Redmount concludes his remarks on this case with this pithy summary: "Her lifelong adjustments seem to represent *less an attempt to accept reality and more of a protest against it*" (110; emphasis added). Redmount hardly concurs that this protest is viable. His ultimate aim would be to help the patient avoid "her own self-destruction" (111). The use of the female pronoun throughout these cases, plus the ubiquitous comments on the normal physiological condition of these patients, indicates the psychologists' beliefs that these patients are delusional. Endocrinologists might defer to the patient's desire for treatment based on the likelihood that a physiological etiology for their condition would eventually be uncovered. The psychologists could only view their patients as at worst deluded, and at best strategic.

Surgical Logic of Treatment:
Reconstructive versus Cosmetic

The history of plastic surgeries and their use-value for nascent FTMs depends upon a similar logic of treatment whereby some bodies are made treatable and others are considered healthy and not treatable.

With a firm grasp on this logic of treatment, it will be relatively easy to understand how surgeries became available to nascent FTMs. Yet the history of surgical procedures is more complex because there are many different surgeries that FTMs pursue. In popular belief systems, "sex changes" are thought to be a one-stop procedure, like walking through a machine in a doctor's office. This perception relies on the assumption of the primacy of the phallus. In actuality, sex reassignment/confirmation has always been a multi-stage process consisting of life-long hormone treatments and multiple surgeries including chest reconstruction, phallic reconstruction, scrotal reconstruction, and partial or total hysterectomies.

For a variety of reasons, FTMs pursue surgery less vigorously than they do testosterone. The multiple surgical procedures, although highly desired by FTMs, are out of financial reach for many and are considered inadequate, functionally and aesthetically, by most. Hormones have carried greater importance than surgeries for the history of the emergence and consolidation of an FTM identity.

History of Surgical Techniques

Both chest reconstruction and hysterectomy have their roots in the medical treatment of "disorderly" female bodies. Mastectomies were performed as early as 1669 (Maliniac 1950, 6) for hypertrophic, pendulous breasts which put women physically at risk. These early plastic surgeries were as risky as the condition itself. Anesthesia, advances in blood flow control, and antiseptic all contributed to the safety and success of surgery, especially non-critical procedures, in the nineteenth and twentieth centuries. From the 1890s onward, improvements were made in the techniques of mastectomy, leading to better results for nipple grafting or transposition, minimization of scarring, and increased sensation. Aside from pendulous breasts, mastectomies were often performed during the twentieth century for women diagnosed with cancerous lumps or illnesses related to the mammary glands. These female bodies commanded surgical attention because they were ill bodies.

The practice of hysterectomies has a long history as well. In 1809, Ephraim McDowell reported on a case in which he removed the ovaries and fallopian tubes of his patient. In 1869, Robert Battery did an ovariotomy that he later used on unspecified "abnormal females." By 1878, the first total hysterectomy had been performed (Dally 1991, 141). Hysteria, originally believed to result from a "loose womb," was most frequently treated by hysterectomy.

Phalloplasties, unlike mastectomies and hysterectomies, were first developed for male bodies. Veterans injured during World War I received the first phalloplasties. John Hoopes's 1969 review article provides an overview of the development of these techniques. Harold Gilles, a British surgeon who was instrumental in the formation of plastic surgery as a field of medicine, created an "abdominal flap" procedure in 1916.[8] This most popular technique creates a "suitcase handle" attached at both ends to the abdomen and eventually released on one end.

Surgeons struggled with two functional difficulties presented by phallic reconstruction—urinary and sexual. Hoopes (1969) reported that, in the 1940s, Frumkin, Maltz, and Gilles all tried various means for constructing a urethra that would not be eaten away by the toxicity of urine. The problem of producing a phallus that could become rigid enough for sexual intercourse and flaccid for everyday life remains unsolved. Various attempts from 1940 onward have included rib cartilage grafts and synthetic materials. Preservation of sensation for FTMs was improved by the use of the enlarged clitoris as the "peg" upon which the phallus is constructed (Munawar 1957).

Scrotum was first grafted for men in 1957 by Gilles. As late as 1969, Hoopes wrote about FTMs: "utilization of the labia majora would seem an appropriate procedure . . . however they do not provide tissue of sufficient bulk to construct an acceptable scrotum" (Hoopes 1969, 344). More recently, techniques have been developed for expanding the labial tissue and inserting saline implants not unlike the procedures for female breast augmentation.

Reconstruction or Cosmetic Surgery?

Kathy Davis writes that plastic surgery became more oriented to *cosmetic* improvements than to its original goals of *reconstruction*. Cosmetic surgery, from rhinoplasty to breast augmentation, has been questioned from the start because of the moral problem of judging beauty.

Since standards of beauty are considered conventional, rather than immutable, the choice to pursue cosmetic surgery has been considered suspect.

Reconstructive surgeries were not morally problematic in this way. Especially because many of the reconstructive surgeries discussed above were related to illness, war, or industrial accidents, these procedures and the patients who wanted them were considered morally innocent in a way that cosmetic procedures and patients were not.

Cosmetic surgery was considered a voluntary procedure that was merely motivated by psychological unhappiness with one's appearance in the world. This discontent was a mind problem that needed to be addressed psychologically. Just as the psychologists considered transvestic inversion to be a mind problem, cosmetic requests indicated an unhealthy mental adjustment to a physical reality. Reconstructive surgeries, by contrast, were not considered voluntaristic or vain. They were mandated, instead, by disobedient bodies that were unhealthy to the patient. This illness model located the problem in the body in order to justify medical intervention within its proper domain of action.

From the start, cosmetic surgeries were more popular among women than among men (Davis 1995). Reconstructive surgeries were developed in response to industrial and war-time activities, which affected more men than women. There is not only a moral distinction between reconstructive and cosmetic surgeries, but also a gendered distinction between them. In light of these distinctions, it is unsurprising that nascent FTMs invoked the reconstructive, rather than the cosmetic, logic of treatment. In order to obtain surgeries while minimizing the stigma attached to their lives, nascent FTMs sank their problems deep into their flesh.

In ethnographic interviews, FTMs uniformly use the language of reconstruction to discuss the procedures they want or have had. For example, instead of "mastectomy," they say they had "chest reconstruction surgery." Instead of a "sex change," they had a "sex confirmation" surgery that *repaired* their bodies in much the same way as a man might have a reconstructive surgery after an industrial accident or a war. By positioning themselves as innocent accidents of nature, they located their problems in their bodies and deferred the stigma associated with voluntary surgery. This made them treatable bodies, like other men who were heroic and manly victims deserving of medical attention.

Conclusions

The history of the emergence of an FTM subject position is the history of the "proliferation of perversions" in the twentieth century.[9] Inversion, a category that referred to both gender/sex and sexual "deviance," split into discrete categories, each with its own diagnosis and logic of treatment. Endocrinology played a crucial role in this process. The growth and legitimacy of this field were established by studying the normal and pathological effects of "internal secretions" on sexual characteristics.

Some scholars of transsexualism have suggested that medical gatekeepers forced transsexuals to develop a purely strategic justification that deceived physicians in order to gain access to hormones and surgeries.[10] While transsexuals had to marshal new discourses in order to make themselves recognizable as transsexuals, this was not a purely tactical claim. Though some transsexuals have instrumentalized the logic of treatment in order to qualify for treatments, chapters three and four present evidence these FTMs have written this story not only for that instrumental purpose, but also for their own sense of themselves. For example, the belief that they have a hidden male physiology, a chromosome out of place, or a hormonal imbalance, is not only instrumental, but also provides a narrative that makes sense of their identities. As much as these claims substantiate the logic of treatment and provide a rhetorical justification for treatments, they also represent FTMs' attempts to theorize the circumstances that confront them, to put their enigmatic existence into words, and to relieve themselves of the constant queries about who and what they are.

The development of a differential diagnosis for transsexualism helped to constitute an FTM subject position, but identities are not reducible to their diagnoses, nor to the discourses of the medical and psychological experts who have treated these bodies. George Chauncey writes:

> [I]t would be wrong to assume, I think, that doctors created and de-
> fined the identities of "inverts" and "homosexuals" at the turn of the
> century, that people uncritically internalized the new medical mod-
> els. . . . Such assumptions attribute inordinate power to ideology as
> an autonomous social force . . . they belie the evidence of *preexisting
> subcultures and identities* contained in the literature itself (Chauncey
> 1989a, 87–88).[11]

The same can be said of the emergence of female-to-male transsexualism. While there is considerable value in a genealogy of medical
discourses, the emergence and consolidation of an FTM identity cannot be reduced to the development of a diagnosis without simultaneously reducing these subjects to "medical dupes."[12]

Because of the interdependence of transsexuals and their medical
care providers, the tendency to overemphasize the role of the doctors is
not easy to resist. However, because transsexualism is both more and
less than a medical condition, history must also acknowledge the subcultural discourses that contributed to the production and mainte-
nance of these identities. Therefore, it is necessary to examine the tension between male-identified inverts and the subcultural discourse of
the lesbian-feminist revolution during the 1970s.

Chapter 2

Border Wars: Lesbian and Transsexual Identity

■ Early data on transsexualism indicated that it was an overwhelmingly male disease. By a significant margin, there were more biological males who identified as women than biological females who identified as men. From 1940 to 1970, reports ranged from a two-to-one ratio (Randell 1959) to an eight-to-one ratio (Benjamin 1966). The most commonly cited data claimed a ratio of four-to-one.[1] Scientists and scholars have persistently sought out the meaning of these uneven numbers. Psychiatrist Leslie Lothstein addresses this question in one of the first book-length treatments of FTM transsexualism:

> Not only do researchers in different countries disagree, but there is also disagreement among researchers working together in the same clinic. Some of the confusion and disagreement may stem from the fact that gender clinics tend to have their own unique identities. . . . Richard Green et al (1969) has also documented the fact that transsexuals are viewed negatively by the medical profession, and many female transsexuals may avoid reputable gender programs in hospitals for fear of being stigmatized. . . . In sum there are no currently available reliable data of female transsexualism (Lothstein 1983, 310).

For Lothstein, the ratio differential may be interpreted as a problem of medical culture. The reason for the sex discrepancies among transsexuals is the lack of standard definitions of FTM transsexualism. This explanation of the different attitudes toward medicalization among transsexuals has some merit. However, it assumes that FTMs have always existed somewhere "out there" as fully constituted subjects. This positivism does not concern itself with the formation of an FTM identity. Nor does it take into account how subjects construct identities using historically specific categories.

Lothstein's interpretation reflects some of the diagnostic chaos discussed in chapter one. However, it still relies on the positivist assumption of a unique type of individual that can be properly classified once a standard definition is in place.

By 1970, it was widely accepted that the ratios were narrowing. Sexologists and cultural critics tried to make sense of this demographic shift: Dr. John Money, heralded expert in the field, suggested that "during the early seventies, almost as many women [sic] as men [sic] [were] seeking surgery" (Raymond 1979, 25). The 1970s are considered by medical practitioners to be a "boom" time for FTMs, but they are often at a loss to explain why this is. The sudden increase in the number of FTMs is the subject of this chapter.

The rates between MTFs and FTMs narrowed in the 1970s, not because of changes in the MTF population, but because of an increase of the number of FTMs. Therefore, to explain this rise in the numbers of female-to-male transsexuals, one must examine the conditions specific to the FTM side of the ratio. The rise in the numbers of FTMs in the 1970s is the unintended consequence of identity work in the lesbian community. Over the course of that decade, internal debates about the essence of lesbian identity helped to sharpen the lines of demarcation between woman-identified female bodies and male-identified female bodies. This distinction consolidated a lesbian-feminist identity that could sustain a burgeoning feminist movement and at the same time contributed to the consolidation of an FTM identity.

The consolidation of a female-to-male transsexual identity was a secondary product of the formation of the revolutionary subject of second-wave North American feminism, the "woman-identified woman." This revolutionary subject was created by obscuring important differences between heterosexual women and lesbians. These differences were class-based and gender specific.

In forming this revolutionary subject, as with all identity formation, something fell outside of its boundaries. This revolutionary *excess*
consolidated itself as female-to-male transsexualism, giving male-
identified individuals another subject position to inhabit. The significant rise in the numbers of female-to-male transsexuals and the narrowing gap between MTFs and FTMs in the 1970s were more than
merely coincidental with the formation of the feminist revolutionary
subject. Though much of this history has been presented in the context of sexuality studies, the implications of these border conflicts for
gender identification has been studied only peripherally.[2]

Becoming Woman-Identified Women

> I have been crossdressing to some extent since age 12 (I am now 34).
> I also came out as a lesbian around the same time. Most of the lesbi-
> ans I met at that time told me not to play the "male" role even though
> I felt more comfortable that way. They told me roles weren't neces-
> sary anymore and I could just be myself. The problem was (is) that I
> did (do) not know what that meant. I guess what I'm asking is how did
> any of you decide that your gender identity was male rather than fe-
> male? And why did you not decide that you were lesbian? . . . I have so
> many questions and I don't really know how to ask them or who to
> ask. I have never felt comfortable with my female body but I am not
> sure having a male body is the answer. How do I know? (Derek, in
> *FTM International Newsletter* 1993, 7).

When Derek came out in 1971, lesbian culture was at a crossroads.
"Old gay life," the time prior to the lesbian-feminist revolution, had
revolved around bar cultures and butch/femme gender roles. This life
was now being challenged and lesbian-feminism was becoming hegemonic. Borders that determined who counted as a "true" lesbian were
changed by second-wave feminism. The effects of this shift on people
like Derek were far-reaching. Derek was told to just be "herself." This
seemingly simple thing to achieve became, paradoxically, Derek's
ambition for twenty-two years and counting. In the context of this
lesbian-feminist world, stripping away all facade and transparently "be-

ing yourself" meant doing away with all gendered roles, especially butch and femme, that had previously provided structure to particular lesbian worlds. The question that motivated Derek to write to this transsexual/transgender newsletter in 1993 is what one should do when cross-dressing and male identification are a central part of the self that is now commanded to express itself in ungendered terms. Derek's situation begs the question of the relationship between identities and communities. The lesbian-feminist scene of the early 1970s dictated the limits of a lesbian identity: be yourself, unless you happen to be a male-identified cross dresser. What was the horizon of possible responses that Derek could have chosen from to satisfy this self-thematizing imperative? Is Derek a lesbian or a transsexual, and how does he know it? How do we know it?

The Lavender Menace

In May 1970, at the Second Congress to Unite Women, Rita Mae Brown and the Radicalesbians rushed the stage in what been recorded as the Lavender Menace Zap, forcing a confrontation between lesbians and heterosexual feminists. The Second Congress has also been referred to as the "Congress to Divide Women" (Echols 1989, 214) because of the hostilities toward mainstream housewives that emerged within the women's movement. One woman, anonymously quoted in the alternative magazine *The Rat*, summarized the flavor of the Congress: "They should call it Congress to Unite White, Middle-class Women" ("Women's Liberation" 1970). Class privilege and heterosexism were two of the most contested issues throughout the weekend. The Radicalesbians forced the Congress to face the secrecy and homophobia that had been a source of tension. The confrontational nature of the Lavender Menace Zap effectively brought these issues into the open and the Congress responded by passing lesbian-friendly resolutions.[3]

A new definition of lesbian identity resulted from this and similar conflicts. The history of the Lesbian Menace Zap is presented here as just one episode in a dense web of socially mediated relationships and was not the only means of effecting the shifts in the borders of lesbian identity. The Congress is being privileged only as a hermeneutic tool, not as the sole causal moment of these changes. Examining this moment can illuminate some of the mechanisms by which lesbians were hegemonically constructed as "woman-identified" and transsexuals were hegemonically constructed as "male-identified."

The Lavender Menace Zap is ubiquitously noted and valorized in historical accounts of women's liberation.[4]

> On May 1st, at 7:15 p.m. about 300 women were quietly sitting in the auditorium, waiting for the Congress to Unite Women to come to order. The lights went out, people heard running, laughter, a rebel yell here and there, and when those lights were turned back on, those same 300 women found themselves in the hands of the LAVENDER MENACE ("Women's Liberation" 1970, 12).

The Menaces wore purple T-shirts, self-stenciled with their reclaimed name, first bestowed upon them by Betty Friedan. Friedan claimed that the lesbians within the women's movement were a "menace" to it, a "lavender herring" that gave the media and the public an easy reason to dismiss the women's movement. They passed out copies of their now canonical essay, "The Woman-Identified-Woman," and spoke informally from the stage about being women who loved women in a culture that was both heterosexist and patriarchal.

This event has been considered a singularly important moment in the "lesbian-feminist revolution."[5] Lesbians began to stand up and counter popular myths about their lives. Their goal was acceptance in the women's movement and in the larger society. The Congress, not the Stonewall riots, has been represented as the birth of the Lesbian Nation.[6] By denying the participation of butches at Stonewall and by locating the Congress to Unite Women as the moment when lesbianism dared to speak its name, historians of lesbianism are making claims about who counts as a lesbian and what counts as rebellion. Though this is the dominant narrative of lesbian-feminism, it is not the only story that can be told about lesbians in this historical moment. There were other portions of the women's movement and other lesbian communities that treated one another differently.

However, this type of interchange between lesbians and feminists was most common. Therefore, it is important to ask who the partici-

pants at the Congress were and how they reached a mutual understanding. What had precluded their alliance up until the Congress and
what were the effects of the alliance once it had taken root? What can
this tell us about the "nature" of lesbians as it was understood by cultural participants in 1970? Most important for the study of the consolidation of an FTM transsexual identity, what were the secondary
effects of this alliance on those who no longer fit into the category of
"female homosexual"?

The Lavender Menace Zap found a means of uniting an increasingly factionalized women's movement. This new alliance was founded
on a reconstructed version of lesbianism that quickly became hegemonic. This "new and improved" lesbianism became the vanguard of
feminism. Historian Lillian Faderman narrates, "Developing along-
side of that revolution of gays was the other revolution of young women
who loved other women and wished to make a political statement out
of their love but denied that they were 'gay.' They insisted on being
called lesbian-feminist" (Faderman 1991, 205). The lesbian feminists
were "women who loved other women," and they distinguished
themselves from gays. "Gay" referred to male homosexuals, or to
women who were still living "old gay life."[7] This distinction between
"old gays" and lesbian-feminists hinged on matters of class and gender
identity.

The second wave of twentieth-century North American feminism
developed in the late 1960s out of a culture already buckling under a
multi-front assault. Civil rights struggles and a sexual revolution, ho-
mophile and counter-cultural rebellions, Black Power movements and
Gay Liberation, drugs and anti-war youth resistance all fertilized the
landscape that bore the fruit of feminism.[8] Many women who participated in these movements reported that the sexism and misogyny that
characterized the parent culture of the 1950s and 1960s were just as
prevalent in the early struggles against it.[9] Great increases in levels of
education for women, coupled with the limited career options after
graduation, created a body of women dissatisfied with their life oppor-
tunities. The women who revived the dormant feminist tradition have
been demographically categorized as being institutionally educated at
colleges and universities, in their middle to late twenties, just starting

to make their own decisions about their futures, white, and middle class with liberal, but not radical, backgrounds.[10]

The early feminist activism of these women was subject to harsh criticism from families and friends, comrades and colleagues. The methods employed to deter the "women's libbers" may seem predictable, but at first they confounded the feminists. Ti-Grace Atkinson recalls her early confusion at the slanderous jeers of "lesbianism":

> Men have been countering all accusations of injustice toward women with the charge that these accusations were being made by "just a bunch of lesbians." For the first year, I couldn't understand the connection. . . . It would bounce off me, without comprehension, and fall to the ground (Atkinson 1974, 83).

Two things are immediately apparent from Atkinson's recollections. First, lesbian-feminism, now thought to be a completely natural alliance, is a product of an elaborate process that bound the two together. Prior to the 1970s, though they were conflated in the eyes of outside observers, feminism and lesbianism shared no political or moral agenda.[11] The creation of this alliance was an achievement, not a natural bond. In order to achieve it, a common terrain had to be carved out. This was the eventual outcome of the Lavender Menace Zap and their article, "The Woman-Identified-Woman." Second, Atkinson and other heterosexual women tried to neutralize the lesbian menace by distancing themselves and denying the existence of lesbians in the movement. Rita Mae Brown, as a vocal young lesbian, writes about her initial experiences with a member of N.O.W./NY:

> I questioned her on the Lesbian issue and she bluntly told me that the word Lesbian was never uttered. "After all, that is exactly what the press wants to say we are, a bunch of lesbians." She then went on to patronizingly say, "What are you doing worrying about Lesbians, you must have lots of boyfriends." Okay, sister, have it your way (Brown 1976, 126).

As described in *Sappho was a Right-On Woman* by Sidney Abbott and Barbara Love, "The Lesbian issue would never have been forced out into the open without the initial persistence of an attractive and fiery young woman named Rita Mae Brown" (Abbott and Love 1972, 111). In January of 1970, Brown and two other women resigned from N.O.W./NY in protest of the "middle class club women [who were] not ready to think about issues of race, sexual preference or their own class privilege" (112). Brown went on to form the Radicalesbians.

> Their meeting was historic in that it was the first meeting of radical young Lesbians without gay men, the first time Gay Liberation Front women had met with Lesbians from the women's movement, and the first time Lesbians from the women's movement had met each other as Lesbians. One woman remarked later, with tears in her eyes, that it was the first time she had met other Lesbians "in the light" outside a Mafia bar (113).

It was through this group of women from cross-sections of the white women's movement that the issue of lesbians was finally addressed. The Radicalesbians collectively penned the groundbreaking essay, "The Woman-Identified-Woman," and immediately decided that it would be the centerpiece of their demonstration as the Lavender Menaces at the Second Congress to Unite Women. Jennifer Woodul, a Vassar undergraduate who had been active in the many mini-zaps that Brown had organized, remembers the genesis of the phrase "woman-identified-woman" which became the name and central ideology of the revolutionary lesbian-feminist of the 1970s.

> I was there when the ideas for "Woman-Identified-Woman" were beginning to take shape. We were trying to figure out how to tell women about lesbianism without using the word lesbian, because *we found that at these conferences we kept freaking people out all the time.* And I believe it was Cynthia [Funk] who came up with this term, "woman-identified." At least, that was the first time I had ever heard it. So what we were trying to do was make women realize that *lesbians were not so different from other women in any sort of strange way* (Woodul, in Echols 1989, 216; emphasis added).

The phrase "woman-identified" could be turned in many directions. It could refer to one's gender identity ("I am a woman") or to one's political alliances ("I place my political allegiance to women above all others"). When, however, these two meanings were combined in the phrase "woman-identified women," there were troubling consequences for any subject whose gender identity was male (including both male-bodied men and female-bodied gender inverts), as well as for any subject whose gender was in line with patriarchal notions of womanhood (femme lesbian, feminine, and heterosexual women).

Before Brown left N.O.W., she made efforts to convince them that she was a normal and moral young woman. Her womanhood substantiated her normality.

> One women jumped up and declared that Lesbians want to be men and that N.O.W. only wants real women. After about one hour of being the group freak and diligently probed, poked and studied, these ladies bountiful decided that, yes, I was human. Yes, I did resemble a young woman in her early twenties. (I had long hair and was in a skirt.) (Brown 1976, 127).

Brown realized that the women at N.O.W. assumed all lesbians were the rough and tumble working-class butches from the bar scene.[12] To dispel their middle-class apprehensions Brown told them that butches were not immoral or abnormal, but had simply identified with their oppressors to gain the privileges of men in a patriarchal society.

> There are good reasons why many Lesbians have no political consciousness of woman oppression. [It] is the other side of the male-identified coin; heterosexual women live through their men and thereby identify with them, gaining heavy privilege; some Lesbians assume a male role and thereby become male identified (Brown 1976, 131).

Despite Brown's own working-class history and her continuing struggle against class privilege in and out of the women's movement, she disavowed the legitimacy of the working-class butch culture. This model charged male-identified bar dykes with false consciousness. This fit smoothly with middle-class conceptions of the working classes as uncultured and in need of political tutoring. The collusion of feminist ideologies and the middle-class tendency to infantilize laborers provided a coherent, but ultimately invert-phobic and class-bound, explanation for the butch phenomenon.

As an alternative to this male-identified lesbianism, the Radi-calesbians posited the lesbian-feminist. The "Woman-Identified-Woman" essay rhetorically posed the question "What is a lesbian?" and the answer became the bridge between heterosexual feminists and feminist lesbians: "A lesbian is the rage of all women condensed to the point of explosion" (Radicalesbians 1970, 6). In the essay, one key element defines the essence of lesbianism; a lesbian is an independent woman. The straight female readers of "The Woman-Identified-Woman" were exhorted to stop "laying a surrogate male role on the lesbian. . . . For women, especially those in the movement, to perceive their Lesbian sisters through this male grid of role definitions is to accept this male cultural conditioning and to oppress their sisters" (7). Translation: lesbians are not virile butches lurking at feminist meet-ings, spotting their sexual prey to devour at any moment of vulnerabil-ity. Lesbians are your sisters.

The Dinosaurs

In order to make a space for lesbians to work with heterosexual femi-nists, the Radicalesbians

> redefined lesbianism as the quintessential act of political solidarity with other women. By defining lesbianism as a political choice rather than as a sexual alternative Radicalesbians disarmed heterosexual crit-ics. . . . [But b]y presenting lesbianism as the political solution to women's oppression, and by invoking essentialist ideas about female sexuality, lesbian-feminists managed to sanitize lesbianism (Echols 1989, 217–18).

According to historians of lesbianism and feminism such as Joan Nestle and Alice Echols, this strategic reconfiguration of lesbianism had dev-astating consequences for "old gays" who had developed a specific cul-ture of lesbian *sexuality* structured by butch and femme identities. This unique form of sexual expression was characterized by two polar posi-tions that fed each other symbiotically in a persistent cycle of desire. The butch was the aggressor who knew how to pleasure her partner. It was the femme's responsiveness to her touch that provided her with her own source of sexual satisfaction. The femme was the woman who

knew what she wanted and found ways of getting her butch to give it
to her.[13]

While much has been made of the *desexualizing* effects of the
woman-identified model of lesbianism,[14] much less attention has been
paid to the inadvertent effects of this reconstructed lesbianism on the
gender identity of old-style female homosexuals.[15] The effects of lesbian-feminism were felt doubly by "old gay" butches and femmes. It
turned sexual contact between two women into merely a secondary
criterion for lesbianism, producing the new phenomenon of the "political lesbian." The severe criticisms that the woman-identified model
leveled against gendered role-playing had a more specific effect on old
gay life. Butches and femmes were seen as self-loathing and falsely conscious—the former for male-identified dress and behavior, the latter
for their pursuit of patriarchally defined beauty and style, as well as for
their supposed weakness. Butch and femme roles were part of the
working-class bar culture and did not carry the same significance in
middle-class or even upwardly mobile circles, so the sanctions against
role-playing had their deepest impact on working-class lesbians.[16]

The Congress was also a site where conflicts over the meaning of
lesbian identity were played out in terms of class struggle. Pam Kearon,
a member of the Class Workshop, which had also staged an opening
night disruption of the Congress, recalls that "in the aftermath of the
second Congress, women would say to her, 'the lesbians are so full of
love and you [the women of the Class Workshop] are so full of hatred'"
(Echols 1989, 219). Somehow, the Lavender Menaces and their
"Woman-Identified-Woman" leaflet had managed to find common,
non-threatening grounds of identity with heterosexual feminists. The
open hostility engendered by the Class Workshop at the same conference is one sign that this alliance was built upon exclusionary class
practices.

The majority of the discussions about class were quickly limited
to leadership questions. The media blitz was making celebrities out of
some of the more educated and middle-class feminists. The Class Workshop tried to demonstrate the ways that this reproduced the class divi-
sions within the movement. While this led to ingenious, though somewhat ineffective strategies for redistributing power in the movement

(Freeman 1973, 286), it also shifted the terms of the discourse away from class differences toward leadership and status elitism. The open hostilities toward the women of the Class Workshop at the Second Congress represented both a real resistance to the issues of class differences within the women's movement and an expression of their escaped class anxiety about the newly formulated lesbian identity.

These definitional battles were far from being settled at the Congress. Lesbians from the Daughters of Bilitis of New York still had to defend themselves from insults made by the prominent feminist Susan Brownmiller. Brownmiller had been invited to speak to the D.O.B. convention in New York, but according to Brownmiller's feminist cosmology, these lesbians did not yet qualify as full sisters. She wrote the organizers a letter decrying butch and femme roles. Abbott and Love sum up Brownmiller's sentiments: "Gay women had made passes at her, she said; they were overconcerned with sex and were generally oppressive in their maleness. Come and march with us if and when you want to, she continued, but our fight is not the same. You have bought the sex roles we are leaving behind." The lesbians were eager to demonstrate their feminist stripes and the more radical among them refused to be categorized in such a "backward" fashion. They "were incensed. Role-playing was a vanishing part of Lesbian life, they felt, disappearing much faster than the roles in heterosexual life" (Abbott and Love 1972, 117). While acknowledging butch and femme roles as part of "old gay life," they claimed that these roles were endangered dinosaurs. Like the extinction of actual dinosaurs, or of any species, this process was not merely one of "natural selection." Instead, it was the result of active relationships between the endangered "old gays" and their environment. These events represent the visible points of identity formation. The creation of the revolutionary subject was simultaneous with the production of a revolutionary excess: the male-identified-traitor-to-the-cause.

Even practices of inclusion, such as the forming of the relationship between lesbianism and feminism, can have an exclusionary effect. Although this new version of lesbianism became hegemonic, it did not fully eradicate the dinosaurs from the previous era. The responses male-identified subjects had to this lesbian-feminist revolution were varied. The woman-identified woman was now the hegemonic definition of lesbianism. Male-identified, female-bodied subjects had to find new ways to make sense of their lives.

The woman-identified woman was something that had to be actively created. She went on to sustain the political agenda of the decade. She was the woman who nursed and supported the battered women at the shelters. She womanned phone lines at the crisis hotline and walked in the demonstrations. She went off to live and farm on the land with her sisters. She opened the women's spaces, those restaurants, cafés, and other entrepreneurial endeavors that sprung up around the nation. She filled the pages of theory and the classrooms at universities. She made art and made love. The story of these achievements cannot be told without acknowledging these earlier moments when the pressures from outsiders and enemies threatened the movement. Realizing the danger of these external forces, the most prescient among the activists cultivated the similarities between lesbians and heterosexual women. For this, they relied upon their common female-bodied experiences—their womanhood. This sameness provided a seemingly stable and coherent basis for political action. However, one of the side effects of this internal stability was the devaluation of previously honorable members of "old gay life."

Climbing *The Ladder*, Riding *The Tide*

Shortly after the Second Congress to Unite Women, *The Ladder,* the longest circulating publication of the modern lesbian world, announced to its readers that the magazine was changing its editorial focus.

> The most fundamental and far-reaching of all social upheavals, the women's revolution has begun. . . . With this issue THE LADDER, now in its 14th year, is no longer a minority publication. It stands squarely with all women, that majority of human beings that has known oppression longer than anyone (Laporte 1970b, 4).

In her piece for this issue, "Women's Liberation Catches up to *The Ladder,*" Gene Damon opens this new era by commenting on the similarities between the first cover of the new feminist magazine *Up from*

Under and one of the earliest covers of *The Ladder,* both of which represent a queen from a deck of cards. For Damon,

> this points out a significant fact: that women must band together, all women, or human freedom as dreamed of by all men and women, heterosexual and homosexual alike will never be possible. . . . Our cover, we feel, also points out how little separated Lesbians are from women as a total group (Damon 1970, 4).

In 1974, a Los Angeles lesbian publication decided to remove the word "lesbian" from its title and rename itself *The Tide.* The editorial board wanted to reach more women and felt that the word "lesbian" prevented fearful potential readers from purchasing *The Lesbian Tide.* What precipitated these changes at both magazines, and how did the readership respond? Was this change more than superficial? Did it go beyond editorial announcements and cover art? What do these changes tell us about the members of the movement that claimed these two magazines as their soapbox? Who were the new readers of *The Ladder* and *The Tide?* The readers of *The Ladder* were enthusiastic and unquestioning about the change to their magazine; there was an immediate and severely negative response to the decision at *The Tide.* What is the significance of this difference? Finally, to what extent do these two cases represent the spectrum of community responses to the alliance between lesbianism and feminism?

The Ladder

In the four issues prior to the new lesbian-feminist *Ladder* there was a sudden increase in the number of articles that addressed the relationship between lesbian life and the feminist political agenda. The magazine became a forum for debating the advantages and disadvantages of joining the feminist movement. In "Out from Under the Rocks—with Guns," Leslie Springvine begins to make the connections that would eventually resonate in the lecture halls at the Second Congress.

> For the sake of her own skin [the lesbian] had better discard any feeling of aloofness and give the women's rights movement all she's got, shoulder to shoulder with her heterosexual sisters. In this one effort

she should forget personalities, forget that she is a lesbian, and remember only The Enemy—the White American Male (Springvine
1969/1970, 10).

Springvine argues that the lesbian is socially and economically better
positioned than heterosexual women for this fight. She has no ties to
family, father, husband, or children. She has already been supporting
herself on a woman's income in a family wage system. However,
Springvine states that this support must be unilateral: "It is unrealistic
to expect the organization [N.O.W. in particular, women's liberation
in general] to identify with the Lesbian to the extent of publicly back-
ing the Lesbian fight. That would give the public one more weapon,
and a lethal one . . . with which to fight the organization" (10). She
adds that she views women's issues as distinct from all other concerns
such as race or class. She writes, "I think *any other issue* should be
incidental to a clear-cut fight for women's rights. The rights of any and
all Negro women, for instance, should be the concern of NOW, but
only because they are women and not because they are Negroes" (11).
She claims that non-professional and non-college women would be
frightened away by the presence of out lesbians because she assumes
that all lesbians are from the middle-class and that all laborers are un-
prepared to deal with lesbians. Finally, Springvine suggests that it is for
the safety of all lesbians that the closet door remain closed in hostile
organizations such as N.O.W.

The next issue of *The Ladder* included a response to these claims
from the D.O.B./SF chapter president Rita Laporte.

> Leslie Springvine's article might better be called STAY UNDER THE
> ROCKS. Traditionally a woman was expected to help everyone but
> herself. Is this requirement henceforth to be limited to the Lesbian?
> . . . I am not saying that Lesbians should desert NOW. This network
> of undercover agents is, under present societal conditions both wise
> and useful. But I would wish that every Lesbian understand that DOB
> is her best hope and that DOB welcomes ALL Women. . . . I appreci-
> ate Leslie's concern about frightening off the little housewives of NOW.
> But even if NOW could cleanse itself of all Lesbian impurities and
> maintain total silence with DOB, this would not prevent men from

> screaming Lesbian. Nor need this be a lethal weapon. When men hurl
> what they fancy to be devastating epithets women should accept them
> with wild enthusiasm. Why of course all of us NOW women are Les-
> bians, so patent an absurdity that this "lethal weapon" fizzles into a
> joke (Laporte 1970a, 3).

Laporte criticizes the easy kowtowing to the lesbian-baiters. She urges
all women to embrace lesbian sisterhood. Laporte does not anticipate
the wave of new lesbian converts that appears to have been the product
of this strategy.[17] Instead, her strategy is based on an absurdly obvious
difference between the two communities. This contrasts with
Springvine's strategy, which is intended to eradicate the differences
between lesbians and feminists in order to build a united front. Laporte,
a butch, was invested in such differences. She saw that these differences could be effectively used against lesbian-baiting.

Masculinity stood out as one of the key differences between the
feminist and lesbian communities. In response to the political opponents of feminism and the moral opponents of lesbians, lesbians at *The
Ladder* reexamined their formal and informal membership requirements. Butch identity was increasingly discredited. In her essay, "Confessions of a Pseudo-Male Chauvinist," Martha Shelley, a former member of the Gay Liberation Front, sought absolution for her sins as a
male-identified woman.

> After I became involved with Women's Liberation, I began to notice
> something about myself that embarrassed me, I didn't really like
> women. In bed, yes—but all my friends were men. In rejecting the
> woman's role, from knitting to cooking to wearing mascara, I had also
> rejected women. In short, I was a pseudo-male chauvinist. . . . By iden-
> tifying with the male oppressor class, I didn't become male or get any
> more privileges than other women. . . . Now before you go around
> beating yourself over the head for being a pseudo-male chauvinist, or
> even worse, button-holing some other woman and accusing her of
> the same, remember that most of our sisters haven't had too many
> choices (Shelley 1970, 18–19).

Unfortunately, Shelley's good advice to refrain from flogging butches
for their male-identification was not heeded by members of lesbian-

feminist communities. As Derek's letter at the start of this chapter indicates, butches were routinely admonished in the name of feminism to give up those identities that seemed most natural to them. Masculinity was increasingly demonized and equated with sexism. The growing significance of this issue is reflected in the titles of many articles that ran in *The Ladder* soon after the switch to its lesbian-feminist orientation: "The Woman-Identified-Woman," "Can Woman Unite?" and "The Butch-Femme Question."

This last essay, also written by Laporte, criticizes the anti-butch/femme trend in stark language. Laporte criticizes feminists who were new to lesbianism and had found their way to the life over the "woman-identified" bridge.

> In their new found Lesbianism they proclaim butch-femme must go. They are hopelessly confusing the heterosexual relationship per se with its almost universal tendency to be a master/slave relationship and then to transfer this reprehensible aspect of heterosexuality over into Lesbianism. . . . It is very bad that they are assuming that all old patterns of living and loving are wrong. The mutual love of a butch and femme is a very old pattern, and for some of us, the happiest (Laporte 1971, 7–8).

This bold counter-argument was rarely defended as the new feminist construction of "lesbian" became hegemonic.

The (Lesbian) Tide

In 1973, a regular columnist for *The Lesbian Tide* made the following humorous commentary on the trends she observed in lesbian-feminism. Radical Rita Right-On prefaces her piece by writing: "The following is a partial transcription of a meeting I attended last week. I felt it was very important, so I am printing it instead of my usual column on advanced political theory."

> CHAIR: The general meeting of the Radical Revolutionary Anti-racist, Anti-capitalist, Anti-imperialist, Anti-discrimination, Anti-smog [it was L.A.] Lesbian Feminists will come to order. [Today's meeting is devoted to] a discussion of the topic: How do we reach the masses? . . . The chair recognizes Susan Savedwoman.

SUSAN SAVEDWOMAN: [T]he name of our group. It turns a lot of new people off, and most don't even come at all. For example, a lot of bar people don't like the word "Lesbian." They prefer the word "gay." I propose we make a change.

CHAIR: That's a very good idea . . . [after much democratic posturing] The name of our group has been changed to the Radical, Revolutionary, Anti-racist, Anti-imperialist Gay Feminists.

NANCY NOTTASLAVE: Yes, I think our problem is that we ignore new people who come to this meeting. . . . I see two new women sitting over in the corner who haven't said anything at all. . . . I'd like to hear from them: why they're here and what they'd like to see this group do.

NEW PERSON: My name's Nicki and my old lady, Suzie, and I thought we'd come and see if you guys can help us out. I got fired yesterday from my job as foreman at a factory because they found out I'm gay, and I want to know what I can do to fight it.

FRANCES FREEDOM: You do have a problem, but more than you think. First off, calling your lover, "old lady" is very sexist and monogamous. Secondly, we are not "guys" we are women. And thirdly, you couldn't have been a foreMAN because you're a woman. Now what were you saying?

NICKI: What? Oh. . . . I was saying I want someone to help me get my job back. . . . Look, I need a job to pay the rent NOW. If you don't want to help, we're splitting now.

FRANCES FREEDOM: Suzie—wait! Don't leave with Nicki. Don't you realize she oppresses you?

CHAIR: Order please! Let them leave. They obviously have no consciousness. Now who has some other ideas on how we can reach out to the masses? (Right-On 1973, 23–24).

The chairwoman's call for order is more than the exercise of Robert(a)'s Rules. This call represents a demand for the ordering of the bodies and identities in the field called the women's movement. Radical Rita describes the ways that this call for order excluded some of the members of the lesbian community. Nicki and Suzie are driven out of the meeting because of their roles and their false consciousness. They no longer fit the *order* of the lesbian community. The irony is in the depiction of a community of women expressing a desire to "reach out to the masses," while simultaneously driving out a working-class butch and femme. The staff of *The Lesbian Tide* was already witnessing the class and gender exclusions that were the consequence of the inclusionary practices of lesbian-feminism.

The (Lesbian) Tide had previously been the D.O.B./LA newsletter, but was cut free from this organization by its editor, Jeanne Cordova. Cordova influenced an eclectic staff of feminist femmes, bisexuals, former navy women, and anti-racist white women. In Cordova's words, *The (Lesbian) Tide* "helped me survive lesbian-feminism. . . . Somewhere in my gut I knew feminism both saved me and shoved me back into the closet. Feminism rescued women, but it subverted lesbianism" (Cordova 1992, 288). From its inception, *The (Lesbian) Tide* was a safe place for those who were too activist-oriented to fit neatly into the "old gay life" and too butch or femme to suit the new lesbian-feminist paradigm.

The (Lesbian) Tide ran articles that questioned the equation of lesbianism with feminist principles. For instance, in "Get in Straight," Rita Goldberger reviews a recent community event, the Gay-Straight Dialogue, she attended. Goldberger calls the discussion a success because it helped participants feel better about each other and come to a mutual understanding, but asks, at what expense?

> I felt that I had been involved in justifying my lesbianism through feminism which resulted in insulting the straight women and in not supporting non-feminist gay women. . . . I felt that the reason no one challenged the straight women was because of an unspoken belief that runs through the mind of most feminist lesbians: that heterosexuality cannot be justified today by a feminist, and that loving other women is a necessary part of a feminist consciousness. [But i]f I "justify" my lesbianism through feminism—through the explanation of roleless, free relationships—does not this condemn my gay sisters who are not into feminism, many of whom are into roles? . . . Feminist movement or no feminist movement, I am gay, and stand with all my gay sisters in their choice to defy society and choose this alternative (Goldberger 1972, 7).

Goldberger was profoundly critical of the justification of lesbianism through feminism. She recognized that this justification could alienate heterosexual women from feminism and/or possibly exclude butches and femmes from lesbianism. Goldberger was acutely aware of the exclusionary counter-effects of these inclusionary practices. While Laporte was a minority voice of dissent at *The Ladder,* Goldberger's opinions were dominant at *The (Lesbian) Tide.* The staff writers at *The (Lesbian) Tide* recognized a need for feminism, but sought grounds on which they could make the alliance without sacrificing important aspects of their specific culture and members of the community who were part of "old gay life."

Though *The (Lesbian) Tide* was more wary of the pitfalls of the synthesis of lesbianism and feminism, it, like *The Ladder,* eventually declared itself a magazine with "Something for Everyone."[18] The decision at *The (Lesbian) Tide* followed within a year of another major conference, the first lesbian-feminist conference at UCLA. These meetings were as tense as the Second Congress to Unite Women had been. The dotted lines between woman-identified lesbians and male-identified others had become bold-faced borders.

These borders were structured and maintained by a relentless repression of unacceptable bodies and desires. At the conference in L.A., the new lesbian paradigm collided with the presence of a "being-with-a-penis," Beth Elliot, a male-to-female transsexual lesbian and entertainer from San Francisco (Forfreedom 1973, 4). From the journal of one of the organizers, reprinted in *The (Lesbian) Tide:*

> This woman is insisting that Beth Elliott not be permitted to perform because Beth is a transsexual. Beth was on the San Francisco steering committee for the conference, a part of the original group that gave birth to the idea. . . . She's written some far-out feminist songs. That's why she's here. No. We do not, cannot relate to her as a man. We have not known her as a man. "He tried to rape me four years ago! He is not a woman! He is not a lesbian!" . . . "You're wrong! She is a woman because she chooses to be a woman! What right do you have to define her sexuality?!" "He has a *prick* ! That makes him a man." . . . "That's bullshit! Anatomy is NOT destiny!" . . . There is a contradic-

tion here. Do we or do we not believe that anatomy is destiny? Just WHERE do we draw the line?

The Gutter Dykes call this "the most bizarre and dangerous co-optation of lesbian energy and emotion [they] can imagine." . . . Now I see The Gutter Dykes' objection to transsexuals is that they have or had been *socialized as men, male identified,* and therefore oppressive to women. Well what about the dykes who have been socialized as men, either by their families or that portion of the gay community which has (and had exclusively) in the past emulated straight society and its sex-role stereotyping? What about the former, and current BUTCHES? (journal entry 1973, 36–37).

The anonymous author of these passages questions the lesbian-feminist perspective on transsexuals. She points out that the principles of woman-identification cast out some community members as garbage undeserving of the love accorded to other sisters. Though the author does not mention female-to-male transsexuals, she makes a connection between the anxiety directed toward Beth Elliot, an infiltrator, and toward butch "traitors."

On the last day of the conference, a "sister spoke and said she had been planning to become a transsexual, female to male. But after being in a woman's consciousness raising group, she began to realize that 'she didn't have to be a man to be a human being.' She denounced transsexualism as both sexist and a rip-off" (Forfreedom 1973, 5). This woman found a niche for herself as a woman in the lesbian-feminist world. Others did not. In this context, transsexualism appears as a rejected route, one that should be discarded once a butch becomes woman-identified.

By 1973, border disputes over the relationships between lesbian-ism and feminism were far more settled. In L.A., there was less category confusion at the socio-cultural level, but still some confusion about how subjects would place themselves in relationship to these newly constituted identities.

Inhabiting an FTM Transsexual Identity

In 1970, an article by an FTM named Karl Ericsen appeared in *The Ladder.* Considered within the context of the early events of the women's liberation movement, Ericsen's testimony in "The Transsexual Experience" proved important to the consolidation of an FTM identity. Coinciding with the Lavender Menace Zap, Ericsen's essay does the kind of identity work that differentiated woman-identified lesbianism from male-identified transsexual identity. Reminiscent of Dr. Michael Dillon, he writes, "In every aspect of [the female-to-male transsexual's] life he is male except physically. He prefers and seeks male company and feels out of place with groups of females, is interested in male vocations and avocations and falls in love with females (usually heterosexual)" (Ericsen 1970, 25). These are the criteria that define transsexual men. Note that Ericsen's definition rests ultimately on an individual's own convictions that he is male-identified. "Something inside lets him know from the onset of conscious thinking that he is a male in the 'wrong suit of clothes'" (25).

Ericsen acknowledges the slippery quality of his definition, especially with regard to those Dillon termed "mannish" lesbians. In "old gay life," it was common for butch lesbians to claim that they had "got mixed up in the wrong body" (Davis and Kennedy 1993, 349). Transsexual men and lesbians share a history of childhood tomboy behavior, romping with the active boys in their neighborhoods, climbing trees, playing sports, and even claiming an identity as a boy in games or otherwise.[19] Ericsen also recognizes that many females, straight and gay alike, hold the belief that it is a man's world. Using similar phrasing, Blue Lunden, a butch lesbian who came out in the mid-1950s, recalls, "When I came out in the bars of the French Quarter, I was coming from a place of being mad as hell that I was a girl, because clearly it was a boy's world. Later on I was falling in love with other girls and thinking of myself as a man trapped in a woman's body" (Lunden 1980, 32).

Ericsen's ambition is to draw an unambiguous line between transsexuals and lesbians. To do so, he is compelled to find an unequivocal standard of judgment. He tries, therefore, to find unequivocal criteria. He offers several promising measures: a difficult sex life, stormy relationships or celibacy due to an alienation from the body, the experience of leading a dual life, and feelings of relief at the thought of radical mastectomy and hysterectomy. These surgical procedures are "very traumatic experience[s] to most females because it completely takes away any chance to procreate. A true transsexual could only come away elated and with no regrets" (26). Lastly, a strong internal conviction of manhood defines the transsexual, whereas "the lesbian always knows she is female. A transsexual is constantly at war unless a sex change can be obtained" (25).

Despite his attempts, Ericsen's criteria are far from definitive since each explanation could be emphatically applied to either transsexuals or to female homosexuals from "old gay life." In that period, stone butches, who never allowed their partners to touch them during sex, often experienced a far-reaching alienation from their bodies that precluded any direct sexual stimulation (Davis and Kennedy 1993, 209). An awareness of dual life permeated the pre-feminist, pre-Stonewall period. "Saturday night" butches had one set of friends, mannerisms, and clothes for their gay lives and another set that they used for their families, employers, and co-workers (Lynch 1985). Passing women kept their womanhood a secret from intimates and outsiders alike (Lyle 1970). The subjective experience of manhood was not uncommon among bar dykes from the working class. Furthermore, as feminism pointed out, not all women could be defined by a procreative imperative. Some women experience relief at the end of their reproductive careers. However, by 1970, it was clear that such experiences no longer fit the hegemonic model of female homosexuality.

Ericsen's article in the 1970 issue of *The Ladder* spotlighted the fault lines beneath the categories of sex, gender, sexuality, and class in the twentieth century. Ericsen's "The Transsexual Experience" represents a transition from a single deviant identity, the invert, to multiple deviant subjects, now determined by either sexual or sex/gender inversion. The rise in the numbers of FTMs during the 1970s is one result of this "proliferation of perversions" (Foucault 1980, 36–49). By the 1970s, FTMs had become much more clearly distinct from lesbians.

Confrontations with Identities-Under-Construction

The connection between the lesbian-feminist revolution and the consolidation of an FTM identity is illustrated again in the letters respond-
ing to Karl Ericsen's article. Three letters appear in the issue of *The
Ladder* following its appearance; each expresses a personal confrontation with nebulous identities-under-construction. Tommy and Beth
Baer write separate letters about their long relationship and the ways
that Tommy's gender identity structured their life choices. Tommy summarizes the experience:

> I can well understand [Ericsen's] feelings, and appreciate his wish to
> become a man. I would have done the same, had it been possible
> years ago. Of course, it wasn't, and I had no choice but to live as a
> female. . . . It is hard for me to say whether I would have the opera-
> tion if I were in my 20s today—knowing what I do, I suspect I would
> have it. . . . I still prefer masculine clothes, masculine occupations and
> the masculine role—such as it is. . . . The fact that I have found a con-
> genial life companion helps of course (T. Baer 1970, 45–46).

Tommy's gender identity is not evident; Beth refers to Tommy as a
woman and as "she," but Tommy avoids any grammatical opportuni-
ties for identification. Is Tommy a female homosexual? Tommy and
Beth are a long-term couple who read *The Ladder*, yet Tommy conjec-
tures that if a sex change had been available, their marriage might have
occurred sooner. What about Beth? Is she a lesbian or a heterosexual
woman? Though she carries the same last name as her lover, she also
forcefully argues, in a manner that recalls the lesbian-feminist con-
demnation of transsexuals, that "changing one's sex, when one doesn't
like the one to which one is born, seems to me to be another of those
easy cop-outs which I view with some alarm" (45).

Roberta Albert, the third correspondent, remembers a "boyhood"
that paralleled Ericsen's description, including "something inside that
let me know that I was a boy inside a girl's body!" (Albert 1970, 46),
and she explains that she loved women, not men. Roberta's parents
intervened, shaming her into what they considered appropriate femininity. Finding the gay life provided her with a sense of herself as a
lesbian. Yet, her final words speak volumes about the position of gen-

der inverts in 1970: "What if I had had the option of a sex change? What if . . . ? Is there really such a big demarcation between the transsexual and the Lesbian? But then I wonder about many things . . ." (46). Roberta's wonderment parallels my own. Is Roberta now Robert? As the redistricting of lesbian identity took effect, what were the responses of individuals to this newly circumscribed field? What individual factors distinguished the adaptive behavior of the butches in these shifting times?

More than a few male-identified butches, like Blue Lunden, changed their social presentation and found a community of women who embraced their strength and independence. Lunden remembers:

> When I got involved in the movement [1972] I was real afraid that I would be attacked by lesbian-feminists for my past role-playing. . . . I did very slowly go through a whole process of change. Being around a community of women who felt really good about themselves showed me for the first time that there were all kinds of reasons why I would want to be a woman. To some extent, some of the changes in the ways I behaved at first were conforming, rather than actual change—conforming so as not to be rejected. One thing that's really amazing to me was to note how very little my clothing habits have changed over all these years (Lunden 1980, 41–42).

To what extent these male-identified butches changed in order to accommodate themselves within the new model of lesbianism is hard to ascertain. Some maintained their masculinity and their lesbianism in resistance to the newly hegemonic woman-identified model, while others altered their gender presentation considerably. Lunden's claims that she has not changed her style much are belied by pictures included along with the interview quoted above. These indicated a fairly dramatic change in personal presentation: Lunden goes from butch in tie and jacket, wingtips, and slick hair to a version of lesbian-feminist androgyny. The change is not only in the way that her community has accepted her.

Other male-identified individuals, like Rene, may have sought out transition technologies in order to survive.

I am writing this letter because there are some trends in the gay women's movement today that to me are very disturbing. In the not so distant past, I was one of your sisters. I thought I was a lesbian because I loved women and I did not fit the picture of the feminine personality society constantly forces us to measure up against. I attended your meetings, felt the anger and fear you did about sexual roles yet when the speaker came to the part where she said something like "we are all proud to be women, we don't have to be butch anymore, or play at being men, we don't have to imitate their roles but love women as women," I was confused. Women as women? The meaning of woman and perhaps the search for a pat definition of different, unique experiences is as senseless and futile as peeling off an onion skin looking for an onion. . . . I know for a fact that currently the lesbian community looks down on what they consider bar-stomping dykes and when you say out loud that your lover feels comfortable being supportive and domestic and that you are fulfilled feeling the stronger of the two, you really get shat upon for "playing roles"! . . . Perhaps years from now, in your grandchildren's children's lifetime there will be a state of consciousness in gay and straight society that will breed freedom of personalities. Transsexual changes are expensive and painful in all ways but very necessary right now for some (Rene, in *The Lesbian Tide* 1973, 27).

According to Rene, the "gay women's movement" relied too heavily on an essential and universal female identity. Rene's letter gives shape to that excess space now outside of the lesbian domain. Rene emerged as a likely inhabitant of a transsexual position, a distinctly different identity. She gives the criteria by which she had known herself to be a lesbian: desire for other women and a gender non-conforming, non-feminine personality. Rene recalls the dysphoria that was produced when she heard a woman condemn working-class butch dykes. Most importantly, Rene draws an explicit affinity between the trends in the community and the transsexual position. When she writes, "I was one of your sisters," the past tense indicates that Rene was now beyond the bounds of lesbian sisterhood. For Rene, a transsexual change seemed to be a necessary, if historically contingent, response to the changes in the meaning of homosexuality in the 1970s.

Enough of these male-identified individuals pursued sex change technologies that the overall numbers of female-to-male transsexuals rose significantly and the previously uneven ratios between FTMs and MTFs narrowed radically. These trends caught the attention of some of the leading experts in the field (Benjamin and Ihlenfeld 1970).

The positivist approach to the rising numbers of FTMs might assume that these men were always "out there" waiting to be discovered by better diagnostic categories. By contrast, this genealogy suggests that the numbers of FTMs rose because of the meager options for self-thematizing their gender in the new paradigm of lesbianism. Nascent FTMs became recognizable qua transsexual men once lesbianism became woman-identified in the 1970s.

Conclusions

Having presented the foregoing historical analysis of the importance of lesbian-feminism to the consolidation of an FTM identity, I would like to make some final remarks to clarify the thrust of my argument and to avoid some common misinterpretations of the analysis presented above. I pursued this history because I had a theory about the historical consolidation of a distinct female-to-male transsexual identity. In preliminary conversations with potential transsexual research participants, and in just over half of the group of men I eventually interviewed, FTMs reported that they had at one time identified themselves as dykes, temporarily aligned themselves with the gay world, or, as they described it, "hid out" in the lesbian community. While the FTMs I interviewed provided their own explanation for their lesbian trajectories, I wondered whether there could be a historical reason behind all of them.[20]

These lesbian careers are indicative of category confusion at the cultural and individual levels. Around 1970, changes in the definition of lesbian identity made it difficult for male-identified gender inverts to situate themselves as lesbians.[21] This category confusion resolved itself by the consolidation of two distinct identities, male-identified transsexual men and woman-identified lesbian women. The idea of category confusion provides a non-positivistic explanation for the sudden rise of the numbers of FTMs and the narrowing gap between MTFs and FTMs.

Objections have been raised to the account I am giving of the consolidation of an FTM identity on the grounds that not all transsexual men are sexually oriented toward women and not all FTMs have had lesbian careers. Some have thought that this history does not account for gay FTMs, but this apparent absence only confirms the account I have given. Initially, gay FTMs were excluded by medical and psychological authorities. Sexologists assumed until the 1980s that all FTMs were heterosexual. Medical and psychological authorities agreed that all true FTMs took women, usually feminine women, as their sexual object choice. Of the few case reports of FTMs from 1940 through 1980, none included an FTM with sexual desire for another man. For example, in Christian Hamburger's report on the 465 letters he received from transsexual men and women after Christine Jorgensen's very public transition, he notes, "It is remarkable that not one single woman admits to heterosexuality [sic]" (Hamburger 1953). Not a single case in 108 had another man for their sexual object choice.[22]

While gay FTMs have recently been "discovered," to use the positivist term, an FTM identity was first constituted by the medical and psychological experts as hegemonically heterosexual. The medical communities were not convinced of the existence of gay FTMs until the 1980s. This meant that gay FTMs would have to wait another decade before the medical community would recognize them. It took the substantial efforts of Lou Sullivan, a gay FTM activist who insisted that female-to-male transsexuals could be attracted to men.[23] The medicalized consolidation of female-to-male transsexualism was first based on an inverted gender presentation and an inverted desire for (feminine) women—inversions that had also characterized the gender presentations and desire of some female homosexuals. The medical and psychological resistance to the existence of gay FTMs, along with the lesbian-feminist revolution, was the main propeller for the consolidation of the hegemonically heterosexual FTM identity.

Not all FTMs have had a lesbian career. Yet, the historical thesis can maintain its explanatory power. At this point, close to thirty years after the consolidation of an FTM identity, there is enough category clarity at the socio-cultural level for FTMs to make fewer mistakes or to be mistaken less frequently than in decades past. Charges of false consciousness in either direction, from FTMs against lesbians for being men in denial or from lesbians against FTMs for being women in denial, indicate that some category confusion continues to structure this identity work, though significantly less than it did thirty years ago. The charges of false consciousness should be taken as further evidence of the historical category confusion between these identities and the tremendous identity work that is still necessary for both FTMs and lesbians.

This kind of category confusion is also indicated by the almost universal tendency in recent popular articles to make claims about whether FTMs are really lesbians or about whether lesbians want to be men. For example, the uproar that erupted surrounding the Brandon Teena murder case while I was conducting my research indicated that there was still some cultural confusion about the border between lesbian and FTM identity categories. Brandon Teena, the Nebraskan youth who suffered humiliation and death for his gender presentation, was alternately claimed as lesbian or as transsexual in popular media and community-based representations of the murder.[24] Competing community claims on figures like Brandon Teena, Billy Tipton, and Radclyffe Hall confirm the history outlined here.

Almost any report on FTMs in the clinical or experimental literature today will compare FTMs and lesbians. Medical practitioners will often pull a quote from an intake exam in which the FTM patient distinguishes himself from lesbians. Physicians will inevitably include a discussion of the different diagnostic criteria for FTMs and contrast these with lesbian diagnostic categories. One example of this medical practice is Stoller (1975). Stoller reports that he believes "female transsexualism looks more 'homosexual' than does male transsexualism." Stoller tries to identify a criterion for distinguishing butches from female transsexuals, claiming that among transsexuals (as opposed to butch lesbians), "one does not sense competitiveness with or anger (or studied denial of anger) at men for their maleness" (Stoller 1975, 224–25). Finally, Stoller seems to settle on the notion of a continuum for females that he does not posit for male transsexuals and homosexuals (242–44).

These claims are neither true nor false. They are the legacy of the history described in this chapter. Whenever lesbians and female-to-male transsexuals confront one another, they distinguish themselves through a process of disidentification. The hostility of these interactions signifies the great stakes both have in these identificatory projects. This continuous identity work recreates and maintains the new boundaries between sexual inversion and gender inversion carved out over the course of the twentieth century and consolidated in the 1970s.

Chapter 3

Betrayed by Bodies

■ Ed: There's the difference—there's tons of butch dykes who could so far tell you almost the exact same story. I finally decided what it is. It's that butch dykes are comfortable enough with female parts and FTMs cannot have that. They would rather die or do something drastic or get help.

In these comments, Ed makes a distinction between himself and butch women based on the specific discomfort he experiences with his female body. Like other FTMs in this study, Ed explains that there are real and empirical differences between FTMs and lesbians—these differences are historically constant and positive. From their perspective, the experiences of comfort or discomfort with one's body, especially one's gendered parts, differentiate these identities.

Ed assumes that even very butch women are more comfortable in their bodies than he is in his. Some butches, especially those who came out before the lesbian-feminist revolution, contest this assumption. Anthropologists like Gayle Rubin and Esther Newton suggest that butches share many predilections and dilemmas with FTMs, including a preference for male names, pronouns, and clothes including undergarments; great discomfort with their bodies; and related difficulties in their sexual lives.[1] These scholars theorize a continuum between FTMs and butches. In this usage, "butch" is a noun.

Against this continuum thesis, most of the FTMs in this study see themselves as distinctly different from butches. They signify this by calling lesbians "butch women." In their lexicon, "butch" is an adjective that modifies the noun "woman." Ed hesitates when telling me that he "finally decided what it is" that distinguishes him from butch women. It has taken him some time to come up with something that he feels answers the question with certainty. Ed's criterion is the one most FTMs in this study prefer: the tension he felt between his body image and his material body. His male body image came into conflict with his anatomy and with how others interacted with him. It is not enough for him to pass as a man in the world or be able to do the things that men do. Ed locates the difference between himself and other females, especially butch women, in his body.

FTM difference claims are unsurprising if we consider them in light of the history of chapters one and two. By articulating a difference between themselves and lesbians, these FTMs are drawing on a discourse that has successfully obtained desired medical procedures in the past. FTMs today make these same claims though it is less difficult to convince physicians to treat them. These claims about their bodies are, therefore, not just means for dealing with physicians; they also provide meaning to their enigmatic lives. Each FTM in this study felt a need to construct a biography that legitimates his seemingly strange life choice. That choice has to make sense to him as the only rational thing to do in such circumstances.

The history of becoming treatable bodies is echoed in the words of the FTMs who speak here about their bodies during childhood and adolescence. Their comments reveal their experiences of betrayal by their bodies. They also demonstrate how their perception of difference from lesbian women establishes them as treatable subjects. FTMs frame adolescence as a persistent conflict between their male body images and their feminizing material bodies. This tension between body image and material body points to the general importance of bodies to a sense of self.

FTMs describe adolescence as an extraordinarily difficult time of life when they risked and often lost their senses of themselves. They divide their lives into two halves: a "before" and "after" puberty. After puberty, as the process of sexual development took over their bodies, they felt simultaneously disembodied and acutely aware of their bodies. They become, in the words of one FTM, "social zeros."

In adolescence, these men used their experiences of disembodied awareness to reinforce their sense of difference from others with female bodies. This difference helped them consolidate their identities as (transsexual) men. They claim that their experiences of puberty were uniquely different, either quantitatively more painful or qualitatively different in kind, than that of most other adolescents. By positing that difference in their changing bodies, they provide a logical reason for modifying those bodies.

Although some may suggest that such difference claims are not empirically valid and that all teens experience this kind of distress, the experience and the claims of such difference are what is important here. Whether this difference can be proven empirically is less important in this context. The experience of difference is one way that these men determined the direction, and interpret the meaning, of their lives. By anchoring this difference in their bodies, as Ed does in the quote that opened this chapter, they could legitimate their transitions from female to male.

Body and Self

> Jake: After I got [breasts], and in order to fight off the glances of the boys, I made myself as invisible as I could, which is why I never made friends in school. I totally became a *nothing* almost. It really angered me if the boys gave attention to me because I know they weren't giving it to me.
>
> Henry: What were they giving it to?
>
> Jake: The breasts. [laughs] Or some illusion or this new outfit. A physical outfit. This thing that glued on me. It was no longer me the way I liked it and it's not the way I wanted it.

All of the confusion, fear, and wonderment of puberty was complicated for Jake, as it was for other FTMs, by the secret knowledge that he was not a girl or a woman. Jake, a gay man who has always been attracted to males, characterized his adolescence as lonely, mostly due to his lack of place within the gendered world of junior high and high school. He became a "nothing." Jake looks back on the new sexual attention he received from his pals with frustration, not pleasure, because the boys no longer recognized him as one of them. As his body developed the cultural signs of womanhood, he became increasingly aware that he identified as a boy on the verge of manhood. He was not the only female-bodied person to grow uncomfortable with the sexual attention given to breasts, but Jake found this attention difficult to receive because it meant that he was no longer able to socialize with others on his own terms. The problem, he says, was not exactly that he was treated as a sex object by his neighborhood chums. Instead, it was his sense of complete misrecognition based on physical cues that are culturally identified with womanhood.

For Jake and for most of the guys in this study, puberty marked the first significant "before" and "after" of their young lives. Before puberty, while their bodies still cooperated with their identities, they were able to convince themselves and others that they were, or at least were like, boys. As their bodies began to look significantly different from other boys, they had more and more difficulty being recognized for their true male selves. It became increasingly difficult to sustain a male identity as their bodies began to resemble the bodies of adult women. Breasts made it impossible to deny that they were female-bodied. Before puberty, when their bodies were unencumbered with breasts, they were able to ignore, hide, or minimize the few physical signs, like genitalia, that marked them as female. Relative to adolescent bodies, the bodies of children are less identifiably sexed. Girls' and boys' bodies are more similar than the pubescent or fully developed bodies of women and men. This is especially true with regard to breasts, which are the most visibly gendered features of the mature human body. This relative lack of sex markings on the bodies of children made it possible for the FTMs to see themselves as boys.

Many of the participants say that before puberty they simply knew that they were boys. Others remember only a persistent sense of difference that had no name. While the former group was clearly beyond the borders of normal female-bodied subjectivity, this latter group remained just on the border of the socially prescribed roles for girls in Western culture. As youths, many of them inhabited the ambivalent position of tomboys.[2] Texas Tomboy appropriated that moniker when he got older, but it had always been a part of who he was.

> I liked being referred to as a tomboy growing up. But I always played with the boys and rode BMX and built ramps and I was the only girl in my neighborhood that liked to play like that. I remember wishing I could wear boy's underwear. I would be really persistent. I don't know what my arguments at seven years old were, but I got my way.

Texas is still persistent. He is a video artist, a part-time hustler, and a short guy who "always exceeded people's expectations . . . with strength and intelligence." Texas's attitude represents one FTM's response to being called a tomboy. For him and those who responded similarly to the term, "tomboy" was an adequate label for who they were and what they liked to do in their childhood. For a short time, it gave them a place in the social order. They were different from most girls, but their sense of that difference could be explained in the deviant identity of the tomboy.

The tomboy identity comes with an implicit normative expectations that the child will grow out of it. Tomboys who do not grow out of their tomboy preferences are stigmatized. Many female-bodied individuals do grow out of their tomboy stages and become unproblematically identified as feminine women. In addition, women athletes are more acceptable today, so even very athletic females are tolerated. Other tomboys grow up to identify as gay women or lesbians. Some FTMs called themselves tomboys until it became apparent that they were expected to grow out of it.

Other men in this study immediately grasped the normative assumptions behind the minimal tolerance granted to tomboys, knew that their experiences were more than a phase, and felt patronized by the tomboy label. They understood that a tomboy is a girl who is *like* a boy, whereas they knew themselves to be boys. Jack and Wolfie both express their dissatisfaction with the tomboy label. They each feel that the tomboy label undermined their sense of difference from girls and trivialized their sense of themselves.

> Jack: I wasn't a tomboy. I was a boy. I would rather just be called a girl than to be called a tomboy. Because that's totally dismissing. That's acknowledging what I'm doing, but saying it's a phase and I'm going to grow out of it.

> Wolfie: I was very conscious of patronizing attitudes towards children and that was one part of it. A tomboy is like a "boyette."

These men were more isolated almost from the beginning of their lives. Their way of being in the world was completely unrecognizable to others. They resisted the tomboy label because they did not want to be mistaken for girls, but by refusing this label, they completely cut themselves off from the social order.

The non-tomboy FTMs classify FTM tomboys as "secondary transsexuals," whereas they see themselves as "primary transsexuals." For this group, the early recognition that they were not girls of any sort is an unequivocal sign of transsexual identification. (Likewise, the FTMs who never had lesbian careers think of themselves as "primary" and those with lesbian careers as "secondary" transsexuals.) The non-tomboys express an absolute discomfort with their female bodies. The tomboys struggle longer to become certain that they are men. Another small group in this study was not tomboy-identified and was more comfortable doing activities that the culture associates with girls, such as doll play and house play. Looking back, these men identify with other "sissy boys" and feel sure that many of their childhood and adolescent boyfriends and pals turned out to be gay men like themselves. Under the cover of heterosexual normativity, their behavior as "sissy boys" looked like normal femininity to others. This "normal" female behavior did not mean, however, that they were girls, at least not in their own minds. They report that they felt like they were boys growing up, but they were not interested in culturally hegemonic activities of "normal" boys.

Before puberty, the guys had disregarded or actively ignored what few markings indicated the sex of their bodies and identified themselves in one of three ways: (1) they were *boys* (with bodies that approximated the bodies of other boys) who liked to do typically boy activities, (2) they were *tomboys* who felt a distinct, yet not quite definable, difference from others with female bodies, or (3) they were *boys* who, because of their preference for activities associated with girls, evoked little suspicion from others although they knew themselves to be different from girls. The first group was more stigmatized than the other two and suffered deeper social consequences for their refusal to conform to the identities their bodies were assigning them. The second group had a temporary place in the cultural landscape of childhood, but it was a place that eventually evaporated as they matured. Finally, a twist of cultural logic gave the men in the third group a hiding place that aroused few suspicions, but made their path after puberty particularly misunderstood by others—if "she" liked doing "girly" activities and preferred men as sexual partners, why change "her" sex?

Once their bodies developed female features, all of them were forced to realize that they were unlike the boys they had considered their natural cohorts. The bodies they inhabited disfigured their essential male selves.[3] They were faced with a choice of maintaining their male identities at great risk of social stigma or "going underground" and playing the role dictated by their female bodies. After puberty, the social difficulties they had experienced increased exponentially as their bodies changed from relatively ungendered and asexual into female bodies. Three things—menarche, breast development, and hair growth—made them physically uncomfortable and socially alienated.

Menarche

Most female-bodied people can point to the onset of menses as a physical threshold that marks one as a grown woman. The capacity to fulfill the childbearing role remains the physical and hegemonic criterion for adult womanhood. For FTMs like Ed, this benchmark of adult female status was greeted with gritted teeth.

> I remember the next day going to school and telling someone and this girl was like, "Isn't it great?" and I'm worried about it and I felt very ashamed that I was not happy at all.

Ed wants to distinguish himself from the typical transsexual portrayed on television talk shows, describing himself as "any other long-haired, some facial hair, black T-shirt guy." In the story that he tells of his first menstruation, he emphasizes the difference between his female friend's response and his own. This difference is one piece of evidence that Ed assembles to legitimate his male identity.

Shadow was born in South Dakota, which is the home of the Santee Sioux and the Lakota Sioux Native American tribes. He was given his name in a ritual by a Native American man, an older friend, because it captured the sense that he was a part of both the light and the dark. As he grew up and assumed this name, he began to frame his shadowy existence as a conflict between his body image and his material body.

> My belief about my process growing up is that what I was going through during puberty was estrogen poisoning. I will swear by that now that I've started the testosterone. The way I functioned in life was taken from a point of anger. In my early twenties the violent rages were frequent. I'd say like once a month. Imagine that. [laughs]

This is an emphatic statement of the difference between a young girl who is approaching maturity with ordinary discomfort and a trans- sexual man as he endures his menstrual cycle.

Like several of the guys in this study, Shadow ties his body alien- ation to his angry and violent youth. For him, the body became his "first clue" in his search for a way to make sense of his dilemma. Most of the other men understand this kind of anger as a social reaction to a difficult situation, but Shadow believes that estrogen poisoning caused his violent outbursts. Shadow's story of estrogen poisoning counters to the hegemonic cultural belief that testosterone is the likeliest cause of male rage. He does not claim that estrogens, in and of themselves, are poisonous. Rather, he explains his rage as an incompatibility be- tween his body image and his female endocrinology. Shadow recalls visiting doctors and becoming frustrated with their inability to fix the problem.

> Going to different doctors and [hearing], "Sorry dear, you're a healthy, young female. Just growing up. This'll pass. It's just what women have to go through." Bullshit! I don't care what you say, this is not normal. Then my other female friends are going through this. I knew there was something different going on.

Like the others, Shadow also used the experiences of the girls around him to sharpen his own self-understanding. These guys went through the normal body changes that are part of female adolescence.[4] However, they insist that their responses went far beyond ordinary teenage angst from the rapid and uncontrollable physical changes. Texas describes it as "a tragedy." James recalls becoming embarrassed of the body he had previously loved because "it could do great things." Francis remembers a loss of self-confidence, crying a lot, and becoming acutely self-conscious. Dani calls it "a shocking experience . . . mind-boggling."

For many of the FTMs in this study, the experience of starting to menstruate brought on intense shame and embarrassment. Several of them, like Julian, say that their shame resulted in an extended silence that isolated them.

> It felt like something so private and so humiliating and so shameful and I already was very private and secretive. Not for a second did it occur to me to go tell the gym teacher, certainly not my mother, certainly not a peer. . . . I don't even know if I could've said the word at that time. I don't know if I could've even said "period."

Not telling anyone about their first periods and not using sex-specific language to refer to themselves were last-ditch attempts to maintain their bodies as they were "before." By choosing to conceal the start of menses, these female-bodied people willfully refused to situate themselves linguistically as women. Partly as a reaction of disgust and shame, partly as a strategy of resignifying the material body, these men took care not to acknowledge their material bodies.

Their unwillingness to use language that refers to female bodies and female processes demonstrates the extent of their discomfort. One important strategy they deploy for preserving their sense of self is the use of euphemistic and indeterminate language to specify body parts that are abhorrent to them. They almost always use articles, rather than possessive pronouns, to refer to their female body parts. These body parts have become independent agents acting in defiance of the disembodied self. Such threats are linguistically neutralized and effaced via grammar.

As Julian notes, this kind of failure to acknowledge one's body required persistent monitoring of that body and the deployment of multiple strategies for maintaining one's gender identity.

> I dealt with it by using these wadded up toilet paper things and of course, this was something else for my brain to monitor. It lasted about four to five days, every night I would go to bed and I remember just saying over and over again to myself like a mantra, "three more days, three more days." I would say "three" in all the languages that I knew how to say "three" in. That's all I could see. That was the focus of my life, getting through the days, until my period ended for that month. Sometimes I would take a pad or two from my mother if I thought I could get away with it. Or I'd use my lunch money to buy a pad in the locker room, in the girl's locker room, but I'd only do it after school so that no one would see me buying it.

Julian goes on to describe the inevitable problems that resulted from his "primitive methods" and the elaborate cleaning rituals he engaged in so that nobody would discover his secret. Though he remembers all of this, he recalls being unclear about what he was doing and why.

The initial arrival of that "dreaded visitor" made other guys aware, sometimes for the first time in their lives, that they were not the boys they thought they were. Francis explains:

> I mean I didn't think about it consciously, "Oh, I wish I was a boy" or "I wish I had a penis." It was just less conscious. It was just I knew who I was. No problem with that. And then one day, right around when I was having my first period, I realized that I wasn't. It was kind of sad. [voice drops to a whisper]

In these memories, Francis recalls a time "before" when he had no problems and he knew who he was. The FTMs in this study likened this unawareness during their childhoods to the unawareness of non-transsexual boys who are at ease with their bodies. The word "carefree" comes to mind when listening to their childhood stories.

Many of the guys in this study remember this easy existence and frame their puberty as an interruption of it. Though several of them think that it would be nearly impossible to recapture the unconscious ease of being their gender, they characterize their transsexual transitions as a return to that interrupted developmental age and a new chance to grow up. Others say that their transsexual transitions promote the sense of ease in their genders that non-transsexual men have, to the point where they no longer consider themselves to be transsexuals.

If menstruation stands out as the mark of womanhood, then it comes as no surprise that these men regarded it with suspicion, hostility, anxiety, and frustration. Some stubbornly refused to allow the material body to define them. For many others, this foreign body convinced them to try to live for a time as women. Those who attempted to do so claim that they were unable to perform femininity adequately and suffered through long periods of depression. Some report an inability to recall whole segments of their lives, suggesting that they withdrew from the world in order to preserve their identities. Several say that they chose to isolate themselves from others as a way of asserting themselves and preventing others from treating them in ways that offended their sense of self.

Breasts

> James: I was embarrassed by my breasts. I tried to cover them up a lot. My posture was bad as a result. It was just difficult sometimes to acknowledge my body.

A writer and an executive, James tells me that he transitioned so that he could finally grow up. James's anguish came from the difficulty he had seeing himself in a body with breasts. Some FTMs on the brink of transition prioritize their breasts as the most important aspect of their appearance that they would change. The chest is the body part most likely to block them from living full lives. It inhibits them from living full-time as men and causes the most discomfort when they look in the mirror. Some start binding breasts from their first appearance and others take up the practice as they age and become more distraught. The men bind the breasts down using everything from control-top nylons with the legs cut out to ace bandages, even duct tape and specially made jerseys. A few choose not to bind because it is too ungainly or too hard to breathe. Another strategy for minimizing the conflict between the body image and the material body is to wear two or more shirts, even on the hottest of days.

By some accounts, breast size could be a relevant factor in determining who can live with their female parts and who cannot. Others said that size made little difference to them. The simple fact of the existence of the breasts was unbearable to most of the men in this study. During adolescence, Texas recalls, he had such a strong antipathy to the mere idea of the breasts that he believes he influenced his development.

> My mom told me because she had really huge breasts in high school that I would, too. I really feel like I willed them away. I really didn't want that. I don't know, it was really hard. I really didn't like going through puberty at all. [close to tears]

Others, like Francis, who never developed or who developed later, report wanting breasts and being envious of the larger girls around them. Their typical explanation for this contradictory desire was a wish to be "normal." Having breasts would confirm their femaleness and magically eliminate those "abnormal" thoughts about being a guy. These guys seem to feel that their wishes backfired, and at least one man suggests that all that wishing got stored up in his body, eventually producing large breasts. These wishful refusals provided the strength to sustain a transsexual man's sense of his essential self while his body was betraying him. As with menstruation, the FTMs felt that their responses to the development of breasts were anomalous compared to the experiences of the young women who were assumed to be their cohorts.

This perceived difference contributed to their isolation. Jack recalls the feeling of not being accepted for who he was.

> They loved to have someone to pick on and I happened to be that person. Thank God for my mother. Every once in awhile I'd go, "I just don't want to go to school today." "Okay." It was so horrible. You act like a boy, you isolate yourself from the whole world. Boys don't accept you and girls don't accept you. They'd often walk by in their groups and yell stuff. A lot of things were, "You're so ugly" and being picked

last at gym. Or nobody would call me. That's just the worst feeling in
the whole world.

By falling in line, these guys could reduce the stigma that they faced,
though at a huge cost to their subjective sense of self. Wolfie, like many
in this study, expresses the feeling that he was faced with a choice between staying committed to his body image and subjectivity but being
alone, or capitulating to social pressures and the materialist compulsion to become the woman that his body dictated he should be.

Either you have a chance at a relationship with somebody and go along
with whatever the prevailing dress and behavioral ideal is or you don't.
Sort of a choice between being uncomfortable in yourself or having
other people make you feel uncomfortable.

Either way, they feel that adolescence brought on these choices because of the changes in their material bodies that failed to represent
their subjectivity adequately.

Several men tell stories that narrate their resistance to their treach-
erous bodies or the social conventions associated with those bodies.
John recalls:

My mom went into the section, I kept wandering off. She kept drag-
ging me back there. The saleslady comes up and she's like, "Raise your
arms up." I said "no" three times; finally I did 'cause I decided I'd let
mom buy it and I'd never wear it. I actually wore it to school the day
of the test and watched all the other girls take their shirts off and took
a good look [laughs] and then refused. I never got the scoliosis test. I
got in trouble. That's the only time that thing ever touched my body.
Ever.

John refuses even now to concede that he went into a lingerie depart-
ment. He will say "the section," but a heterosexual man in his social
location would not say he had been in a store looking at women's un-
derwear with his mother. He refused the saleswoman's attempts to put
the garment on his body three times. Conceding to take it home was a
passive move that allowed him to defer wearing it. The single time that
he wore a bra became an adolescent locker-room escapade, a covert
kind of panty-raid that allowed John to exercise his heterosexual, mas-

culine desires for the girls in his cohort. Instead of a story of joy at this event, or even a certain modest embarrassment that a non-transsexual child might express, John's tells of maintaining his male gender identity despite outside attempts to discipline his body. In fact, the heterosexual masculinity of this story helps him to consolidate his gender identity.

These offending body parts contributed to a chronic state of mind that is difficult to imagine. Gregg says he oscillated relentlessly between a constant awareness and a disembodied feeling toward his body. It was as if two radio waves were trying to come in through the same position on the dial.

> You end up basically just seeing yourself from the neck up. You don't even want to look at the rest of your body. You feel detached from your body. It's just your head going through life.

These teenagers now had a perpetual stream of sex and gender to monitor while unable to fully inhabit either their bodies or the social world.[5]

These experiences confirm the idea that we have a body image, an embodied sense of our selves that may not coincide with the material body itself. "Agnosia" is the term used by phenomenologist Merleau-Ponty to designate the condition of a *reverse* "phantom limb." Agnosia is "the nonrecognition of a body part that should occupy a position within the body image" (Grosz 1994, 89). FTMs become disembodied selves who refuse to recognize their breasts. Transsexual men perpetually monitor their breasts because their flesh does not coincide with their body image. Agnosia, in this sense, is an assertion of a self rather than a delusional condition.

After having had their chests reconstructed, many of the guys report that they could not remember what their bodies looked or felt like before the procedure. They say that this effect occurs within weeks of the surgery. This observation shows that their bodies now conform to their body image and their sense of self.[6] No longer agnosic, FTMs in this study feel as if they are now "tuned into one station." The alignment of body image and material body restores, to some degree, the carefree embodiment that characterized their youth.

A few of the guys noted that their disembodied awareness shifted after chest reconstruction to other, less obviously gendered body parts like hips and buttocks, as they began to be able to inhabit the upper halves of their bodies. Some report an increased desire for penis reconstruction after their chest surgeries, or increased frustration with the limitations of phalloplasty and other surgeries for penis reconstruction. These desires and frustrations indicate that the physical body remains, to some degree, out of sync with the body image and that a disembodied awareness may continue to structure their lives.

Hair Growth

Though it stands out to a lesser degree than the other two signs of female embodiment, patterns of body hair are a significant marker of gender in this culture. While breast development and menstruation are strongly resistant, though not impervious, to willful manipulation, hair patterns are a quality of gender expression that is more easily modifiable. Hair is

> almost always groomed, prepared, cut, concealed and generally "worked upon" by human hands. Such practices socialize hair, making it the medium of significant "statements" about self and society and the codes of value that bind them or don't (Mercer 1990, 248–49).

Unlike their breasts and their periods, these FTMs could and did modify their hair as a means of self-expression during adolescence. Creatively marshalling their resources, they asserted themselves through whatever means were available.

Hair length and style are important indicators of self. In his drug-addicted youth, when he was in the deepest withdrawal from the world, Matt had the standard feathered look of a teenage girl in the 1970s. In his late teens, after he came out as a lesbian, Matt took on the cutting-edge, defiant flat top style that signified his young, white, urban rebelliousness. Ed chose a severe, short hairstyle to emphasize his toughness and masculinity at the very moment when his body was becoming the most female. He explains, "Back then I wanted shorter hair especially, probably because I had a female body and I wanted to like take away [from that] as much as possible." In his childhood, Ed, like many of the other guys, was forbidden to cut his hair, which predisposed him to wanting it short, though he now prefers it long to show that he is a metal-head rocker or to signal his Native American heritage.

The men would often capitulate to social expectations about the female-bodied, working on their hair to look like the young women they were assumed to be. James remembers:

> My mother was ashamed of the hair that I had. She made me bleach the hair on my upper lip. She made me very self-conscious about my arms . . . so that I would never wear short-sleeved shirts. I also had trouble with girls. "Well, you'd be so much prettier." Sometimes I would actually give in. It was horrible. I wanted them to be my friends. I thought maybe they were right. Maybe if they did my hair it would all be straightened out.

While John's story about the time his mother bought him a bra is full of resistance, James's is more common. Standards of beauty were mobilized by others for the purpose of disciplining them. Their shame at being called ugly or being offered more subtle criticisms of their appearances led to self-doubt and attempts to fit in, make friends, and appease their mothers. Though some managed to approximate the behavior, mannerisms, and attitudes culturally associated with female bodies, they say that this always felt like a performance to them and that they were "passing" as women. This performance allowed them to participate in social life, to be accepted among friends and family, and to have important relationships. Nonetheless, it felt inauthentic.

Betrayal

It became apparent to James and the other men that things would not be "straightened out" by a hairdo, a purse, or learning to walk "right." Every one of them express the same sentiment about their bodies during their adolescence. Universally, each man felt betrayed by his defiant physical body. Prior to puberty, their bodies had not troubled them in quite this way. Though their pre-pubescent bodies were never particularly useful when it came to communicating who they really were inside, they had not been the cause of the extreme agnosic response that puberty generated. With the onset of menses and the development of breasts and female patterns of hair growth, these men were faced with bodies that were actively betraying them. James remembers:

> I was always very physical as a child and very much enjoyed my body. My body betrayed me when I was an adolescent and I grew embarrassed by my body. I eventually became embarrassed by almost anybody's body.

This comment, typical among the men in the study, indicates that the alienation James experienced was not due to stereotypical notions about what a woman's or a man's body could do. It was due to his embarrassment and discomfort at what his own body had become. Others in the study suggest that the betrayal was similar to that which a "normal" boy would experience if his body suddenly sprouted breasts or if he began bleeding through his genitals.

What are the guys implying when they characterize their female development as "betrayal"? Treason is a violation of an internal allegiance, to king, country, or, as in this case, to one's self. The betrayal of this self by the body is the horror that splits their lives into a before and an after, an outside and an inside. As Matt puts it, "That's like trying to compare my insides to everyone else's outside. It never works. The way I feel on the inside has always been different from the way I look on the outside." This inside/outside metaphor represents Matt's sense that his body image, his interior sense of his gendered self, matched neither the outside of his body nor the outsider's view of his material body.

Accepting the notion that the body could betray the *I* means privileging the subjectivity of these men and depathologizing their agnosia. These are not women with mental problems, in denial about their female bodies. They are, instead, men whose bodies have erupted in a vicious mutiny against them. They are not engaging in an irrational project meant to change them from women to men. They are restoring a trusting, loyal, and faithful relationship of representation between self and body. At the least, they hope to return to the minimal discomfort of their youth. If they are lucky, they will produce a new level of harmony between their minds and their bodies.

Legitimating Transition: Located in the Body
and Different from Girls

When I ask how or if their adolescent experiences were different from those of the girls around them, several respond that they do not know because they were mortified at the thought of discussing the issue with girls or their mothers. Many think their feelings were extreme versions of a girl's reaction to her development, while others say there was a qualitative difference between their discomfort and a girl's excitement. Matthew, a gay, suburban parent of an adolescent girl, claims a qualitative difference.

> I'm watching her go through puberty and I'm coming to understand how a girl hitting puberty, that this is a wonderful, exciting thing, and I wasn't horrified by it, but I certainly wasn't thinking it was a wonderful kind of thing. Inconvenient.

Despite their claims that their experiences were different, in quality or severity, their descriptions of this time share some commonalities with girls'. In *Blood Stories: Menarche and the Politics of the Female Body in Contemporary U.S. Society,* Janet Lee and Jennifer Sasser-Coen suggest that girls are ambivalent about their periods. Expectation and excitement are joined with great shame and fear. However, the transsexual men had none of the thrill of becoming women reported by the girls in *Blood Stories.* They took no pleasure from this event and report that their responses were uniformly negative. Their experiences of betrayal by their bodies, however, were echoed in the narratives of the "normal" girls. This commonality was something I asked the men about directly. If distress at menstruation was a sign of being a transsexual, how do they explain this experience among "normal" girls? How do they explain what seemed like a commonality between themselves and adolescent girls? They insist that their experiences were uniquely awful, not at all ambivalent or tempered by positive emotions.

Because these FTM experiences are framed retrospectively, many years after the experience itself, it is impossible to validate these claims of difference. We cannot, in any empirical sense, definitively confirm or deny these claims of difference. We can suggest, however, that the claims of difference between the FTMs and the girls are meaningful claims that do important identity work. These difference claims are a significant way of legitimating their transitions and a valuable way of making sense of their lives. Though these differences may not be empirically confirmed or denied, they are experienced, and told, as real. As with the comparisons that the FTMs draw between themselves and lesbian women, their focus on difference legitimates their identities as transsexual men.

Lee and Sasser-Coen's findings provide a useful point of comparison for assessing the shared experiences as well as some differences between FTMs and girls. The girls in Lee and Sasser-Coen's study felt shame and embarrassment about their periods. They represent themselves linguistically as split subjects through impersonal pronouns and other grammatical forms of non-ownership. Lee and Sasser-Coen suggest that girls use language that splits off and personifies their menses. Impersonal pronouns designate that something was "happening 'to' them, as something outside of themselves, rather than something that was a part 'of' them" (Lee and Sasser-Coen 1996, 94). The FTMs also indicate a fragmented or split self by using language of non-ownership about their bodies. The FTMs and the girls were at risk of a loss of self around the time of their first menstruation. Both have a language for maintaining their selves while their bodies betray them.

The similarities stop there. While the girls developed solidarity with each other, the FTMs became isolated. An additional difference between the FTMs' reports and the girls' is the focal point of their embodied alienation: FTMs resist becoming women, but the girls resist becoming a certain type of woman. Girls and women are sexualized and objectified in this culture, especially at puberty. Menarche "is a site where individual girls produce themselves as women and gender relations are perpetuated" (Lee and Sasser-Coen 1996, 36). Their entrance into adult female status comes with concomitant pressures that some girls anticipate and resent. The girls' alienation is a result of social relations of objectification and sexualization, but FTMs do not want to be or cannot be women even if their bodies are accorded the respect and dignity deserved by every woman. Their discomfort stems, not from the type of women our society demands female bodies to be, but from being a female body at all.

In the following story about menstruation, Julian points out this different locus of their alienation.

I was in a graduate seminar on "Men and Masculinity" and we read an article about a boy who was morphologically male and didn't know that he was intersexed until puberty at which time he began to menstruate through his penis. I just remember the men in the class were absolutely mortified. "Oh, that must've been the most humiliating thing." They really just felt like it was something really tragic and horrible. Like they wanted to feel this boy's pain. I just remembered thinking that's exactly how I experienced it. At first I was really just pissed; it's kinda like if a man gets raped that really humiliating, but if a woman gets raped, it's kinda bad, but . . . not as bad as . . . Maybe it's bad if you're a girl, but if you're a boy, it's like, how tragic! But that's how I experienced it. How these men expressed they imagined this boy must feel. I certainly experienced it that way.

This story illustrates the different locus of Julian's alienation. It distinguishes his alienating experiences from how a girl might feel betrayed by her menses. He disidentifies from girls by establishing his likeness to the intersexual boy in the story who began to menstruate through his penis. For the intersexed boy and for Julian, menstruation was surprising, tragic, and humiliating—not for lack of information or the shame of being sexualized and objectified, but because it signified that they both had an anomalous bodily condition.

The responses of the men in the class demonstrate that men hold a double standard about menstruation, like they do about rape. Though he wants to acknowledge this double standard, it also serves to mark Julian's difference from women. He felt the same horror at menstruation as did the men in the class and the intersexual boy, and this similarity helps to establish his male identity. Where teenage girls may want to escape the sexualizing and objectifying demands of hegemonic womanhood, these men wanted to escape their female bodies altogether.

In light of the history of the emergence of a discrete FTM identity, a story like Julian's illustrates the importance of bodies, especially intersexed bodies, for establishing an FTM's differences from girls and his likeness to boys or men. The logic of treatment for gender inverts, from 1940 until 1970, required a physiological reason to intervene. Female-bodied, male-identified patients could, by positioning themselves as a type of intersexual, convince doctors to confirm, or "change," their sex. The intersexual body, the anomalous body, is a treatable body.

Claims of difference from female bodies and claims of similarity to intersexed bodies legitimate the body modifications that seem irrational to others. Whether or not the guys in this study really had different responses to their female puberty than girls is, in the end, not at issue. There are some similarities and some differences. What is important is that these transmen are compelled to make these claims. They choose to focus on the differences in order to explain the "unidentifiable feelings of dis-ease" to themselves. They feel an existential need to make them, and feel that these claims reflect their experienced reality.

Chapter 4

Transsexual Trajectories

■ The process of becoming an FTM does not end with the early childhood identification of a male self. FTMs may feel like boys from the start, but they still need to formulate a specifically transsexual identity. This often happens during puberty or young adulthood. The questions this chapter addresses are: how do nascent FTMs begin to identify as transsexual? When and why do they choose to modify their bodies and/or live as men?

The process of consolidating a transsexual identity is called a "transsexual trajectory." The concept of a trajectory is borrowed from sociologist Barbara Ponse (1978), who develops Irving Goffman's notion of a "career." Goffman writes:

> Traditionally the term *career* has been reserved for those who expect to enjoy the rises laid out within a respectable profession. The term is coming to be used, however, in a broadened sense to refer to any social strand of any person's course through life . . . [t]he regular sequence of changes that career entails in the person's self and in his framework of imagery of judging himself and others (Goffman 1959, 127–28).

In Ponse's schema, a "trajectory is a non-sequential route to an identity with five stops": (1) experiencing a subjective feeling of difference, (2)

finding the appropriate category and assigning the feeling of difference a meaning in relationship to that category, (3) accepting the category as descriptive of one's experience, (4) seeking a community, and
(5) engaging in relationships. The first four stops in this typology have
explanatory power for transsexual men. In transsexual narratives, Ponse's
fifth stop, relationships, is actually subsumed by the process of accepting the category of transsexual. A better definition of the fifth stop in
transsexual trajectories is "making transition choices." Transition choices
are the choices about body modifications and other means of present-
ing oneself as male.

Matt sums up the rudimentary experiences that he eventually categorized as transsexualism:

> I didn't have any language when I was fourteen years old to talk about
> the fact that I felt different. There was an unidentifiable feeling that
> there was something different. Unidentifiable feeling of dis-ease in my
> life.

Like many of the other men in this study, Matt's feelings of difference
as a fourteen-year-old made him uncomfortable. In response to this
"dis-ease," he began an unofficial search for knowledge that would
help him name and organize his feelings. Finding self-knowledge as
FTMs helped Matt and the other guys accept themselves as transsexuals, make transition choices, and live their lives as men.

In their search for self-knowledge, FTMs often compare themselves with the portrayals of sex and gender found in books, TV, folk
wisdom, or common stocks of cultural knowledge. For example, Ed
recalls one moment when he discovered the category of FTM and made
a comparison to his own feelings of difference:

> I remember one day Joan coming into work and saying that she was at
> a bar hanging out somewhere in L.A. and this guy came up to her and
> introduced himself as this woman. He used to be this woman that she
> went out with.

Ed's co-worker was the first one to pass along a story that informed
him about people who change their sex. After discovering the category

of FTM, Ed still had some way to go before he associated that category with his own experiences.

> I remember going, "That's the first time I ever heard of that." And again it didn't go, "Oh, that's what I am." It was just like it was filed away in my head . . . but I still didn't think that's what I would want to do. I didn't even really consider it myself, but it was again one of those things where it wasn't a whole thought process, it just sorta sunk in.

At the time, Ed did not yet identify as transsexual or believe that he would want to do what the FTM in the story did. He remembers filing away bits of information that he later assimilated into his own experience. These fragments of knowledge just "sunk in." "In" is the operative word here: Ed feels that his self was like fertile soil absorbing nutrients that would allow him to grow. Having the category of transsexual and knowing that it was possible to change one's sex were important moments in his transsexual trajectory.

The process of comparison with significant others helps FTMs describe their experiences and associate those experiences with the category of transsexual. By "significant others," I do not mean only boyfriends, girlfriends, wives, husbands, or other romantic partners, but also any significant person within the social orbit of the nascent FTM who helps them in their identity formation. As chapter three points out, one set of significant others are playmates and mothers. During adolescence, many FTMs feel that they are different from their friends, sisters, or other girls. They may want to be in a different kind of relationship with a man or to wear different clothes or to do different things than the girls they know. These feelings of difference become meaningful as these FTMs are introduced to the category of transsexual.

In their trajectories, some compared themselves to MTF and FTM transsexuals they knew. Dani says that he had been friends for a long time with someone who then transitioned from female to male. This friendship and the long talks that they had helped Dani figure things out: "Well, my friend, he started going through this process. . . . We talked. And I would think about stuff that he would say."

Gregg remembers that he and one of his friends talked until 5
A.M.:

> We're talking about our dreams. "Who are you in your dreams, do
> you see yourself as being male or female?" And I said "male." She said
> "me too." She said, "That's how I identify." Then it just took off.

Gregg and his friend were both in the dark together, finding their way
out.

Others, like Matt, identified themselves as FTMs because they
knew other female-bodied individuals who were already living as men.

> I met several FTMs at the International Mr. Leather conference. . . . I
> was like "Hi, duh. . . . I think I need to go have a cigarette now" and I
> fuckin' bolted out of the room. . . . It was really intense. It was really
> scary. Of course, I did the normal thing and I followed them around
> like a puppy dog all week. It makes sense to me. "Oh, I think these
> people are like me. I must follow them around."

Matt's first response, to go off and have a smoke, demonstrates the
immediate need he felt to make his body relax or even numb while he
contemplated his likeness to them. He remembers feeling drawn to
them like a puppy dog that resembles his person-owner.

For Jack, who found out about transsexuals from the 1970s television program *Three's Company*, it took a small reversal of logic and
some Scotch tape to get from MTFs to FTMs.

> I always thought I was stuck like this forever. I saw an episode where
> Mr. Roper was asking his wife Helen, they were talking about Jack or
> something, about sex changes, male-to-female and he was saying, "Now
> I could understand how they cut things off, but how do they put 'em
> back on?" I'm watching this intensely and I'm thinking they can't. And
> Mrs. Roper said, "With Scotch tape, Stanley." I thought, "If she's mak-
> ing a joke about it then it must be possible." From that moment on, I
> just knew, "Oh my God, it's possible."

The sense of being like other transsexuals and knowing that the technology was available made it easier for the guys to identify as transsexuals. Going to support groups, informational meetings, or confer-

ences, or just knowing one other transsexual person was a major factor in organizing their identities.

Significant others who help FTMs confirm their identities can also be found in romantic relationships. Helpful partners encourage FTMs to live their lives authentically. A few transmen consider special female partners as "mothers," and some of their female partners conceive of themselves as "giving birth" to FTMs. More often, the process is characterized as "othering." For example, Ed talks about his preference for women who use cosmetics: "I can't exactly already explain the make-up thing, but mostly that it represents something different than me." Ed prefers women who use make-up because it emphasizes their difference from him. This difference allows him to consolidate his identity.

Male partners of FTMs aid a transsexual identification in three ways. The FTMs in this study see their husbands and boyfriends as (1) sexual partners, (2) models of masculinity that they patterned themselves after, and (3) vehicles into gay life. Husbands and boyfriends are vehicles for moving in gay or bisexual circles and for fulfilling homosexual desires. Several of the gay FTMs in this study, like Jake, found their way to their transsexual identity by hanging around co-ed gay groups with their husbands, as married couples.

> They all thought he [Jake's husband] was gay or bisexual because he looked that way. When I brought him over, the guys would flirt with him, not me. But I also kind of used him as my ticket to get to all the guy things. We would be invited to guy get-togethers, the two of us.

They used their husbands as "beards," allowing the groups' members to think that they were supportive wives accompanying their closeted husbands into the gay world. In fact, they were there searching for their own place in the gay world.

Male partners are often seen as the men that FTMs might like to become. Desire and identification are often mapped onto each other. Jack saw his sexual involvement with boys during his youth as an opportunity to see, touch, and imagine a penis of his own: "I just wanted to see their penises. So I didn't care at all. I just wanted to see it and touch it and have it be mine, I think." Jack nonchalantly dismisses the question of how the boys' attention to his female body made him feel, saying he did not care at all. This statement indicates the denial of his female body, but it also suggests that during these sexual sessions, Jack identified with the bodies of the boys with whom he was sexual.

Jake reports that "playing boys" with his husband was a gateway to his identity.

> I got the guts to tell him I want to pretend that we were both guys. Because it was part of this fantasy thing and we'd done all sorts of other fantasies, he said okay. That's when I allowed that male thing that I was holding back and not really letting out to fully come out and I had the best sex of my life and that's when I realized that I never want to go back to anything different than that.

Jake's narrative demonstrates the mapping of desire and identification for FTMs with male partners. Jake continued to ask his husband to "play boys" until it became a problem in their relationship.

Sometimes, specific sexual practices clarified the FTMs' identities. Ed recalls:

> I thought that you should have it like fifty-fifty lying down sex, and I was never into penetration. . . . I thought it was like a selling out thing. The first time I ever used a dildo and a harness was with her. That was a huge breakthrough. . . . All of a sudden I was like, "That's how I like to have sex!" . . . That's when I started realizing that I really like to fuck women. For some reason I assumed that I had to let people do this to me.

Realizing that he liked to be, in the words of another FTM, "the fucker, not the fuckee," channeled Ed's identity and took him one step closer to transition. Ed's previous affairs had been unfulfilling because the sex had been "fifty-fifty": mutually penetrative or his partners had done to him what he had done to them. He says that sometimes he let his partners touch him the way he touched them and that he did this only because he assumed this was the only way for two female-bodied people to have sex. He mentions the politics of sexuality that guided his earliest sexual encounters with women: penetration was selling out. He eventually discarded this ideology and started to have sex that suited him. Ed appreciated one particular partner because she did not expect to penetrate him or to stimulate him in the way he had touched her. Penetrating his lovers and giving up fifty-fifty sex were some of the ways that he began to assume his identity as a transsexual man.

Many of these same factors necessary to FTM identity formation can inhibit it as well. For example, Shadow remembers discovering the categories of transsexual and homosexual at the same time. His relationship with his parents compelled him to discard the label "transsexual," at least for an interval of about fifteen years.

> I basically had the word transsexual, I found that word when I was fifteen. When I turned eighteen, "Okay, I have to tell my parents something about who and what I am. To try and explain some of this. So I think I'm finally getting a handle on it. Which of these two words do I give 'em? Do I give 'em homosexual or transsexual?" At that point and time, there were some big question marks for myself as well. And I figured the least of the two would be homosexual.

Surprisingly, Shadow suggests that his parents were much more accepting of his transsexual identity than of his initial identification as a lesbian. Shadow eventually abandoned his lesbian career, but this passage demonstrates Shadow's own confusion of "homosexual" and "transsexual" categories. It also points out the pressure from significant others in his life to formulate a coherent identity.

Partners who resist the idea of FTM transition and who subtly mark the boundaries of acceptable self-presentation are one of the strongest barriers to FTM self-acceptance. This limiting behavior of lovers and significant others puts pressure on the FTMs and prevents a full acceptance of who they really are. Jake recalls how "playing boys" became a problem in his marriage:

> What started happening is over time, and that did not help our relationship, is I kept asking for that [playing boys] and then when he would ask for his fantasies, if they happened with me being the female, then I couldn't do it. *I started becoming impotent in performing as female.* That would anger him. He's like, "Well, I'm doing something that's absolutely unnatural for me, then why can't you do something that is natural for you?"

It became apparent that Jake and his husband would have to divorce. He started to work at a specialty store for male-to-female cross dressers and made friends with an MTF transsexual who supported Jake's view of himself and condoned his transsexual trajectory. Jake's marriage is representative of the paradoxical relationships the FTMs in this study had with husbands or girlfriends during their trajectories. Several feel that their relationships eventually hindered their self-acceptance or their transition choices.

Wolfie, who has chosen not to transition, seems unbothered by his husband's critical remarks: "I think in a way he thinks I'm making a fuss over nothing and that I really can dress any way I want. I'm too conscious of what other people say. This is probably true." Wolfie is trying to accept who he is, but on the other hand, he feels that his marriage is something he values more than living full-time as a man. "Well I really, being married I don't feel that I really can transition. I feel a responsibility to him, too. I know he would be very unhappy about it." Many FTMs choose not to transition for financial, political, or medical reasons. Others choose to preserve their relationships in lieu of total self-acceptance or living as a man full time. It might be helpful here to separate transition choices from self-acceptance issues. Wolfie is on the verge of self-acceptance, despite the trivialization he suffers from the significant others in his life. If he attains self-acceptance, he may or may not pursue transition. Some FTMs see Wolfie's choice to preserve his marriage as a kind of denial of who he is. Wolfie may really agree with his husband that cross-dressing is no big deal or that he is not really a man. Only time will tell what the truth is in this case, as Wolfie takes his time sorting out what he wants to do.

Therapeutic experts, whose authority is hard to overthrow, can also prove to be a barrier to identification. Several of the FTMs report extreme therapeutic measures. Michael, an artist and community activist, says that he went through thirty years of therapy, most of which was spent avoiding or negating his real identity.

> Her response was, "Okay [patronizing tone], that's nice." Initially, she said she was supportive. She would say things like, "I support you in this. I will help you in this." But when I began to make changes, she

resisted that all the way. For instance, I chose a male name and she wouldn't call me that. I asked her to call me by the male pronoun and she wouldn't do that. At different points, she'd say things to me like, "Well when you go back to being a woman, you'll feel much better about things." On the surface she was saying she would support me, but the underlying messages from her were, "I'm doing anything but supporting you here."

The difficulty of finding therapists who are willing to take an FTM at his word and to help him negotiate his identity trajectory is a recurring theme in the narratives of FTMs. As Jack relates, the cost of therapy and the dissemination of misinformation can also be prohibitive.

Ninety dollars a session. I couldn't pay for that. There was no way, I was making minimum wage. I paid for a couple sessions. She gave me some misinformation and said that "you're not allowed to do any of this. No reputable doctor will start you on hormones until you're twenty-one." And I believed her because here we have Johns Hopkins, they must know. So I didn't pursue it. I'll just wait. That's the second big regret, because that's not true. But I didn't know any better.

The power of an institution like Johns Hopkins intimidated young Jack into accepting his fate, at least for a short time longer. For those like Jack, who are still legally dependent on their parents, the selection of a therapist and the conditions of payments to therapists are limited by their non-cooperative parents: "My father would not give me one penny towards this therapy because they saw it as condoning what I was doing."

FTMs internalize the skepticism of others. Doubts about identification or transition result from a number of situations. Pregnancy and childrearing are top among these. For Alex, the desire for his first child stood as a kind of diagnostic test.

I'd been trying for awhile and had a couple of miscarriages before and [I thought] maybe I shouldn't really have a kid, because I'm really not a woman in certain ways.

Eventually, Alex separated his gender identity from his gender role. He decided that his desire to have a child did not mean he was a woman. Alex suffered physical discomfort for his greater goal of having a child.

Matthew also thinks that being a parent is distinct from the experience of bearing a child. But, unlike Alex's, Matthew's pregnancy was not physically problematic. He said that the benefits of pregnancy were feeling physically healthy and having everyone's support. Matthew, who was always outside the boundaries of appropriate gender behavior, treasured this kind of support, but his feelings about motherhood remain vexed.

> I felt absolutely nothing even closely resembling maternal instinct. I was like, "This is a baby and I'm taking care of it, it's my job right now." I never felt any of that bonding kind of stuff that people describe. I felt kinda fond of my new baby and attached to it maybe the way a father would.

This lack of "maternal instinct" was another confirmation for him of his gender identity.

He recalls the Baby M surrogate mother case and remembers his response as a testimonial to his lack of great maternal instinct.

> I got into a conversation with another of my female co-workers. Based upon my feelings about having given birth to a child, I made the statement to this group of women that I didn't think it was any big deal to be a surrogate mother. You make a baby, you have the baby, and you give it away. What's the big deal? And they're going, "Oh how could you give away something that's part of you?" and "You would feel like a part of you was being ripped away."

The contrasts Matthew and others draw between themselves and women in incidents like this one help to consolidate their identities and justify their transitions.

Some of the FTMs who came into contact with male-to-female transsexuals have initial difficulties identifying as transsexual. Contrary to popular belief, there are no natural affinities between FTMs and MTFs. For example, some MTFs try to live up to normative gender ideals and FTMs who know MTFs of this sort are sometimes put off by the hyper-femininity that these women embrace. Many FTMs are trying desperately to escape the feminine imperatives required by their female bodies. The combination of these factors can lead FTMs to assume that they are not transsexual.

FTMs also compare themselves with other men to see if they are like them. Many FTMs wonder if all men are jerks and are disturbed by hegemonic masculinity. This becomes a significant barrier to achieving an untroubled identification as a man. They do not want to become the demonized man that is represented in some feminist ideologies. Others wonder if they measure up to hegemonic masculinity. Are they strong enough, tall enough, virile enough? Do they have to wear ties and jackets to be men? What constitutes being a real man and will they ever be authentic? Alex speaks to this issue in reference to the kind of clothes he wants to wear:

> Even dressing, if I would wear my Birkenstocks, it's like is this ambivalence on your part or is this my idea of a guy? I could be a guy who wears Birkenstocks. I could be a guy who wears a pink shirt. I can't be a woman who wears a pink shirt. But I could be a guy who could wear a pink shirt and be okay about that.

Wearing Birkenstock sandals instead of construction boots could be a sign of ambivalence about his gender identity or it could just be Alex's version of manhood. Because he was atypical compared to some men that he met, Alex was uncertain for a while about his identity. Ultimately, he decided that a man can wear pink and still be a man. He also points out that as a woman he could not wear that color because it emphasizes femininity. Becoming a transsexual man allows Alex to break hegemonic gender ideals.

These FTMs' worries about being "real" men increase when they encounter FTMs who embrace hegemonic masculinity. This disidentification delays their total identification as transsexual men. Alex recalls his struggle with this dilemma:

> There's this one guy who was like beer belly man. Oh my gosh, I don't want to be that. I didn't really want to be a guy, this straight guy . . . who would want to be? It wasn't something that I aspired to at that point. It seemed limiting in a lot of ways. . . . I said, "Look, I don't want to be just this regular guy." A lot of them, the other [FTMs], really

were very polarized. For me, there are lots of different ways of being a guy. Like some could be more academic, some could be more truck-driver guy.

What it means to be a man has to be thoroughly problematized. Un-conventional expressions of masculinity in dress, career choice, and sexual object choice are a barrier to assuming an identity as an FTM. It requires intellectual and emotional work to separate one's gender iden-tity (who one is) from one's gender role (what one does). Like women who redefine womanhood—women who do not wear make-up, who play sports, who become electrical engineers, or who have sexual rela-tionships with women—FTMs have to redefine the meaning of being a man.

The last stop in a transsexual trajectory is transition choices. Hav-ing found the category of transsexual, assimilated one's experiences within that category, and accepted that category as an identity, the FTMs in this study still had transition choices to make. Transition choices are a significant site of contestation within the FTM commu-nity. Although the dominant norm is to transition to an unambigu-ously male presentation, a transsexual trajectory is not necessarily a linear process with a clear end. Skipping "steps" or not transitioning is often regarded within the community with skepticism. This hegemony, however, is being challenged.[1]

Changing one's sex is a multi-step process rather than a single walk through a "sex change" machine or one trip to a surgical unit. Transi-tion consists of a variety of procedures. An array of factors may enable or derail transitions: financial cost, general health, ideological beliefs about what makes a man, and the limits of transition technologies for FTMs at the time. Weighing these factors, each FTM in this study makes his own transition choices. Despite differences in transition choices, each of the research participants considers transition to be a part of his transsexual trajectory.

Disidentifying Work: Consolidating an FTM Identity

Female-bodied individuals of all kinds are among the most significant others against whom FTMs judge their own experiences as different.

In particular, lesbian others perform this function in a way that is unique and worthy of special attention.

FTMs' reiteration of their differences from lesbians is persistent, independent of the nature of the experiences FTM men have with lesbians. FTMs seem to be driven by an inexhaustible need to repeat their differences from lesbians, even after reaching the point at which they are indistinguishable from other men. Some FTMs have lesbian careers and some do not. Whether or not FTM men have a previous lesbian career has a distinct effect on the intensity of the identity work necessary to differentiate themselves from lesbians. Figure 4.1 summarizes the relationship between lesbian careers, sexual object choice, and identity work.

The function of this disidentification work is to consolidate an FTM identity. These difference claims have the force of truth for FTMs. In the interviews, and in community responses to my research, I was often reprimanded for not drawing a clearer distinction between FTMs and butches. These slaps on the wrist pointed to the need these men have to distinguish themselves from lesbian women. By highlighting that these difference claims are a kind of identity work, I do not intend

Figure 4.1. *Intensity of identity work varies with sexual object choice and physical or conceptual proximity to lesbian women.*

Sexual Object Choice	Lesbian Career	Intensity of Identity Work		
		Low	High	Highest
Male Sexual Object	NO	Gay FTMs		
Female Sexual Object	NO		Straight FTMs	
Female Sexual Object	Yes			Straight FTMs

Note: Though some of the FTMs in this study reported that their sexual object choice changed over the course of their transition from female to male, they have been categorized in this typology according to their sexual object choice *prior to transition*. The sexual object choice prior to transition was the greatest determinant of the intensity of identity work that each man performed to differentiate himself from lesbians.

to discredit either their truth-value or their use-value to the FTMs in this study. Whether these claims are empirically true is not my concern.[2] I only want to show what purpose such claims serve for those who make them.

FTMs without Lesbian Careers

Less than half of the FTMs in this study do not have a previous lesbian career. Before transition, these guys confronted the possibility that others might misrecognize them as lesbian. Some had to figure out why they felt gay, but were not attracted to women. The work that they did to distinguish themselves from lesbians is a significant part of their stories, though not as prominent as the same kind of identity-work performed by FTMs with lesbian careers.

FTMs without lesbian careers can be divided into two types: straight men and gay men. These different sexualities result in different types of identity work. Because their bodies were female and because they were assumed to be women, straight FTMs were sometimes presumed by others to be lesbian women, while gay FTMs were presumed to be heterosexual women.

The fact that they are sexually attracted to women makes it important for straight FTMs to differentiate themselves from lesbians. They have to articulate a specific version of lesbianism that clearly does not apply to themselves. The paradigm they created to do so sounds a lot like the lesbianism-feminism of the 1970s. By this definition, all lesbians were women first. Since straight FTMs are not women, they cannot be lesbians even though they have sexual desires for women. Francis's story is a good example of this dilemma.

> I always had crushes on these girls. But it was only in my head. I didn't identify then and I don't identify now as a lesbian. And even when I found out what that was, I never felt that I was one. 'Cause I was never identified as a woman or a girl who was in love with, had a crush on another girl. Deep down inside I knew I was a guy. In my fantasies, I was the guy with them.

Gay FTMs have sexual desires for men and therefore have no reason to consider themselves lesbians. Still, many feel the need to distinguish themselves from lesbians. For example, Jake attended a co-ed gay group with his husband for some time, and was attracted to the gay men in the group. He ran a test to make sure.

> I got a dream about kissing one of the lesbians that was there. For that split second after I woke up, I said to myself, "That's really weird, girls never appealed to me, but just to make sure, I want to kiss her for real." So we did and that closed the door for me. I haven't questioned that after that.

Gay FTMs have to explain their feelings of kinship with gay people, despite having what appears to be a heterosexual object choice. These FTMs are faced with the task of claiming a gay identity that is not reducible to "lesbian." On the one hand, FTMs like Matthew feel a kinship with gay people.

> I felt kind of a kinship with other gay people that I met. Somehow one of them. The same way you might feel if you were in a place where there weren't very many Jewish people and you met another Jewish person. Whether you like them or not personally, you might feel that kind of kinship, like you were another Jewish person.

On the other hand, they know they are not attracted to women.

> As soon as I knew that gay people existed, I was absolutely convinced that I was one of them. I had absolutely no attraction to women. I couldn't explain why I felt I was gay. . . . I didn't understand that if I was gay that meant I must be a lesbian. So I had to figure out why I kept thinking I was gay.

Because these gay FTMs were sexually attracted to men, they figured they could not be gay. Yet, they persistently sensed that they were like gay people. This paradox structured their search for identity. They sought out gay people and groups and participated in gay life, but with confusion about their place in that world. The other members of these groups were also confused and tried to fit these FTMs into established categories. Matthew says, "They couldn't figure me out at all. Because there I was married to a husband, not in the process of getting a divorce."

While Matthew's marital status caused confusion in his group, Jake says his wedding ring foreclosed the question of his identity. The group thought Jake's husband was in denial about his bisexual tendencies. In either case, Jake and Matthew both enjoyed the company of the lesbians without identifying with them.

In addition to their sexual attraction to men, these gay FTMs without lesbian careers recalled having childhood friends whom they believed had turned out gay. For them, this was a diagnostic sign that helped to make sense of their position in the gay world. Jake recalls such a friendship:

> I remember when I was twelve there was a boy that liked me a lot. He was gay, but he didn't know it. I knew it. I didn't really know it either, but a lot of other kids knew it. They would say, "Why are you walking so funny?" or he would say to me, "I don't know what to do, I don't know how else to walk, that's the way I walk" and he was so sincere. And I would just tell him, "Don't worry, you're fine the way you are" and we would develop these bondings. We wouldn't date or anything, but the only friends that I would make would be those kinds of boys that were totally outcast because of the way they walked or moved.

Having gay friends or crushes on boys who were effeminate confirmed their sense of being gay themselves. The boys they had friendships or relationships with did not treat them as heterosexual men treat women. These relationships were between two effeminate boys, one of whom happened to have a female body.

Gay FTMs often assume that they represented the total population of FTMs without lesbian careers. In fact, there are straight FTMs without lesbian careers. This assumption tells us something about how gay FTMs think about themselves and the kind of identity work they do. Male sexual object choice is the primary way that gay FTMs disidentify from lesbians. Their desire for men is the most important factor in consolidating their identities.

Gay FTMs without lesbian careers are less threatened by whatever characteristics they share with lesbians. They have less of an intense urge to define what a lesbian is or to explain why they are not like lesbians. This group of men has the least amount of identity work in order to perform to make sense of their histories: their sexual object choice was considered appropriate for their female bodies. This allowed them to be sexually active without stepping outside of hetero-normativity. Pre-transition, these men were less scrutinized for uncon-ventional choices. Jake explains:

> Because I think we could get the boyfriends, even if we didn't like what we were getting. If you start as lesbian, it's harder to get the girls because it is hard to find someone who likes girls. But because we did like guys, most of us lasted a lot longer before going insane and be-cause we could close our eyes and pretend something. Take enough medication and still get what we need. It was easier to disassociate and float. 'Cause we were at least getting our partners, even if they weren't what we wanted.

However, as Jake points out, this small privilege changes after gay FTMs transition. Becoming gay and giving up their heterosexual status is difficult to do and hard to justify. It involves taking on a stigmatized role from a previously unstigmatized position.

Of all the FTMs in this study, gay FTMs without lesbian careers had the least conceptual proximity, or closeness that comes from simi-larity at the level of categories, to lesbians. Gay FTMs are often more *socially* proximate to lesbians than are straight FTMs without lesbian careers. They socialize with lesbians in political clubs, gay bars, and other sites of gay life. However, their sexual object choice makes them less proximate *conceptually* to lesbians than are straight FTMs, since both straight FTMs and lesbians date women. The sexual object choice of gay FTMs precludes the possibility that they will be mistaken for lesbians, either by themselves or by others. In their transitions, they have the least intense need to disidentify from lesbians. This is re-flected in their tolerant attitudes toward lesbians.

Straight FTMs without lesbian careers have to do more intensive identity work than their gay counterparts to distinguish themselves from lesbian women. Both lesbians and straight FTMs have women as their sexual object choice. This makes the need for disidentifying work greater. Like FTMs with lesbian careers, these straight FTMs have to make clear that they are different from lesbians in other ways. Their conceptual proximity to lesbians makes it necessary to explain how they know that they are not homosexual women. The main way that they do this is by articulating a specific notion of lesbianism: lesbians are woman-identified women who love other women and celebrate being women. Lesbians are, in their view, the most female of all women. They are female-bodied and comfortable with their female parts. Most importantly, lesbians are not uncomfortable being sexual with women as women. Though this last piece of the definition of lesbianism is often shrouded by euphemism, straight FTMs will often imply that lesbians are not uncomfortable being penetrated or having sexual attention paid to their breasts and genitalia by their female partners. In separate interviews, Jack and Gregg summarize their concepts of what a lesbian is and why they knew they were not lesbian.

> Jack: There was *no way in hell* I would ever go into anything that would look anything remotely close to a lesbian thing. I mean that was just so far away from me. 'Cause that's like being girl-girl-girl. That's as close to girl as you can get. So there is no way in hell I'd do that stuff. . . . I knew I was male. Like I said, being lesbian is the female of all females. It's like you can't get any more female. That's so far away from what I was.

> Gregg: They still see themselves as women, and celebrate themselves as women. "I am a woman!" These women want to celebrate being women, but still identify as lesbians. I don't want to celebrate being a woman. . . . They would want that done, but then they'd want to have some type of gratification, too. Orally. I didn't want them doing the same thing to me that I was doing to them. That I enjoyed doing to them. Not at all. Don't even touch me there. They like breasts. I like them on other people, don't touch mine. I'll stay fully clothed.

These conceptions of lesbianism are based on the post-1970s paradigm of female homosexuality. The straight FTMs without lesbian careers often have little experience with the gay world and do not acknowledge the possibility of male-identified lesbians. For example, John visited a lesbian bar with a transgender acquaintance and was surprised by what he saw there.

> [My friend] took me to that dyke bar, the first time I met him. That was the first time I've ever been in any situation like that. I said to [my friend], "If these are all lesbians, why do they dance with this guy?" He said, "That's a woman." "That's a woman?" He's like, "She's the hottest one in the place. Everyone is after her." In my mind, I thought it was a guy. Looks like a guy. Acts like a guy. Dances like a guy. Deals with them like a guy. Why are they so hot for this person? If they like women, why are they after this person who looks like a guy? I didn't understand the whole scene.

John's confusion about the butch lesbian at the bar reflects his belief that lesbians are womanly women who love other womanly women. His friend explained that the women at the bar would have been interested in John, but only on the condition that he "out" himself. For John, this re-established his sense of difference from the dykes at the bar because he would never consider "outing" himself.

John and the other straight FTMs without lesbian careers also establish their difference from lesbians by reporting a pure dating history: they have only dated and will only consider dating straight women.

> They were both totally straight. They both dated guys before. And after me. No. I've never, ever, ever dated a lesbian. Honestly, I could not understand it. Because there's no way in hell I ever would've been called that. The girls I dated, well I dated straight girls. If they ever dealt with me, I never had one, but if they had dealt with me as a woman in any way shape or form, that would've been it. I would've been out of there.

For John, the purity of his dating history confirms his heterosexual manhood, as well as his transsexualism. Several of these guys refused all sexual contact with women until after their transitions. Abstinence is the only acceptable option for men who feel that any sexual contact between two female bodies is lesbian sex. Refusing to engage in sex with another female body is a way of maintaining difference from lesbians and substantiating heterosexual male identities. For example, Jack abstained from sex with women before his transition because he believed that his body would prevent his female lovers from treating him like a man.

> I knew I was not lesbian. There was one point where I could've kissed her, but no, I'm not going to, because this would be lesbian sex. I'm not going to do that. I can't do that. I won't do that. Not in this body.

Jack's emphasis on his body is not unusual. The agnosia that many straight men without lesbian careers locate in their bodies is a fundamental way to distinguish themselves from others with female bodies. These straight FTMs restricted their own sexual activities to fantasy until after transition, when they were no longer female-bodied, so that their sexual behavior would not be misinterpreted as lesbian. Gregg says

> At that time, I had no sexual experience because I didn't want to. No, I'm not interested in . . . letting a female touch me the way that women want to be with each other.

Being read as lesbian is more upsetting to straight FTMs like these than to gay FTMs without lesbian careers. Being mistaken by others as lesbian is a major cause of concern for them, whereas the gay FTMs expect this possibility and are not nearly as disturbed by this reading. Wolfie, a gay guy, reports that he is "at the point where obviously I know I look female, so I certainly wouldn't feel offended to be taken for a dyke at all." In comparison, Jack felt absolutely horrified when this occurred.

> Once when I was walking through a mall, these two scummy guys walked by and said, "You look like a dyke," and that was the only time ever. It just made me so mortified that people saw me like that. God, that was like the worst of the worst. I'd rather them see me as a frilly little girl than to see me as a dyke.

While being misread as a lesbian at the mall could be traumatizing for the day, being misread in romantic relationships has higher stakes. John's wife had married him knowing his past history, but eventually left him because she believed that their marriage was really a lesbian affair. When

John's wife began to consider their marriage "lesbian," she pointed to his female body as evidence. In order for John to resist his wife's account of their marriage, he had to demonstrate that he had the wrong body.

> I don't know at what point she decided, but three months before she left she told me that she didn't think that we were really married, because I was born with this body. God's always seen me as a female. So she decided I was a female so our relationship was a lesbian relationship. I can't even say that word.

The end of his marriage came as a result of being misread as a lesbian by his wife. Like several of the other straight FTMs, John has practically stopped dating until he can afford the phalloplasty that will complete his transition and foreclose the possibility of misrecognition.

John says that his need to distinguish himself from lesbians is not motivated by homophobia. He remembers with fondness a gay friend with whom he shared his secret. He points to the several gay FTM friends he now has as proof that he is not homophobic.

> Chris turned out to be gay and I didn't. I held his wallet for him when he met his first guy. I didn't have any problem with other people being gay. Or guys liking guys, or girls liking girls, but it wasn't me.

FTMs with Lesbian Careers

More than half of the FTMs in this study had a lesbian career that preceded their transsexual trajectory. Their lesbian careers were ultimately abandoned and explained away as a wrong turn they made while searching for their true identity. Making sense of these lesbian careers is central to the consolidation of their transsexual identities. The disidentifying work that these FTMs do is at the highest pitch of intensity due to the conceptual and social proximity they have to lesbians. The identity work they do is similar to the work that straight FTMs without lesbian careers perform. The latter only need to contradict the mistakes of others, but straight FTMs with lesbian careers must confront their own "mistakes." These have the most intensive disidentifying work to do.

An FTM who had a lesbian career may doubt his own transsexual identity. This self-doubt makes it necessary to construct explanations for the lesbian careers. Straight FTMs with lesbian careers must explain why they dated lesbian women, participated in lesbian communities and culture, and assumed a lesbian identity.

As Shadow explains in the earlier quote, many FTMs in this study discovered the category of lesbian and figured that was what they were. These are a few of the reasons FTMs give for their "mistaken" lesbian careers: they had sexual desires for other female bodies, they found that being a lesbian was a means of being "mannish" or approximating their gender identities, or being a lesbian was one strategy for getting out of the position of "woman" in heterosexual relationships. While some straight women probably want to escape their position as women in heterosexual relationships, FTMs say that this is a different feeling. For example, Julian says, "I always just hated being the 'girl' to anybody else's 'boy.' Sex just makes that very salient. It was one area that. . . . I was a woman in a way probably more acutely than other situations." FTMs do not want to be women, whereas non-transsexual women do not want to be subordinate.

These explanations for a lesbian career are framed as mistakes. Other FTMs with lesbian careers say they "detoured" through the community, dating women without claiming a lesbian identity. In either case, these FTMs claim that they have always felt they were different from lesbians. Those who detoured through the lesbian community often said they were just "hiding out" among lesbians. They have fewer investments in their past and less to explain. Those who made "mistakes" claimed a lesbian identity at one point, but eventually feelings of difference and unease returned. The return of difference generated another search for identity in a transsexual register, ultimately resulting in what one FTM calls, "a better fit." Those with a case of mistaken identity have the most to explain about their histories.

Some FTMs with lesbian careers initiate efforts to maintain their lesbian careers, stretching the definition of lesbian in order to enclose themselves within it. Some choose to "stay gay" and begin relationships with men as men. Some straight FTMs reframe their romantic and sexual relationships to women, reidentifying as straight. In any case, these FTMs eventually exit or re-evaluate queer life.

In that gray area between acknowledging their difference from lesbians and consolidating their identities as transsexual men, some of these FTMs attempt to extend their lesbian careers. They now view these extensions as last ditch attempts to live as women before embarking on transition. The feminist analysis of female bodies helps to minimize their differences from women. The ideology of feminism, with its radical critique of patriarchal hatred for bodies in general and women's bodies more specifically, provides some temporary relief for these men.[3] Many of the men report well-meaning attempts to reclaim their female bodies from the scorn of society. In these attempts they tried to make sense of their own struggles with their bodies as internalized self-hatred, as a form of self-surveillance, or as a pernicious result of patriarchal disdain for female bodies. Ed remembers his efforts to use this political analysis to explain the agnosia that arose during menstruation:

> I felt very ashamed that I was not happy at all. I guess there was enough feminism around. Even though I felt like this is not right for me, this is awful. . . . I felt ashamed and it got more focused as I got older. So I tried to believe, "Okay, this is a gift." But I hated it.

Ed tried to frame his relationship to his body within a feminist analysis like the women around him. He now says that this attempt failed.

Ed, like the others, claims he had more or different discomfort with his body than women. Doing the work of disidentification, Ed draws on his persistent agnosia to mark the difference between himself and lesbians. From his point of view, the reemergence of a sense of difference signaled the end of his lesbian career.

A second strategy for maintaining a lesbian career is to change geographic location. But geographic relocation eventually fails because of a persistent sense of difference from lesbians. Some FTMs with lesbian careers moved to a larger and more diverse lesbian community, with several different lesbian styles and cultures, in order to extend their lesbian careers. Shadow went to San Francisco.

Then I moved here. There were so many [more] different facets to a
dyke community here than Minneapolis could even think about having. There was just a lot more freedom. *It gave me a little bit more time
to get to know myself and about that.*

FTMs with lesbian careers have to make sense of their desire for
women. Many explain that they used to think "lesbian" was the de-
fault category for female-bodied desire for women. This is the pre-
dominant reason that FTMs in this study give for their lesbian careers.
Using the "lesbian" category allowed these FTMs to organize their sexual
and romantic affections for women.

Julian says that, when becoming a man was not yet imaginable, he
called himself a lesbian.

Maybe it seems kinda stupid but it took me awhile to sorta realize,
"Oh my God, I could actually be with a woman and not be a man."
Like I could be with a woman anyway, even though I'm a woman. At
that point, I just started claiming a lesbian identity, even before I'd ever
even kissed a woman. I started telling all of my friends that I was a
lesbian. I just sorta kinda made it up.

At the time, identifying as a lesbian was the logical way of framing his
desire for women. It was something he "made up," rather than something that came out of his experiences with women.

Whereas some straight FTMs without lesbian careers choose abstinence, some FTMs with lesbian careers prefer to pursue women,
sacrificing their male identities. Others do not see their interim lesbian
identities as a sacrifice, but rather as a means of approaching their male
identity. Alex says:

I could sorta fit in. I didn't have to dress in a way that didn't feel comfortable to me. I didn't have to pretend that I was straight. I didn't
have to worry about pronouns. In a lot of ways, it felt comfortable.

The lesbian community provides a place for these guys to creep up on
their masculinity. Being among those lesbians who do not wear make-
up or shave their legs, who encourage their cross-dressing or butch
behavior, makes it safer to be themselves. These men know lesbians
who were not the "most female of all females," but were rather doing a

kind of female masculinity. Acknowledging this version of lesbianism, these men approximated a version of themselves within the lesbian category.

Nevertheless, they say a sense of difference ultimately reopened the question of who they were and where they fit in. Alex explains, "What happened was that increasingly I became I aware that I really didn't belong there, because I really didn't identify as being a woman and I never really did." Though Alex knows some "mannish" lesbians, he still considers them women and, by comparison, he is neither a woman nor a lesbian. This is the same type of disidentifying work that the straight FTMs without lesbian careers employ to consolidate their identities.

Transition Again

Transition choices are one place in transsexual trajectories where the contests over the meaning of being FTM become obvious. Most of the FTMs in this study think transition starts with hormones and proceeds through chest reconstruction, placing less emphasis on hysterectomy and testicular implants, metaoidioplasty ("freeing" of the enlarged clitoris), or phalloplasty. Those who have not physically transitioned are divided between those who plan for some future modification and those who do not. Among those who do not plan any modification, there are also two subgroups: one group of those who are comfortable and satisfied with their present physical condition and another group of those who are uncomfortable and dissatisfied but are stopped by external obstacles. Transitioning, or at least a desire to transition, is hegemonically regarded as the truest sign of a transsexual identity. Decisions not to transition are regarded skeptically, although more leeway is given to those who want to transition but cannot due to reasons beyond their control.

In response to this skepticism, a few of the FTMs in this study voice the opinion that transition is an emotional, not a physical, change. The emotional component of transition involves acceptance of oneself as a transsexual and as a man. This "non-op" or "no-hormone" route challenges the dominant FTM trajectory. It has the potential to throw some individuals into doubt as to whether they are FTMs. Soon, an FTM identity may not be predicated upon the desire for body modifications.

Men who have physically transitioned mention that emotional acceptance is an important part of their process. Nonetheless, they continue to believe that this acceptance will automatically lead an FTM to make modifications to his body. Those individuals who are not modifying their bodies express skepticism about their own choices and their status as FTMs.

Within this debate, there are smaller debates about the different aspects of physical transition. For example, attitudes toward "bottom" surgeries are less rigorously policed within the community. Without a feasible phalloplastic option that is reasonably priced, aesthetically pleasing, and fully functional, there is a greater range of opinions about which choice is best. Hegemony is not as strongly established in the case of phallic reconstructions as for other transition choices, notably hormones and "top" surgery.

Julian and Alex mention that the lack of a satisfactory phalloplastic option is a significant limitation on their decision to transition. A majority of men in this study are indefinitely postponing that step until new procedures are developed. Others have worked out ways of being a man without a penis. Julian says that this was a severe concern of his: "If you're a man to not have a penis that works—kinda a drawback. [laughs]" He goes on to discuss how the penis question is usually answered by other FTMs.

> I do agree to some extent that "man" is a social category. If one is culturally legible as a man. As one takes on or has the role that men have in our society, then one is a man. Gender is interactive. Obviously, the penis doesn't make a man. I do agree with that. I think that you *can* be a man without a penis. But who'd *want* to?

Julian believes he can be a man without a penis, indicating that manhood is not anatomically defined. Yet for him, the desire for a penis represents the importance of bodies for self-definition.

Most of the FTMs in this study say that they want a penis in order to date and have sex without complication or to urinate in public bathrooms or shower in locker rooms. These are all social settings where some nudity is expected and it troubles the men in this study not to be able to live this part of life without taking extra precautions. For Julian, and some of the others, the problem of not having a penis is more than a social problem that undermines his gender presentation. Not having the right anatomy undercuts Julian's sense of self. He wants a penis for his own pleasure and as a tool for completing the consolidation of his identity.

> To me, a dick is a thing I would like to satisfy myself. [laughs] A dick is a thing I would like to have and to look at and to see in the mirror and to touch and to wank and to just to touch it. Oh my God! To me it's like the mirror inverse of the feelings that I have about my breasts—a constant monitoring awareness in a negative way. I imagine having a penis, for me, I imagine it would be just the opposite. This constant awareness—"Yeah, my dick, I feel my dick, I feel my dick in my underwear, I love my dick. I got a dick, I'm gonna touch my dick, I love my cock."

Though he is read socially as a man, he is dissatisfied without a penis. Not because of what this lack might say about him to others, but because of his own need for a body that he can be pleased to inhabit. The issue of phalloplasty is related to a larger set of worries about the bodies that could be produced through hormonal and surgical techniques. Julian mentions that he is concerned about several other features of his body.

> I'll always be short. My hands will always be kinda too small. My chest will be scarred, even though it might look all right in a shirt, it's gonna be scarred. Maybe my hips will always be disproportionate to my shoulders and they'll always really be too wide. Which feels like not really quite okay. And to, of course, not have a fully functional penis.

He points out that many FTMs try to cope with these limitations by acknowledging that non-transsexual male bodies come in all shapes and sizes. By placing themselves within the context of all other male bodies, these men can take solace from the range of height, size, and proportions among men. Hoping to undercut the problem of surgical addiction, these FTMs challenge hegemonic transition choices.

If body modification has been a component of a hegemonic FTM identity, new challenges to that dominant paradigm include acceptance and acknowledgment of the variance among men. In response, these new approaches have engendered a reaction from some FTMs who do want to modify their body and who resent the belief system of the challengers. They feel that this coping strategy, while useful, can sometimes obscure or deny the pain of living in bodies that are limited in all these ways. They believe that this coping strategy is not much different from the denial they lived in before their transitions. For these guys, "acceptance" is a rhetorical trap that precludes making the body modifications they so desire.

Correlating Historical and Biographical Identity Work

The socio-cultural production of an FTM identity and the biographical work of disidentification are mutually reinforcing, correlative processes. In the biographical work of disidentification, individual FTMs mobilize the same terms by which a historical FTM identity came into existence. FTMs reiterate that they are unlike lesbians and more like intersexuals. The ways that they articulate these difference claims draw on both the medical logic of treatment and the lesbian-feminist revolution, that is, the discursive contexts out of which an FTM identity arose and consolidated itself.

For example, the logic of treatment put an emphasis on the body as the focal point of discomfort. Where female inverts did not qualify for treatments because they lacked a bodily anomaly that could be corrected via hormones and surgeries, nascent FTMs bodies are treatable to the extent that they locate their dis-ease in their bodies. These terms are remobilized at the individual level when FTMs claim that their discomfort is with their bodies as a way of differentiating themselves from other female, especially lesbian, bodies.

The other discursive context, lesbian-feminism, defines female homosexuals hegemonically as woman-identified women who celebrate their womanhood and are at ease with their female bodies. Drawing on this context, FTMs make explicit difference claims to distinguish themselves from other female bodies with sexual desires for women. They are male-identified and uneasy with their female bodies. These difference claims are drawn from a socio-cultural context in which these two identities have become distinct and it is possible to clearly categorize oneself as either a lesbian or an FTM based on these differences.

The echoes of history in the personal narratives of these men represent multiple dialectical relationships. Subjects draw upon the discursive terms of the day to make sense of themselves. The terms they use are not accidental, but are rather due to the socio-cultural discursive horizon of possibilities that gender inverts have for making sense of their lives. Individuals retell their experiences, effectively rewriting their histories as mistakes or "detours" in order to fit themselves within the categories most useful to them.

However, socio-cultural categories of experience are subject to alteration as individuals try to place themselves within those categories. The newly consolidated FTM category is already being challenged by individuals with unorthodox experiences attempting to inhabit it. This is a result of the inadequacy of categories to ever fully capture experiences. Always insufficient for describing experience, these categories are in a perpetual dialectical motion with no final end. Categories of identity always produce an excess against which they maintain a sense of internal consistency. All social formations, including all identities or paradigms of identity, are unstable consolidations that succeed one another without end as individuals confront the limited ability of all categories to adequately capture their experience. The conflicts over orthodox transitions reflect the eternal dialectics of identity. Debates over these choices show how identities, once consolidated, are challenged from within and from without by subjects in pursuit of meaningful lives.

Chapter 5

Always Already Men

■ James: People want to refer to us as women who wanted to be men,
   or women who became men, but as women first. It's true that
   we have had female bodies, but we were not women. It's very
   important to understand that.

James and the other FTMs believe they have always been men, despite
their female bodies. In contrast, in the eyes of most non-transsexuals,
FTMs are born female and grow up as feminine girls who strangely
and without explanation decide to become men. This seems like an
irrational choice to their family, friends, lovers, and the public at large.
Non-transsexuals may even believe that women become men to access
male privilege. Though they do not seem as crazy as male-to-female
transsexuals, who sacrifice their male privilege, FTMs seem calculat-
ing and post-feminist to non-transsexuals because some privileges ac-
crue to them. An FTM may appear to be taking rash personal actions
to address a social problem that would be better tackled by political
action.[1]

But the FTMs were not in pursuit of male privilege. Many suffered serious consequences in their professional lives and intimate relationships. Their goal is simply to become recognizable. Who they are
at heart does not change during transition. Notice that they use the
term "transition" rather than "transformation."[2] Although they do have

to make a social and physical changeover from one sex to another, they are not transforming, like caterpillars becoming butterflies. They are not changing their personality, only the physical package that houses the person inside the flesh. They are not transforming themselves from women into men. They are repairing the link between their bodies and their gender identity.

Sensationalism in the tabloid press or television[3] may account for the "woman becomes man" descriptions that accompany most popular stories on transsexual men. The claim that one has always been male is less easily sold to the public. It also raises some difficult questions about masculinity and men. What does it mean to be a man and what does one have to be in order to count as a man? Why do these individuals assume that they cannot be men without modifying their bodies? These questions about transsexual men also raise general questions that are at the heart of Gender Studies. What are the hegemonic beliefs about maleness, masculinity, bodies, and biology? In what ways do men sustain or subvert these beliefs? Answers that do justice to the life stories of FTMs may also address some of the fears, hesitations, and hostilities about transsexualism raised by feminist and queer authors and activists.

Most of the FTMs make a distinction between maleness (sexed bodies) and masculinity (gender roles). They claim that all men have male bodies, but reject the belief that men behave in any one particular way. Men may behave in an infinite variety of ways, but all men have male bodies. At this point in history, fewer people, FTMs included, associate any particular set of behaviors or social roles with maleness than have done so in the past. However, it remains a cultural expectation among most people, including FTMs, that men have male bodies. The men in this study see themselves as males, though not necessarily as masculine in temperament. This points to the escalating primacy of embodiment rather than behavior or social role for male identity in this historical moment.

Paradoxically, transsexual men believe that all men have male bodies *and* that they are men despite the evidence of their female bodies. They resolve this paradox by claiming a core identity that is obscured by their female bodies. This explains why they alter their bodies: in order to be recognizable to themselves and to others. Their transitions are only a means of making their core identities visible and recognizable to the public. This points to the importance of expressive identities. An expressive identity is a core gender that is situated inside oneself, a gendered soul. Bodies are an expression of that core self.[4]

FTM beliefs about testosterone's effect on their bodies and their behaviors tell us still more about current notions of maleness and masculinity. Most believe that testosterone is the source of physical maleness and some believe that it is also the source of masculine social behavior. These beliefs seem to conform to cultural stereotypes about men and masculinity, and about identity and embodiment. Some social scientists view the stories they share about testosterone and transsexualism as confirmation that transsexuals reify gender (Kessler and McKenna 1978; Raymond 1979, 1996; Butler 1993).[5] In response, other social commentators hold up transsexualism an example of the subversion of gender (Bornstein 1994; MacKenzie, 1994; Feinberg 1993, 1996, and 1998; Wilchins 1997).[6] Transsexualism itself does not necessarily subvert or affirm dominant forms of masculinity. Transsexual men have the potential to generate either alternative or hegemonic forms of masculinity. Altering their bodies to fit this cultural expectation, these men have an opportunity, though they do not always take it, to resignify what it means to behave like a man. Transsexualism is neither essentially normative nor essentially counterhegemonic.

Essentially Male, Not Necessarily Masculine

FTMs in this study have essentialist ideas about what it means to be a man. In order to say "I am a man," each of them has some idea about what a man is and what all men, regardless of their class, status, ethnicity, race, party affiliation, nationality, religion, or sexuality, have in common. They have to associate their core sense of self with the characteristics they attribute to men. They have some absolute criteria they use to define what all men are and that include themselves as men. These men have to define maleness and apply for membership to that group.

For these men, the body is an expression, possibly *the* expression of manhood. The male body is more important to them than a gendered role. These men make a distinction between maleness and masculinity. They believe that all men are male-bodied, but not necessarily masculine. The body is the crucial focus for these men, not only in how they define what it means to be a man, but also in how they fit into this definition. Ed comments:

> I don't feel like a woman although I don't know exactly what a woman would feel like or what a man would feel like. *But I don't identify with my female parts.*

Though Ed is uncertain about exactly what a man feels like or what a woman feels like, he does think that being one or the other has to do with feelings of identification with the sexed parts of one's body.

FTMs are uncomfortable with the equation of maleness with masculinity. They are particularly concerned that the general public thinks that they, as transsexuals, recapitulate hegemonic gender norms.[7] Julian summarizes this common argument against transsexualism:

> "[Transsexualism] reifies gender. Because transsexuals have preferences or styles or behaviors associated stereotypically with the other sex, then they're changing their body and that somehow signifies that they're buying into sex equals gender and that the two must go together or that gender is associated with sex."

In answer to this charge, twenty out of the twenty-two men interviewed distinguish between sexed bodies and gender roles. For them, the essence of being a man has little to do with the privileges associated with men in this culture or a preference for a socially masculine role. Julian explains, for example, that the body dysphoria he experiences is different from the role dysphoria that some women experience. This, more than anything else, motivated him to change his sex.

> It comes down to role dysphoria versus body dysphoria. For me it is so focused in my body. I really want to feel different in my body. I want my body to be different. I want to have big arms. I want big shoulders, I want my beard. . . . I want to have a male body. I've always wanted that. If it were just a matter of being dissatisfied with being forced to

be a second-class citizen because I was a woman, I wouldn't do this unless I wanted a male body.

One strategy FTMs use to make this distinction clearer is to refer to butch women and especially butch lesbians. FTMs think that butches are masculine, but not male. From their point of view, these butch women are masculine females.[8] Ed relates

> I remember talking to some butches who said to me "What? Now I'm not butch anymore, 'cause now there's one step up to being butch . . . taking hormones and you're TS [transsexual] and that makes you more butch than me?!" I'm like, "Hell no." I know plenty of dykes who are butcher than me.

According to Ed, butch women are engaged in "female masculinity" (Halberstam 1992, 1998). The FTMs in this study claim that they are not necessarily hyper-masculine. As Ed says, "I think I'm a masculine person, but I'm not really way way butch."

Few of the men in this study conflate gender roles and sexed bodies. Some of these men do think they are men because they prefer "manly" activities over others. FTMs that are slightly older than the study's median age, like Michael, are more likely to base their identity on their preferred gender roles as well as their desire for a male body. For these men, social roles are linked to embodied maleness.

> I could play all the real sports. Everything else, to me, felt like a copy sport or a sissy sport. Field hockey, I wanted to play real hockey. [laughs] I was very good at the sports that I did do. [The gym teachers] had this stupid points system. They gave us this very pale yellow uniform to wear with little bloomers and a little itsy-bitsy skirt that had pleats in it that had to be ironed with starch. If you came in with your uniform wrinkled, they took points off. I kept failing gym, even though I was one of the best athletes in the school. I'd fail gym, because my uniforms were wrinkled. [laughs] Or my hair wasn't combed. [laughs] Stupid. They could've had a real good player on their hands, and they just blew it.

Part of how Michael knows he is a man is the fact that he enjoys stereotypically masculine activities more than feminine activities. He is naturally good at sports, but not very good at personal grooming and "feminine arts" like ironing. He failed gym because he failed to be a proper girl. These failures and successes are evidence to him that he is truly male.

> I would go through these Sears & Roebucks catalogs and I'd pick out Lone Ranger costumes. [laughs] My mother never let me have 'em. But if I'd had my druthers, I would've been dressed up like Roy Rogers, or Gene Autry, or Lone Ranger, or later on, Davy Crockett. Cowboys I guess. And then maybe later on, baseball players and astronauts. [laughs] Superman. I mean, doesn't every boy want to wear that?

As with his preference for "masculine" activities, Michael tells us that he naturally identified with male heroes in his childhood. Fearless, strong, and independent explorers, these men are the essence of masculinity to Michael and he associates himself with them. This story tells us much more than Michael's sartorial preferences. He is defining masculinity, associating it with males and with himself as he truly is beneath his female body. He universalizes what boys want to wear or to be.

This conflation of maleness and masculinity places limits on the kinds of behaviors that are appropriate for men and women. These limits have been rightly problematized by feminist activists and scholars in the twentieth century. It is this conflation that raises concern among some feminists about transsexualism (Kessler and McKenna 1978; Grosz 1994; Bem 1993; Lorber 1994; Hausman 1995). When masculinity is conflated with manhood, it limits women to stereotypically feminine behavior. This pathologizes women who act "masculine" or men who act "feminine." It narrows the potential range of legitimate behaviors for men and women.

Though some of these FTMs conflate sexed bodies and gender roles, most agree with Ed and Julian that maleness is different than masculinity. The younger men link their core male self only to their bodies. This distinction makes sense if we consider the extent to which gender roles are becoming more flexible. The remaining legitimate differences between men and women are at the level of bodily appearance and bodily functions. In the urban and coastal contexts where this fieldwork took place, gender roles are less dimorphic than in the past. The feelings of dysphoria associated with transsexualism are located more often at the level of bodies. Body dysphoria is replacing gender role dysphoria as gender roles open up.

The Paradox of Male Embodiment

If all men have male bodies, FTMs have to explain their belief that they are men despite their female bodies. The notion of a core self is the main way that these men lay claim to their male identities. The men believe that their adolescent bodies betray the internalized, core sense of self that they have carried with them since childhood. As their bodies changed from relatively androgynous to markedly female, they either suffered social isolation or went "underground" at the expense of their male identities. Those who went "incognito as women" give vivid descriptions of the day they realized they still had that "little boy" buried in the cavernous depths of their bodies. They are now eager to mature and they see their physical transformations as the best way of restoring their broken life cycles. Both the isolationists, who preserved their selves at the cost of social relationships, and the "undergrounders" speak fervently about the absolute intransigence of this core male identity. In lieu of a male body, these men rely upon their core identities and the notion of expressive errors in order to justify their physical transformations.

The idea of expressive errors is the main way that they resolve the paradox of male embodiment. The belief that their bodies fail to express what they are inside is the central tenet legitimating their transitions. This belief depends on the assumption that all bodies should, and usually do, *express* something about the selves that reside within them. This idea has been neatly captured by feminist theorist Judith Butler as the expressionist hypothesis. Expressionism is, she says, the belief that identities reside somewhere within our bodies and are expressed through our bodies.

> It seems fair to say that certain kinds of acts are usually interpreted as expressive of a gender core or identity, and that these acts either conform to an expected gender identity or contest that expectation in

some way. That expectation, in turn, is based on the perception of
sex, where sex is understood to be the discrete and factic datum of
primary sexual characteristics. This implicit and popular theory of acts
and gestures as *expressive* of gender suggests that gender itself is something prior to the various acts, postures, and gestures, by which it is
dramatized and known; indeed, gender appears to the popular imagination as a substantial core which might well be understood as the
spiritual or psychological correlate of biological sex. If gender attributes,
however, are not expressive but performative, then these attributes
effectively constitute the identity they are said to express or reveal.
(Butler 1990, 278–79)

To Butler, the expressivist model is so much a part of the air we breathe
that we can hardly think otherwise. Butler thinks that all people experience their bodies as expressive of their identities, phenomenologi-
cally speaking, which is why it is so difficult to grasp the alternate
model of gender she calls "performativity." It remains unclear to most
of her readers whether Butler is taking a normative stance toward the
expressionist model of identity. Is she merely describing these two systems of identity, or does she hope to substitute performativity for expressionism? Many of her interpreters think the latter, and, following
this model, criticize transsexuals who remain within the expressionist
framework. The FTMs in this study are routinely criticized for their
false consciousness about the ways that they are "doing gender."[9] I
believe that Butler wants us to be aware that the expressionist model is
a fiction that we have created. It is a powerful fiction that cannot be
dismissed simply because we would like it to disappear. It is, in fact,
one that people in this culture cannot do without. In that case, we
might take a closer look at how and why these FTMs draw upon the
cultural idea that all bodies express an internalized core identity that
never changes.

Whereas most individuals feel that they have bodies that adequately
express their true selves, these FTMs all feel as if their bodies are erro-
neous expressions of their core selves. Their bodies fail to express their
internal male identities. An expressive error occurred, severing the link
between their body and their identity. The men in this study describe
a variety of possible errors, ranging from the belief that God had made

a mistake, to genetic mutations, to chemical imbalances, to under-developed or hidden male anatomy. One man believes he was reincarnated in a female body so that he could avoid the draft during the Vietnam War. This occurrence would be fortuitous, but most of the other men are less than thrilled with the mistakes of God or nature. They have always been men, albeit men whose bodies fail to express this to the world.

The FTMs are aware of the expressivist paradigm; they know the difficulty of being recognized as men without a male body. While the primary sex characteristics are usually covered and therefore unhelpful for the gender attribution process, secondary characteristics are crucially important for gender attribution by others. When we encounter a person, we do not categorize them as male or female based on their genitalia. We do recognize, however, a person as male or female depending on other physical cues: hair, breasts, etc. FTMs are motivated to alter their bodies in order to simplify the gender attribution process. Few FTMs modify their genitalia. However, most in this study are planning or have already started hormones and chest surgery because they understand and calculate the importance of physical cues for the attribution of identity.

However, this is not the only motivation for enduring the risks and stigma associated with surgeries and exogamous hormones. The purpose of body modification is also to be recognizable to themselves. It is not enough for the public to treat them as men despite their female bodies. They remain uncomfortably agnosic without bodies that adequately express their true identities. Lacking crucial physical characteristics, they understand that they cannot be recognizably male, to themselves or others, without some approximation of male bodies.

FTMs view hormonal and surgical technologies as a way to correct expressive errors. They believe that their mental and physical well-being depends upon restoring the expressive links between this immutable core self and their more flexible flesh. To resolve the paradox of male embodiment, FTMs say that all men *should* have male bodies. Sometimes men have other kinds of bodies, but these are anomalies that should be corrected whenever such repairs are desired and possible.

Realigning their bodies to their identities may seem to reinstate the culturally hegemonic link between sexed bodies and gender. If one views Butler's claims as normative prescriptions for abolishing gender expressivity, then one is likely to condemn or criticize transsexual men for perpetuating norms that regulate bodies and identities. This is a reductive reading of Butler that leads to a hasty dismissal of the real cultural forces that delimit the ways that one can achieve intersubjective recognition. Such social conventions bring a tremendous amount of pressure to bear on subjects in formation.

We should view the resolution of this paradox in terms that are more complex. The belief in a core male identity is an effective means of attaining the respect typically denied to FTMs. Wanting recognition for who they are inside, these men invoke the hegemonic belief that all men have male bodies[10] and modify their bodies. This is nothing less than an ingenious reinvigoration of these hegemonic beliefs for the project of self-realization and social recognition.

A Sociology of Testosterone

For many FTM transsexuals, surgical procedures are of limited significance. Testosterone and its effects on the secondary sex characteristics play a much more significant part in their lives. There are three reasons for this. (1) The limits to the effectiveness of both "top" and "bottom" surgeries make testosterone into the primary means of their transition from female to male. Phalloplasty is an imperfect set of procedures that normally leave a man with poor urinary and sexual functions, no sensation, and an almost unrecognizable penis-like appendage, which is considerably subject to infection. Significant scarring and loss of some sensation also result from chest surgeries, though these procedures are considered more aesthetically pleasing. (2) FTMs feel that chest reconstruction and hysterectomy only take away offending female parts, while testosterone actively makes the man.[11] (3) Testosterone has a direct effect on the secondary sex characteristics such as voice, body and facial hair, and fat distribution. FTMs realize that the social process of gender attribution is largely independent of the primary sex characteristics, relying upon the secondary sex characteristics instead.

Testosterone is valued because it alters the most important features used in the sex attribution process.[12]

Several interviewees speak of the meaning of testosterone. They point out that testosterone does not alter their identities, just their bodies and behaviors. They are always already men and this biochemical substance does not change their core identity, but see testosterone as the source of male embodiment. Testosterone is the most reliable means of making them hairier, stronger, sweatier, etc. Members of society, including FTMs, interpret these features as signs of maleness. To be recognizable, the FTMs rely upon testosterone and cultural beliefs about male bodies that allow these physical changes to be interpreted as virilizing.

Some of these men believe that testosterone changes their *behavior*. The changes they note in their behavior sometimes confirm and sometimes challenge hegemonic cultural beliefs about masculine gender roles and testosterone. Often, the changes confirm normative beliefs about maleness and masculinity and undercut feminist criticisms of hormonal and biological determinism. All of the guys are aware that their comments have implications for the on-going "nature vs. nurture" debates about sex differences. Most of them are uncomfortable with the deterministic biological rhetoric that justifies unequal and unjust treatment of women in this society. They provide alternate, social explanations for the changes or opt for a mixed approach. Despite these concerns, the men continue to make strong claims about the power of hormones to affect both bodies and behavior. Although they are concerned about the implications of the biologisms running through their comments, they also feel that they cannot deny the effects of testosterone. They think that their experiences make an important contribution to scholarship and they imagine themselves to be living scientific experiments that can shed light on a controversial topic.[13]

Testosterone and the Self

FTMs report that testosterone does not affect their core identity. Only their bodies and their behaviors are changed by testosterone. Testosterone has little effect on who they are inside. From their point of view, they are becoming the men they always already were. They do not claim that testosterone transforms them from women into men. Gregg emphasizes, for example, that he is the same person after testosterone that he was before.

> The inside is still the same. The outside has changed. Unfortunately, some people go through the change and think it's gonna change who I am. Then they find out it doesn't. I thank God I've had a counselor who said, "You need to understand that you have brown eyes, and they're still gonna be brown. You have whatever disease, you're still gonna have it."

In some cases, the belief that testosterone does not affect the core self could sometimes deter transition. Alex wondered why he should bother transitioning if he was going to stay the same person.

> I wasn't gonna change who I was. I'm gonna be the same person. That's really not gonna change. And so people are going to make this big deal, so if I'm gonna be the same person, then why do I need to do it? I'd go back and forth about this. It's like you're really the same person anyway, so why do it?

Alex eventually decided that he was willing to go through the "big deal" of transitioning. He understands that testosterone makes his body conform more closely to cultural norms about male bodies. He knows that the physical changes to his body make him more recognizable to others and to himself. Testosterone raises the possibility of being recognized as a man.

Deciding to inject testosterone still provokes fears that they will somehow become different people. They are often relieved to find that they are, indeed, the same person on testosterone as they are without it. This is how Matt remembers his first shot of testosterone:

> The minute that miracle "vitamin T" entered my body, no fuckin' lightning came down from the sky. I got on my bike, I left the hospital and nothing had changed. Not a fuckin' thing had changed.

From Matt's point of view, only his "outsides" are affected by the testosterone and even that takes time. A few men report that transition changed them, but they deny that testosterone has anything to do with these changes. Matt acknowledges that he has become different, but sees the change as a result of his life history, not of the testosterone. He explains, "I think there's something to be said about being scrutinized on a daily basis and having your identity challenged on a regular basis that changes you."

Testosterone may alter Matt's "outsides" and this affects whether he is recognizable, but it does not change him from a woman into a man. The men believe that the changes that occur are a kind of sloughing off process. They are shedding their female skins.

Testosterone as the Source of Maleness

Though testosterone does not change who they are inside, the FTMs believe that testosterone has the power to change their "outsides." Their bodies now look more like the bodies of men—they are bigger, hairier, denser, and more muscular than most women. These changes to their appearances make them culturally recognizable and more accurately reflect their core identities. All of them hold this biochemical substance responsible for the virilizing effects that make their bodies recognizably male. The men designate testosterone as the source of embodied *maleness*. James describes the process:

> I didn't feel anything on my first injection. A little apprehension, but ultimately nothing. . . . Over a period of weeks I realized my metabolism increased. My physical temperature was warmer. Over a period of maybe six months, I noticed that my body odor changed. I sweated a lot more. My skin was much more oily. . . . Of course I was starting to get facial hair. I guess I started having to shave just my mustache and my chin within a couple of months. It was a good year before I had to shave every day. I could sometimes get by with shaving two times a week. Then it took four years to be able to grow a full beard. My shoulders were getting thicker, my neck got thicker. I had to buy smaller pants and larger shirts. I had to buy smaller pants once . . . and one size change for that. Then I had to buy larger shirts three times. . . . that's what made me have to buy shirts all the time, because I couldn't button them [laughs] or my sleeves were getting too short, because of my shoulder development. I'd have to buy new shirts about every six months.

All the FTMs in this study describe similar experiences. They have become more recognizably male as their size, smell, skin texture, metabolism, temperature, body hair, and genitalia change. They explain that it takes some time to fill out their bodies. The changes are gradual, yet noticeable to James. He notes that his "second adolescence" took about five years. These are subtle changes, minute and unnoticeable on a day-to-day basis. The effects of testosterone are eagerly anticipated by those who inhabit these bodies.

Many of the elders in these communities tell newcomers and outsiders that the changes to one's body will be limited by the genetic composition of one's own family. For example, they warn that male pattern baldness is likely if one's brothers are bald. Similarly, the growth of the micro-phallus is considered to be limited by familial patterns. This advice demonstrates their belief in the power of biology to effect bodily changes.

They experience the effects of testosterone as a real force that alters their physical form. Yet they also take into account the social conventions whereby these changes are viewed as virilizing. They are aware of which male features are necessary in order to be recognized as a man by themselves and by others. They know that this recognition is made possible by the cultural norms governing male bodies. They know "what makes a man."

These experiences highlight the ways that hegemonic discourses about sex can be *reversed* in the name of a project of self-actualization.[14] As in the case of the paradox of male embodiment, FTMs depend upon normative claims about male embodiment and biology to make themselves into recognizable, gendered subjects.[15] They find these norms invaluable to the process of becoming recognizably male to themselves and to others. Though the FTMs in this study are sympathetic to the types of negative effects wrought by normative ideals regarding sex, they are also aware of and thankful for the ways such beliefs can be marshaled for their own life projects. They know that they have little chance of intersubjective recognition and respect without appealing to these norms.

Testosterone as the Seat of Masculinity

Significantly, fewer FTMs believe that testosterone has a masculiniz-ing effect on their psychology or behavior. This minority believes that testosterone is the seat of masculinity. They think that their behavior, and the behavior of others, is directly related to hormones. Androgens and estrogens are factors in the ways that men and women act, not just what shapes their bodies take. Not under the willful control of indi-viduals, actions are instead determined by different ratios of these sub-stances. It is one thing to suggest that human bodies develop di-morphically according to the influence of hormones; it is another to suggest that the behaviors of men and women are due to such causes. Here, one is treading on the unfamiliar ground of the behavioral endo-crinologist or the sociobiologist. These claims are thorny because they seem to suggest that hormones determine the different natures of men and women, and may even be asserted to justify the patriarchal and unequal relations between them.

Criticism of hormonal determinism is common in feminist schol-arship and Women's Studies.[16] The criticism of hormonal determinism is difficult to summarize, but its essence is that the association of gendered behavior with hormones places permanent limits on the kinds of behaviors that are appropriate for men and women. Hormonal de-terminism pathologizes women who act "masculine" and men who act "feminine." While it may be acceptable to acknowledge that men and women have different body types, it is no longer reasonable to suggest that those body types, or the substances running through them, can dictate behavior. Such claims unduly narrow the potential range of legitimate behaviors, activities, professions, etc. appropriate to each gender.

The conflation of bodies and behaviors raises concerns about hor-monal determinism in general and transsexualism in particular. Trans-sexuals are not the only people to give deterministic accounts of hor-mones; other examples of hormonal determinism include the attribution of mood swings to pre-menstrual syndrome (P.M.S.), of violence in body-builders to a surge in testosterone, or of adolescents who cannot sit still in class to raging hormones, and the treatment of menopausal women with hormone replacement therapies.

It is nevertheless worthwhile to pay attention to what these men say about the associations they make between hormones and behaviors. They are sociologically significant. These reports are important because they tell us about the lived experiences of this group of men. As a collective of individuals living in a particular time and place, they share a common course that is rarely taken and uniquely intriguing to those who have not taken that course of action. Their lived experiences are also sociologically significant because they tell us what it feels like to live gendered lives under the influence of hormones.

Moreover, aside from their straightforward sociological significance, we cannot politically afford to dismiss the claims of hormonal determinism made by these FTMs. These claims are ambiguous, polyvalent, and contradictory. As often as they confirm social norms about masculinity and femininity, the changes in their behavior seem to subvert them. Unexpectedly, their reports about behavioral shifts in response to testosterone challenged many of our normative gender ideals. For instance, the idea that testosterone could produce a peaceful state of being, rather than a violent and aggravated mood, could support the idea of manly tenderness. When, on the other hand, these reports do confirm cultural norms, they provide us with invaluable information that must inform the measures society takes to achieve equality and social justice between men and women. Either way, we must come to terms with what it feels like to live under the influence of testosterone, even—or especially—when it seems to confirm our worst nightmares about the inequalities between the sexes.

There were four dimensions of behavioral changes that the men said were affected by testosterone: energy level, emotions, aggression, and sexual drive. The behavioral changes were not uniform, but all of the men said their behavior changed in at least one of these dimensions. Practically all the men who were taking testosterone experienced a significant rise in energy levels. Shadow shares:

> [When] I first started, it felt like a real, like a brand new river. Lots of rapids, quick-paced, very strong. I was very caught up in that. There's so much excitement involved. The excitement lent a certain amount of energy to it. I was really frantic for a while. A lot of people didn't want to be around me. When I watched some of the other people

start, in the first six months of hormones, I don't want to be around them either. "Go get this out of your system. Go race motorcycles!" What we're going through at that point in time, which is relatively universal amongst all of us, is that we do get that extended energy. I think some of it is the excitement. But some of it certainly is the adjustments and the changes that are happening, uh, chemical-wise.

By attributing differences in energy level to testosterone, Shadow knows his experiences could be used to justify the different accomplishments of men and women. Wary of this deterministic claim, Shadow has another account of the increased energy that he and most of the other transsexual men report; he posits that transition as a kind of "peak" experience that gave him a burst of creative energy. This unique experience can make it difficult to separate out the sources of his increased energy, but he is certain that the chemistry had some effect on his energy level and made him behave differently than before.

The second set of behavioral changes is aggression. Testosterone is normatively correlated with aggression and masculinity. Estrogens are more commonly associated with peacefulness and femininity.[17] Their reports are mixed, sometimes confirming and sometimes challenging our normative assumptions about gender. Many of the men said they became more aggressive on testosterone. "Roid rage," similar to the kind that bodybuilders report as an effect of steroid use, was common. Julian recalls:

> I had a week or two of being really really extremely irritable and for awhile I thought it was related to increased aggression associated with testosterone. Part of the moodiness that I've experienced has almost been like a physical irritability where I just feel like hitting anything around me. "Don't touch me," . . . kinda snappy, short. So I thought maybe it was associated with that.

Others comment, counter-intuitively, that they became more peaceful and less easily angered or irritated. A few say that testosterone actually calmed them down and made them less aggressive than they had been prior to transition. Shadow correlates "estrogen poisoning" with his previous violent outbursts. In response to testosterone, by contrast, Shadow reports feeling centered and sane.

> The most significant thing has been the calming effects. Now I don't
> want to make it sound like, "This [testosterone] has made me a strong
> person." A lot of that came through my own self-explorations of find-
> ing out who I am and building on that foundation. *But I couldn't have
> done that on estrogen.*

Shadow makes room for a social argument as well as a biologically
based argument. He suggests that self-exploration and self-acceptance
have contributed to his sense of well-being. Nonetheless, Shadow believes that testosterone has some effect on his behavior. The most interesting thing about this example is that the change he attributes to
testosterone is the opposite of our normal expectations. The amount
of estrogen in Shadow's blood stream has decreased, but he claims that
this has calmed him down. Not all of the behavioral changes that these
men report confirm the normative assumptions about testosterone and
masculinity. When they do make biologistic claims about the power of
testosterone to change their behavior, these FTMs are cautious about
inferring that some behavior is masculine and some is feminine. What
Shadow's story illustrates is the persistent belief that hormones affect
behavior. Hormone imbalances can cause violence, aggression, and
other kinds of dysfunction. These men remain faithful to the normative belief in the effects of hormones on the body, but they have un-
linked traditional associations between testosterone, masculinity, and
aggression.

Not all of the men reverse these associations. Emotions were one
dimension which some of the FTMs linked to testosterone. The physical
inhibition of crying, for example, is one of the most commonly reported changes. For Francis, these things are more hormonally related
than we have even suspected.

> I have no inhibitions about crying. So it's not the fact that now that I'm
> becoming more masculine—"Oh, men can't cry or shouldn't." I used
> to have a great release and a lot of satisfaction in crying. Not like
> crying hysterically—I didn't like that either. I'd put a sad song on when
> I knew I needed to cry. Now that doesn't do a thing for me. I have a
> real difficult time crying. It only happens when I'm extremely upset or
> I think about somebody close to me dying. That's about the only thing

that will really bring a little tear to my eye. Now when I get stressed out at work, I go into the restroom and I pound on the wall. . . . I'm not stressed anymore and I didn't have to cry for five minutes. Then I see these movies with these guys where they get upset and they go into a bar or they go into a restroom and they hit the wall a couple times or kick a bucket or they kick their car. They come out and they feel fine. [laughs] I said, "Jeez, that's what I'm doing." It's hormones.

Francis links his stereotypical masculine behavior to the androgens he is taking. He suggests that he has no qualms with "feminine" behavior. These hormonal changes are out of his control. They determine his behavior just like they affect the behavior of men he knows or sees depicted in films. For Shadow, by contrast, not crying is a socially learned behavior. It is something other men pick up from the movies.

I hear a lot of the guys [other FTMs] say, "I'm a lot more detached, it's a lot harder to cry." There is a certain amount of removal from the accessibility of tears. But at this point in time, I think I cry much easier than I did before. If you look at what little boys get growing up—they fall down and skin their knees—"Don't cry, big boys don't cry." It's in all the music, all the literature. Even at your parents' funeral, it's someone you love dearly, or your spouse's funeral. . . . It's bullshit. I think men cry just as easily as women do. They're just trained not to.

Shadow believes in the power of social conditioning. Yet, as demonstrated above, he does not shy away from the belief that hormones can affect behavior, though he does not think that the social roles of masculinity and femininity are dependent only upon hormones.

The association between gender roles and hormones is most dramatically confirmed by the increase in sexual drive the men in this study report. As they tell it, the experience is unparalleled. James relates:

Getting me to initiate sex was very difficult. Once I got started, then fine. But getting me to get started was generally quite difficult. In my relationship that I had been in for almost fourteen years, we were not having sex with great frequency when I began transition. She said her ideal thing would be to have sex once a week. As it was, we were having sex about once every three months.

> Henry: [whistles] And then what happened with the testosterone?
> James: Then I wanted to have sex every day.

James believes that testosterone has had the effect of increasing his sex drive. This belief is consistent with the dominant assumption that men are more quickly aroused and driven by a harder sexual current than women. His increased sex drive is an effect that James regarded ambivalently; he said that it made him incompatible with his partner. Yet he seemed to enjoy his increased desire for pleasure and the way that it confirmed his male identity.

The experience of a magnified sex drive is not universal to the population of transsexual men. Matt retorts, "You know what? I have no fuckin' sex drive. I didn't have a sex drive before I started hormones. My brother doesn't have a sex drive." Matt rejects the belief that all bodies are determined in the same way by any given bio-chemical agent. However, Matt does believe that his body responds to hormones like his brother's does.

Matt's experience is less common in this research group. The experience of an increased drive is more common. Their explanations of these experiences can be frighteningly similar to those that non-transsexual men use to justify violent or sexual behavior that harms others. For example, Francis says:

> I think I understand men a lot more now. I have a lot more compassion
> for them, what they're going through. Sometimes they just can't help
> it if there is somebody who is extremely attractive to them.

Francis's comments are alarming. He sympathizes with the plight of men who "just can't help it." This belief has been used as a justification for violence against women and other men. It reproduces norms about male lust that legitimate the violation of physical boundaries.

Sociologists should, however, take such reports seriously and consider what they might tell us about testosterone's effect on male behavior. By paying attention to statements like these, it is possible to develop a critical perspective on male lust and violence.[18] If this is a struggle for men, then it is necessary to increase men's ability to find the control that they need to refrain from behavior that violates others. Dismissing this struggle as hormonal determinism will exacerbate the experience of being out of control. Trivializing the experience as fictive will not alleviate the problem.

While some of the FTMs in this study unreflectively reproduce the hegemonic norms that associated masculine behavior with testosterone, others, like Julian, are more uncomfortable with these beliefs and hesitate to connect behavior with this biochemical substance.

> I didn't really believe that it would really happen and in a way, I didn't really want to believe that men had higher sex drives than women, that that's just some inherent thing. But there is *something* that has happened.

These men experienced changes in their behavior that they concede could be correlated with testosterone. These experiences may confirm or challenge hegemonic beliefs. For some, testosterone has the expected result of increased energy, sex drive, and aggression, and decreased emotional access. For others, testosterone has little effect on these behavioral dimensions. Still others report that testosterone has a counternormative effect, such as lessening of aggression, an observation that challenges the association between "male" hormones and masculinity. The likelihood that these men will reproduce the culturally hegemonic ties between testosterone and male behavior is dependent upon the degree of recognition their core identities and new bodies allow them.

Subversive or Hegemonic?

Up until now, it seems as if the most pertinent question about transsexuals is whether they subvert the heteronormative gender order. We view transsexuals only as either revolutionaries or traitors. By speaking of their choices in these either/or terms, we are unable to comprehend their lived experiences and their worldview. This question renders transsexuals as suspicious subjects whose lives are continuously open to scrutiny and scorn. They are either in service to a greater cause or they betray that cause. The cause is the overturning of the present configuration of gender, sex, and sexuality that configures and constrains institutions and individuals. This sort of scholarship has fetishized transsexuals, either as "gender revolutionaries" or as "gender traitors." It refuses to acknowledge that transsexuals are a heterogeneous group. Some subvert gender or sexuality; some do not. Most combine subversion of and conformity to dominant cultural beliefs about gender, sex, and sexuality. The fetishistic appropriation of transsexuals or the critique of false consciousness makes it impossible to grasp the meaning of their social psychological experience.[19]

I propose a ban on the question of whether transsexualism and transsexuals are unequivocally subversive or hegemonic. Transsexual men may confirm or undercut the hegemonic version of normative maleness and masculinity in this culture. Transsexuals per se are neither *essentially* gender normative nor *essentially* gender subversive. Judging transsexuals as a group by their commitment to the gender revolution obscures the heterogeneity among transsexual men.

FTMs are engaged in a whole range of behaviors and beliefs. Some of them challenge our general cultural assumptions about masculinity, embodiment, and identity, while others remain consistent with dominant cultural norms. Some of these men, for example, believe they can be men without a phallic reconstruction, a belief that clearly challenges the cultural belief that anatomy is destiny. Others believe that testosterone raises sexual drive, a belief that conforms more closely to cultural associations of masculinity, embodiment and sexuality. Most of the men I spoke to call upon a mixture of some dominant cultural beliefs and some alternative conceptions of maleness, masculinity, or embodiment and identity.

We must identify the possibilities for inter-subjective recognition that are opened or closed by any given constellation of sex, gender, and sexuality. We can come to terms with them as people in psychological and physical torment, socially annulled, stigmatized, discriminated, and violated by others. We also see that these individuals have overcome the betrayal of their bodies, gained worldly recognition, and restored their sense of self. This kind of knowledge captures the unique ways that each of these twenty-two transsexual men has repaired his life.

We need to focus on the likelihood that these men will remake what it means to be a man. What makes it likely that they will reject patriarchal forms of masculinity and maleness? What might make it more likely that they will create new versions of masculinity and maleness? The most dominant beliefs about sexed bodies and gendered core identities can produce some of the most secure forms of masculinity. The men who marshaled culturally hegemonic beliefs about core identity, maleness, and embodiment were less likely to engage in stereotypical masculine behaviors. Being recognizably male-bodied makes it more likely that FTMs will reject stereotypical versions of masculinity or idealized versions of male bodies.

Threatened Men, Threatening Men

The likelihood that any man will accept male privileges is dependent on the extent to which his manhood is challenged. In short, threatened men are threatening men. This is especially true of FTMs. If their status as men is challenged, they will choose to appear as stereotypically male as possible and behave like the most "manly" of men. Their behavior may be hostile, oppressive, and even violent in ways that deny recognition to women and other men. Conversely, if they are recognizable as men, they will feel comfortable enough to deviate from the dominant types of manly presentation and behavior. The ideals of masculinity have long been criticized for the ways that they perpetuate cycles of inequality, abuse, and oppressive male behavior.[20] FTM men are more likely to engage in these behaviors if they are denied all other means of claiming their manhood.

All men face the pressure to be "real" men.[21] The most stereotypical versions of masculinity are examples of neurotic "splitting." They are compelled to ask themselves whether they measure up to an ideal of manhood. Hyperbolic displays of masculinity are attempts to restore their masculinity or their status as men. Psychologists have suggested that dominant forms of masculinity are defensive reactions to some kind of threat.[22] Any man might react defensively if his manhood is challenged.

Whether it is actually possible to have a form of masculinity that is not built upon a reactionary stance toward this vulnerability has been debated among psychoanalysts and feminists (Layton 1998; Butler 1997; Benjamin 1988; Flax 1990; Chodorow 1978). I believe that reactions to such threats may be defensive or not. It is possible for men to be men without embodying the most oppressive, noxious, and violent characteristics associated with men today. Although masculinity is a tenuous thing, it is possible to come up with alternative versions of masculinity that result in more equal and just relationships with other men and with women.

Two Sources of Threat:
Disfigured Bodies and Core Selves Denied

Paying attention to the sources of these defensive reactions may help limit the likelihood that men, especially FTMs, will reproduce stereotypical versions of masculinity. One of the most important things that allows a man to claim his manhood is his body. If his body approximates the cultural ideal of masculinity, his status as a man will be unquestioned. If a man's body deviates from the cultural ideals about men's bodies, then his social status as a man will be questioned. What counts as a male body is hard to pinpoint, but the FTMs in this study articulate several crucial features including genitals, chests, body and facial hair, straight hips, large hands and feet, tall height, muscularity, and bulk. They hope to embody a clearly definable ideal male body. Most expect merely to approximate this ideal.

Without a male body, a man has a much harder time proving he is really a man. He is likely to be questioned about his manhood and this skepticism may make him defensive. Transsexual men face many of the same risks and threats to their manhood that other men face. They are subject to scrutiny and doubt about their claims to manhood. Like other men, they sometimes respond to this vulnerable position in defensive ways. They may have to compensate more than other men because their female bodies fail them completely. Their burden may be greater in degree, though not in kind. These men face the almost impossible task of being men without male bodies. Others have doubted or denied that they are men because they do not have male bodies. Especially before transition, their female bodies make it necessary for some to overcompensate with stereotypical forms of masculinity. Similarly, incomplete transitions, due to medical conditions, lack of funds, or poor surgical options, may also make it difficult for an FTM to make legitimate claims to male status. Semi-private settings, bathrooms, and bedrooms, can be the site of threats to FTMs who have not had phalloplasty.[23] Without a male body, these men speak of a daily insecurity that makes them more on-guard about their masculinity.

For example, remember Francis's claim that testosterone made him more prone to the feeling of being out of control of his body. Francis made these comments early in his transition when he was not yet living full-time as a man. He was cross-dressing at his job, but his colleagues did not recognize him as a man. He was more likely to make stereotypical claims about his self-control because of his unfulfilled need to be recognized as the man he is inside. FTMs' male identities were most threatened prior to their transitions, when they were still female-bodied. At that point, the only way they secured their male identities was through their core identities. It was difficult to convince others that they were men. Instead, they often acted in stereotypically male ways to convince others of their hidden identities. Like their reliance on short haircuts in their youth, these men depended upon stereotypical forms of masculinity to convey their true selves. As they gradually became recognizably male, their masculinity became less suspect and less threatened. They also became less stereotypically masculine.

While some have claimed that the process of modifying a female body so that it resembles culturally dominant ideals about male bodies is misogyny and mutilation, it is instead a means of mutual intersubjective recognition. Such a process allows an FTM wider circles of recognition, fewer misrecognitions, and greater security about his manhood. This adds up to ample opportunity to create new forms of masculinity.

The second source of anxiety that induces FTMs to act hypermasculine is threats to their core male identity. If a man's core identity is threatened, he will draw from hegemonic codes of masculine behavior in order to secure recognition as a man. When the idea of a core self is denied altogether, as in the case of the post-modernist "death of the subject" thesis, then transsexual men, who rely on their core selves to substantiate their identities, will feel particularly threatened and misunderstood. These challenges lead to stereotypical behaviors meant to serve as "proof" of manhood.

The dominant belief that all men have male bodies makes the idea of a core self crucial for transsexual men. When their bodies fail to be the anchor of their male identities, they substitute a core male self as evidence of their male status.[24] Their belief in a core gender identity becomes the anchor of their claims to a male identity. This substitution makes it possible for them to transition, which makes it more likely that they will be recognized as men.

If a core identity is denied and transition is inhibited, they will need to reiterate even the most offensive aspects of maleness. Stereotypical behavior is the result of their desires to be seen as ordinary men despite their far-from-ordinary experience. Threatened male identities lead to overcompensation and behavior that denies recognition and dignity to those around them. The all-too-easy threats to their masculinity can engender overblown, stereotypical male behavior (Connell 1995).

New Forms of Maleness and Masculinity

We are now in a position to examine the ways these men challenge stereotypical masculinity. Due to their unusual life histories, they are conscious of the hegemonic gender codes. Each found that he could claim a male identity by reassessing what it means to be a man. Some were critical, for example, of the dominant beliefs about masculine behavior that equate masculinity with dominance, power, strength, aggression, sexual drive, lack of emotion, etc. These men found that as they became more recognizable in their new bodies, they could behave in non-stereotypical ways and still count as men. They might be considered slightly off-center or alternative men for rejecting the some masculine behaviors, but their manhood itself would no longer be challenged.

Some of the men questioned the most fundamental of all cultural beliefs about men—that all men have men bodies. What, they asked, counts as a male body? Is it the often unseen genitalia or the internal glands that they do not have? Is it the Adam's apple, which some nontranssexual men have and others do not? Is it straight hips, a particular facial hair pattern, or a deep voice? What combination of these things would be enough for them to be recognizably male to others? More importantly, what would satisfy their strong desire to be comfortable in their own skin? As the men contemplated these questions, each came to unique insights about the importance of bodies to their male identity.

Faced with the limits of their material bodies and modern techniques for altering them, these men acknowledged the range of male bodies. By placing themselves within this differentiated set of men, they essentially remade what it means to be male. These men cope with the physical and technological limits of sex reassignment procedures in creative ways that refigure what it means to be a man.

Remaking Maleness

Despite the results of testosterone on their sex characteristics, the men had to acknowledge that their bodies would only approximate the ideal male body. They would have recognizably male bodies that would be closer to their body image, but always limited by modern surgical techniques and hormones. Many of these men hold tightly to conventional beliefs about men's bodies and are haunted by relentless grief over their own incomplete bodies. They constantly wish that they could have been born with the bodies that they spent thousands of dollars to achieve. Whatever feature of their physique has not responded to testosterone in an ideal fashion is a focal point of anxiety, anger, and sadness over the misfortune of their birth. Whether their hips remain curvy, their voice has not dropped a full octave, or they are under six feet tall with smallish hands or feet, each man views himself in relation to a ideal male body and only the rare man does not come up lacking.

Beliefs about the ideal male body make it difficult to accept their micro-phallus, small hands, and light beards. They have difficulty coming to terms with the limits of their transitions and continue to feel threatened. Their grief has not subsided, and often perpetuates feelings of inadequacy and contributes to the cycle of threatening masculinity discussed above. Many of these men found themselves able to resolve their grief by expanding what it meant to be male-bodied. If they acknowledged the heterogeneity of male bodies, then they could fit themselves within that version of maleness. They did this by look-

ing at men in the media, on the street, or in their lives and recognizing
the wide variety of men. They noted skin-, hair-, and eye-coloring,
height, weight, proportion of body fat to muscle, as well as the size of
limbs, penises, and nipples. They examined and compared their sing-
ing voices, scars, bald spots, and every other conceivable difference.
The harder they looked, the more they realized all the possible body
types that could be called male. Recall, for example, that Julian was
concerned about his height and his hands. These, he acknowledges,
will never conform to his or this culture's male ideal. However, he also
understands that other men are short and other men have small hands.
These people, he realizes, are men despite the fact that their bodies do
not fulfill a male ideal completely. Likewise, Julian reasons, he is a man
although his hands will be small and he will not grow any taller. The
same reasoning can be applied to all aspects of the body that are sex-
differentiated, including hair patterns, fat distribution, muscle and bone
density and structure, sense perception, genitalia, nipple size, chest
scarring, etc. These men contemplated the category "male" and fit
themselves within it by acknowledging the actual heterogeneity of
male bodies. If this culture accepts them as men and if they accept
themselves as men, despite the limits to their physical transitions, then
all those involved are shifting the definition of what it means to be
male.

Remaking Masculinity

These men contributed to the expansion of what behavior is associated with masculinity. As we have seen, the links between behavior
and gender have been coming undone throughout modern history.
Transsexual men can contribute to this undoing if their manliness is
secure. Manliness may be secured by internalizing a core identity and
by modifying bodies in order to approximate the ideals of male embodiment held by this culture.

By modifying their bodies, FTMs relieve the need to repeat, ad
nauseam, the most stereotypical codes of maleness and masculinity in
order to be recognized as men. A core identity makes it more likely
that these FTMs can "riff" on masculinity without compromising who
they are inside. By claiming that they have always already been men,

these men may engage in any behavior and claim that it is appropriate to a man. They can do any activity at all and still be men. For example, Matt says, "When I get nervous, when I get upset, I bake things. . . . I sew. Those aren't things that I have to throw away. I don't have to go learn how to fix cars." If they like to sew, then they are men who sew and sewing becomes a behavior that is socially associated with being a man. Likewise, as Alex says, he can wear pink and still be a man. He could be a man who wears a pink shirt and Birkenstock sandals, but he could never have a female body and wear such items. As a recognizably embodied man, Alex feels less pressure to conform to stereotypical versions of masculinity than he did when he had a female body. When he had a female body, he says, he could not afford to engage in stereotypically feminine behaviors.

The men feel similarly to Ed, who realized he did not measure up to standard masculinity. He did not want to be a typical man. He hoped, instead, to be his "own kind of guy."

> I don't think that a sensitive male is being female. That was a huge breakthrough in my life. I remember saying [to his girlfriend], "Snuggling is really important to me," and I remember saying, "Do you think it would be okay if I could be my own kind of guy?"

Ed could become his "own kind of guy" once his core self had been acknowledged and he had become recognizably male to the public, his loved ones, and himself.

All of this suggests that the possibility of remaking what it means to be a man is dependent upon the notion of a core self that is recognizable in the flesh. To be a man need not depend on stereotypical behaviors associated with masculinity. The transsexuals in this study could expand what counted as a male body and could participate in a wide array of activities and still be considered men, but only if their core identities were recognized. Of utmost importance, the core self is the anchor that secures their desire for body modification and opens up the range of behaviors they feel comfortable doing. The core self provides the security necessary for remaking maleness and masculinity.

Conclusions

It is often the case that scholars, activists, therapists, and others wonder why it is that transsexuals need to endure all those complicated and potentially dangerous surgical procedures and hormone treatments. Why, it is often asked, can't they simply live as men without modifying their bodies? Why not challenge, rather than reinvigorate, the culturally hegemonic belief that all men have male bodies?

> In a society that could tolerate lack of correspondence, there would be no transsexuals. There would be men with vaginas and women with penises or perhaps different signs of gender. . . . We suspect that in a society that allowed men to have vaginas and women to have penises, the biological imperative of gender would weaken (Kessler and McKenna 1978, 120).

The answers given in response to these questions often depend upon justifying such choices in terms of the subversion or normative confirmation of gender by transsexuals. If transsexuals and body modifications subvert gender, many feel they should be allowed to pursue their chosen life course. If, on the contrary, transsexuals confirm gender norms, these same people claim that they should not be allowed to pursue that course.

My answer starts out, instead, from a commitment to intersubjective recognition. This answer emphasizes personal dignity and the right to self-determination, as well as the respectful treatment of one's personhood and individual integrity by others. Intersubjective recognition is the foundation of the rights, privileges, and obligations that come together in the concept of humanism. Their desire for body modification should be supported by the principles of humanism.

There is another reason why FTMs should be granted the opportunity to alter their bodies. If threatened masculinity produces or encourages men who threaten others, then it is in the best interest of society to make it possible for them to secure their masculinity by changing their bodies. If society affirms their physical transitions, transsexual men will feel secure in their manhood and will rely less on stereotypically masculine behaviors to communicate their identities to others. If body modifications are not sanctioned, they will be stranded in a culture like ours, where bodies are such a crucial feature of sex and gender attribution, and be less likely to be recognized as men. Denied recognition for themselves, they will be more likely to engage in the type of stereotypical masculinity that denies recognition to others. Misrecognition of the self is likely to produce other misrecognitions.

Transsexualism is not necessarily either hegemonic or subversive with regard to gender. There is a wide range of ways to be transsexual; some subvert hegemonic masculinity and some do not. Moreover, some dominant cultural assumptions can produce unexpectedly unconventional results.

Body modification is not self-hating misogyny, but rather an attempt to secure intersubjective recognition. If this core identity is dismissed as a fiction, as in some versions of post-modern gender theory, or if body modification is viewed strictly as body mutilation, as in some versions of radical feminism, these men will be denied a valid motive for changing their bodies.

Conclusion

■ This book has been an account of the life stories of a group of FTMs and also a general meditation on identity. At one level, it is an invitation to become acquainted with the unique difficulties and triumphs of transsexual men. They demonstrate extraordinary ingenuity in order to achieve authenticity and recognition. At another level, this book is a broader investigation into the Janus nature of identity. All identities have two faces: they are both socially constructed and absolutely real. Identities are products of particular cultures and times, but no matter how constructed they are, these identities still feel real to those who claim them. Identities are experienced as an internalized core from which we derive our free willing agency.

Transsexual Lives

A Boy's Life

The female-to-male transsexuals in this study narrated lives of betrayal and misrecognition. Their female bodies betrayed them by failing to represent their core male identities. As a consequence, the process of recognition broke down. This betrayal and the need to secure recognition is an FTM's central motivation for changing his sex. While most others view these men as women who have changed their gender, these men feel that they have always been men. They are merely changing their physical form to make their "outsides" match their "insides." They are changing their sex, not their gender.

While most of their childhoods were untroubled and carefree, their adolescences were marked with horror, shame, and embarrassment. They narrated their lives as "before" and "after" stories that mark a radical break that they sought to repair. In their youth, they considered themselves to be boys in the company of other boys. Some felt they were tomboys. Others knew that this term applied to a girl who was "like a boy." Puberty was the crucial moment when their bodies feminized and they lost their most authentic selves. They said that the onset of menses and the development of breasts were traumatic events.

Their descriptions of puberty suggest a disrupted life cycle. Socially, they became "nothings." They were insufficiently socialized due to voluntary social withdrawal and the infliction of social isolation by hostile others. Some went underground, mistakenly identifying as the women that their bodies seemed to dictate they become. This explains, for some, why they lived lives that looked much like the lives of ordinary women; deluded by their physical bodies, they tried to emulate womanhood. This uncomfortable act left them depressed, isolated, and hostile. Their post-pubescent bodies felt dead from the neck down.

Not unlike others with female bodies, puberty is a time of loss for them. However, the FTMs felt that they were unlike girls who were going through the same physical changes. Though girls may be uncomfortable with their bodies and may resist or capitulate to the adolescent process of becoming "normal" women, these FTMs resisted becoming female altogether. Though many had earlier memories of being different or being at odds with the world and their bodies, puberty was often the first sign they had that they were transsexuals. Some felt that their difference from others with female bodies was absolute; they thought that girls were unequivocally excited and happy about their feminizing bodies, while they, conversely, were mortified. Others felt that their difference from girls was of degree, not kind: they knew that girls were ambivalent about menarche and developing breasts, whereas they felt absolute horror.

Their life cycle was eventually restored through a "second puberty" brought on primarily by exogamous testosterone, and by surgical modification of their bodies. Modifying their secondary sex characteristics and having their chests reconstructed make them indistinguishable from other men in all but the most private situations. The physiological changes induced by testosterone are greater muscle tone; decreased body fat; expanding shoulder span; shift in weight from the thighs to the stomach; body and facial hair growth; thicker vocal chords and a deeper voice; growth of the primary sexual organ (one to three inches); change in body odor; skin texture becoming tougher and more oily; skull growth; and possibly slight growth of hands and feet. Changes in behavioral dimensions were noted with some variation between the individual experiences of these research participants. Differences reported were increased sex drive, energy, aggression, and inhibition of emotions.

These men manage their lives so that they do not have to reveal the physical limits of their transitions. After their transitions, they are accorded greater recognition and many do "blend, blend, blend" in just the way that Jack hoped would be possible one day. The extent to which they reveal their life histories to others varies considerably, ranging from totally cloaked, stealth, or private to complete openness and transparency to any and all others. To some extent, their lives are marked by lasting physical and emotional scars. They carry grief over the years lost due to traumatic depersonalization and misrecognition. Social and psychological stigmas can plague them long past transition. Nonetheless, most feel able to participate in the banal joys and disappointments of life. They feel that they have restored their broken sense of self and are now able to pursue other life projects.

Identities-in-Progress

Although they felt as if they had always already been men, transmen did not have transsexual identities from birth. This process of identity formation is called a transsexual trajectory. These men demonstrated, somewhat paradoxically, that they had to become the men that they always already were. Most indicated that they had always been men. The life cycle story of adolescent betrayal is part of the way that they established their essential masculinity. The transsexual trajectory describes how they became transsexuals and the men they always already were.

The transsexual trajectory involved finding the "transsexual" category, identifying with other transsexuals and other men, and disidentifying from women, especially lesbians. They begin a transsexual trajectory by looking for explanations for their feelings of discomfort with their bodies. Unlike "coming out" as gay or lesbian, which creates a kind of visibility, FTMs become invisible as they transition, assimilating into the woodwork. Therefore, the term "coming out" does not adequately reflect the movement from female to male.

The multi-stage process of transition can take place over several years. It can be encouraged or discouraged by significant others, parents, friends, lovers, and acquaintances who model femininity and masculinity. While some of the FTMs homogenized, idealized, and identified with all men, most distinguished between different types of men. They acknowledged that men come in all shapes, sizes, and personalities. Some were role models, while others were noxious. Identification with other men was dependent on the type of man that an FTM encountered.

FTMs also compared themselves to other transsexuals and realized that they were more like them than like homosexuals. From television to newspapers and one-on-one chance meetings, FTMs found other FTMs or male-to-female transsexuals and noticed likenesses in their life stories. Sometimes other transsexuals, especially MTFs, had foreign experiences with which the FTMs could not identify. Meeting with a transsexual they could relate to allowed the men to identify themselves as transsexual. This prompted them to acknowledge heterogeneity within the category of transsexualism.

Women, especially lesbians, were a flash point of disidentification. Most of the participants had universalized the experiences of all women. By comparing themselves to this universal experience, they realized that they were not women. Menstruation was one such site of comparison. Most men felt that their experiences of menarche were absolutely different in quality from the way that they thought women experienced the same event. While they recognized heterogeneity among men, fewer recognized differences among women. Nonetheless, even those who saw diversity among women disidentified with them based on an absolute alienation from their female parts. Comparing themselves to these others made it possible for them to position themselves as men and as transsexuals.

About half of the men had a lesbian career that preceded their transsexual identification process. Explaining this lesbian career as a mistake preserved their belief that they were always already men. Like lesbians, they desired women sexually, but they found they were different from lesbians in too many other ways. They realized their dis-ease stemmed not from their desires for women, but from their agnosia when confronting their bodies. While some feminists, physicians, and psychologists have thought that FTMs are lesbians suffering from internalized homophobia, these men explained that, in their attempts to identify as lesbian, they had confused sexual orientation with gender identity. Learning to distinguish between sex and sexuality was a crucial step in their transsexual trajectories.

Men without a lesbian career could be gay or straight. The gay men felt a general affinity with gay people, but they knew all along that they did not desire women, so they could not be lesbians. In the minds of the straight men, whose desires for women could be confused by others as lesbianism, lesbians were woman-identified women. No matter how butch these lesbians were, they were still women. Transsexuals were different from butch women—they were male, but not necessarily masculine.

Historical Determinants of the Transsexual Trajectory

The terms of lesbian disidentification are historically determined. The emergence of an FTM identity depended upon making a clear distinction between sexuality and sex. In order to qualify for treatment with hormones and surgeries, FTMs had to distinguish themselves from lesbians and liken themselves to intersexuals. Lesbians were women with sexual desires for other women. In contrast, transsexuals were men who had a bodily anomaly that could not yet be detected, but that was surely there to be found once one had a strong enough microscope.

Though these categories are now sufficiently separated, FTMs are still compelled, literally and figuratively, to cite the differences from lesbians in order to make themselves recognizable as transsexual bodies in need of treatment. Literal compulsion occurs when FTMs must undergo a process of evaluation by psychologists or psychiatrists who

specialize in gender disorders. They must meet the standards of a differential diagnosis that discriminates between homosexuality and "gender identity disorder," previously known as transsexualism. The Benjamin *Standards of Care* (1981, 1990) make the requirements for this
diagnosis explicit. They are figuratively compelled to establish difference in that these FTMs must repeat their differences from lesbians in
order to make their identity claims logical to themselves and to others.
This disidentification is compelled by a "narcissism of small differences," which means that the closer the categorical or physical proximity of one group to another, the more stringently will the borders between them be articulated and defended.

Lesbians and FTMs have a historical relationship mediated by
medical specialists and political actors. This relationship has dictated
the horizon of meanings within which these individuals make sense of
their lives. Social forces continue to have a constitutive effect on what
FTMs believe. The experiences of their bodies and their transsexual
trajectories are all made meaningful within the historical terms of this
century.

The experiences of FTMs, however, are no less real for having been
constituted by social forces. Neither their uncomfortable experiences
of their bodies, nor the subjective sense of being male, nor even the
sense of having a core self are fictions. Merely the fact that these experiences or identities are historically situated does not undercut their subjective validity and meaning.

The Cultural Significance of the Body:
Expressivity and Recognition

The lives of transsexual men highlight the cultural significance of the
body. Through FTM experience, we can see the modern relationship
between sexed bodies and gendered identities. Bodies are the physical
medium through which selves interact with one another. In this culture, bodies are expressive representations of a person's soul. We view
bodies as the reflection of a gendered self. These beliefs about embodiment apply to all human beings living within the cultural nexus of the
modern West. They are some of our fundamental truths.

The way that our society treats transsexuals highlights the dominant beliefs about the relationship between the body and the self in modern life. Prior to transition, FTMs are treated as women because their female anatomy is assumed to be an accurate expression of who they truly are. Transsexual individuals confuse people who expect to find a woman within the flesh of a female. FTMs are more likely to be acknowledged as men if their bodies are recognizably male. Acknowledging these hegemonic beliefs, these men altered their bodies to achieve recognition as the men they have always already been.

The dominant belief in bodies as expressive may also be detected in the self-understandings of transsexual men. From the FTM perspective, their bodies are failed expressions of their core selves. Their female parts are scrambled representations of their true gender. Some transmen tried to be the women that their bodies suggested they were. Eventually, it became apparent to them that their identities were obscured by their bodies.

Expressive failures make it difficult for transsexuals to achieve intersubjective recognition. Intersubjective recognition is the mutual process whereby we acknowledge others and are acknowledged as authentic selves. Misrecognition happens when the relationship between the body and the self is skewed so that it does not conform to the dominant modern beliefs about expressive bodies. If they claim to be men without altering their bodies, FTMs are more likely to be subject to suspicion, stigma, discrimination, and misrecognition. By altering their female bodies, these men are taking a logical step in order to be granted human status as authentic and recognizable individuals. Sex changes are rational measures for securing their human integrity and the rights associated with it.

A few FTMs are questioning the relationship between embodiment and identity, choosing instead a transnatural option. Foregoing hormones and surgeries challenges the hegemonic relationship between sex and gender, but makes it more difficult to achieve recognition from others. These FTMs may also continue to feel agnosic.

If bodies were not considered expressions of identities, then fewer FTMs might be compelled to change their sex. If recognition of an authentic self was not valued, then body modification might not be necessary. However, within the present horizon of the modern West, the body has retained its central role as the representation of the self, and recognition continues to depend upon the expressive function of the body.

Concluding Thoughts

At this particular historical moment and in this Western, post-industrial place, people experience themselves as subjects with depth, consciousness, or a soul. At least, that is the normative expectation for us. Historically and culturally determined as we are, we each feel this depth and expect that others also feel it about themselves. If we do not feel it or feel that it has been corrupted or broken, we seek out methods to "get in touch" with it, to "find ourselves," or to "put ourselves back together." We hope to meet another consciousness and to transcend whatever barriers may exist in order to reach an intersubjective moment of understanding and recognition. These principles, that we experience ourselves as subjects with depth and that we hope for the possibility of intersubjective recognition, are the basis upon which the strongest and highest values of this society are built (e.g. human rights, democracies, health). The "culture of authenticity" is the guiding moral, political, spiritual, and social value of our day. The need to self-actualize, or realize the "inner letter" that is written inside each one of us, is stronger than almost any impulse we know.

This need and the experience of having depth cannot be abandoned without negative consequences for the individual and for society. To claim that we can or should willfully transcend these cultural demands is folly. To see that the terms of our identities are social constructs does not translate into the possibility of or the prescription to overcome them. A sense of self is not a will 'o wisp that can be denied, abandoned, or refuted simply because we become aware of its socially constructed nature. As a construct of cultural forces, the deep self is firmly rooted.

The men in this study have thought about identity and embodiment more than most people. In the end, they felt that they had to pursue their sex changes in order to authenticate their deepest self, to feel comfortable in their bodies, and to convey that self to others. They found technologies that could assist them in this task and brought these to bear on their bodies. They acknowledged the immutability of their male identities and pursued the surest way available in this culture to achieve recognition for who they were deep down. In all these ways, they have been following the most culturally determined needs of our age—to find the letter buried within them and follow its instructions. After watching them as they work on this life project, I can only encourage others to do the same.

Notes

Introduction

1. In fact, in the coverage of the true story, Brandon Teena was often referred to as a lesbian, a transvestite, or as "Teena." Because of his untimely death, we will never know exactly what identification Brandon Teena preferred, if any. Brandon Teena's own mother was interviewed after Oscar night and claimed that Brandon was not a man and that Swank's speech was an inaccurate representation of her daughter, who she said was sexually molested by a man and passed in order to avoid further trauma. I have assumed, like most of my research community, that Brandon Teena was male-identified.

2. Less is known about FTMs in the Midwest or non-urban centers. As one FTM from the South commented to me, feminism was unheard of in the small-town bars and softball fields. One of the limits of the materials collected from the archives on both coasts was that they represented urban, usually middle-class, educated, and usually white communities. This limit turned out to be a structuring component to my argument that as feminists and lesbians encountered each other, class differences (coded as "respectability" and "femininity") factored in their alliance-building.

3. As Kessler and McKenna (1978) have shown, the so-called "secondary" sex characteristics are crucial to gender attribution, while genitalia are less important. In their study, drawn figures who were lacking male genitalia would regularly be read as men as long as the figure had just a couple of secondary features associated with male bodies (148–50). While primary features were not crucial for gender attribution, secondary features were. It is especially this reason that leads the FTMs in this study to prioritize testosterone over surgeries. Indeed, these men realized that most people do not need to see their "private parts" to make a male gender attribution.

4. For an excellent overview of the feminist history of the terms "sex" and "gender," which informs many of my definitions, see Donna Haraway's "'Gender' for a

Marxist Dictionary: The Sexual Politics of a Word" in *Simians, Cyborgs and Women: The Reinvention of Nature* (New York, 1991).

5. Eve Sedgwick has flagged this fact and has defamiliarized it by suggesting that sexual orientation might just as easily be differentiated along other axes than is currently the case, such as how often one thinks about sex, how often one has sex, whether one prefers spontaneity or scripted sex, whether one is autoerotic or not, whether one is genital or not, etc. (Sedgwick 1990, 25). Her imaginative list of such differences is offered in this context to suggest that the categories that have been used to articulate non-transsexual desire are not the only ways of categorizing desire, and may not be as useful when applied to transsexual desire. Nonetheless, I have used the standard typology of "heterosexual," "homosexual," and "bisexual" because they remain culturally significant descriptors to both transsexuals and non-transsexuals.

6. Regarding the phrase "gender inverted": to claim that gender inversion is ahistorical is a bit misleading. As Thomas Laqueur (1990) points out in his book *Making Sex*, it is only recently that Western civilization has shifted from a "one-sex" model to a "two-sex" model. Whereas previously only one sex existed in weaker and stronger forms (female and male), now we conceive of the sexes as an oppositional dichotomy. Only in a two-sex model can we think of an individual as being gender inverted—as the opposite of his or her morphology. So "gender inversion" as a category is actually reliant on a historical context as much as is "FTM."

7. That James was distinguished from his community not only based on gender, but also on age (he was deemed a boy, while they were women) dovetails with James's belief that he needed to transition in order to grow up. This desire to grow up is not an uncommon motivation for transition and is further complicated post-transition by the fact that these men tend to appear at least ten years younger than their birth age. Many expressed both joy and frustration at this age-regression—joy at being able to recoup many lost years living in the wrong body and frustration at being read as less mature or less experienced than they were. Alternatively, many suggested that because of their lost years, they had never developed certain social skills. They felt inadequately prepared for their adult lives, but reasoned that they would gain these skills as they progressed through their transitions.

Chapter 1. The Logic of Treatment

1. This promise is intriguing if it is considered in the context of the narratives of contemporary transsexuals. Some FTMs in the present study reported an increased zest for life and an increased sexual drive, while their fertility is undone. In addition, FTMs are notably younger looking than their years, especially if they pass before transition. After administering hormones, many reported consistently being taken for at least five to ten years younger than their birth age. In transsexuals, testosterone treatments remain marked by these formative discourses of vitality and virility. This section documents the organotherapeutic logic of treatment in so far as it foreshadows the youthfulness of FTM transsexuals.

2. Eunuchs, especially self-castrators, were also significant to the logic of treatment because they did not seek to remedy or surpass nature, but instead, they violated nature's own doing. They raised the specter of the taboo against unjustifiable body modification that would play itself out again in the logic of treatment for transsexualism.

3. Synthetic estrogens were put on the market slightly later in 1939 (Oudshoorn 1994, 77).

4. Meyer-Bahlburg's earlier survey (1977) of these studies is intended to historicize the treatment of homosexual inverts in order to provide a scientific counter-argument to more recent endocrine investigations into the influence of the hypothalamus and pre-natal "causes" of homosexuality. He is critical of these investigations and uses the history of hormone treatments to foreground the wrong-headedness of his contemporaries.

5. That this novel has become the subject of controversy in the 1990s as FTMs and butch lesbians debate Stephen Gordon's identity confirms that we have fallen once again into the muddy waters where homosexuality and transsexualism are not clearly distinguished categories.

6. Dillon's repositioning is reflected in the narratives of FTMs in this study who make distinctions between themselves and butches (mannish inverts) based on a "narcissism of small differences." Chapters three and four are replete with examples that demonstrate an FTM's perception of his differences from female homosexuals, especially the mannish, or butch, type. Few of these FTMs will concede that they are like homosexuals in any way, and the rationales they use for distinguishing between themselves and butches are remarkably similar to those Dillon mentions.

7. The narratives of FTMs in the study reflect the same logic of treatment outlined by Dillon (see chapters three and four). Many of them remarked that their bodies had betrayed them at puberty. Several reported thinking that there was a physiological reason for their dilemma. Some have had themselves tested in order to discover the anomaly. Finding none, these FTMs believe that science will one day find the physiological cause of their transsexualism. Almost all of the FTMs in this study privilege their subjective sense of themselves, their psychosexual outlook, their male gender identity, and justify their testosterone treatments as a means for making their bodies fit their minds. Some suggested that they were not changing from one sex to another. They were merely becoming what they already knew themselves to be.

8. Point of historical interest: as noted by Bernice Hausman (1995) and Liz Hodgkinson (1989), Gilles performed Michael Dillon's phalloplasty.

9. In his *History of Sexuality, Volume I*, Foucault implied the idea of "proliferating perversions" in his discussion of the formation of gay male identity and other "deviant" identities that came into being through and against medicalized discourses. He writes, "The nineteenth century and our own have been rather the age of multiplication: a dispersion of sexualities, a strengthening of their disparate forms, a multiple implantation of 'perversions.' Our epoch has initiated sexual heterogeneity" (Foucault 1980, 37).

10. See Sandy Stone (1991) and Ann Bolin (1994) for two examples of the analysis of instrumental reason in transsexual relationships with their health care providers.

11. See also Chauncey's more strongly stated defense of this position in his later article (1989b) "Christian Brotherhood or Sexual Perversion? Homosexual Identities and the Construction of Sexual Boundaries in the World War I Era" in Duberman, Vicinius, and Chauncey. Chauncey refers to the medical discourse on homosexuality as a Foucauldian "reverse discourse" (314). He suggests that the sexologists took the categories and typologies from the subculture.

12. In *Changing Sex: Transsexualism, Technology, and the Idea of Gender* (1995), a recent genealogy of transsexualism (mostly male-to-female), Bernice L. Hausman argues that the mid-twentieth century sexologists *created* the category of gender and the disorder of transsexualism. While Hausman attributes some agency to transsexuals, she also believes transsexuals to be the dupes of sexology and of the sex/gender system.

Chapter 2. Border Wars

1. This ratio is reported by Janice G. Raymond (1979, 24–25) and Leslie Lothstein (1983, 308–11). While I do not share Raymond's moral judgments of transsexuals, nor Lothstein's pathologizing psychology, their books are important historical documents that offer valuable data on the emergence of FTMs.

2. The histories of gender nonconformity among gay women that I draw upon include the work of Davis and Kennedy (1993), Gayle Rubin (1992), Esther Newton (1989), Joan Nestle (1987, 1992), and Lillian Faderman (1991).

3. The resolutions passed at the Congress are "(1) Women's Liberation is a lesbian plot. (2)Whenever the label lesbian is used against the movement collectively or against women individually, it is to be affirmed, not denied. (3) In all discussions of birth control, homosexuality must be included as a legitimate method of contraception. (4) All sex education curricula must include lesbianism as a valid, legitimate form of sexual expression and love" (Abbott and Love 1972, 115).

4. See especially Abbott and Love (1972, 113–15), Del Martin and Phyllis Lyon, (1972, 266). See also a more critical appraisal in Echols (1989, 214).

5. This is Lillian Faderman's term for the changes I am describing here. For a discussion of her evaluation of this era see Faderman (1991, 204).

6. Despite the best efforts of some of the most distinguished historians, the question of the existence of a "mythological" cross-dressed butch at the Stonewall Inn on that fateful night of June in 1969 remains unanswered. According to Martin Duberman's sources, lesbians rarely frequented the Stonewall and the night of the riots was no exception. In fact, in Duberman's presentation of several competing views of the night, this is one matter that resisted a definitive account (Duberman 1993, 190, 196). By this historical record, the origin of the specific fight for lesbian

respect and human dignity is not to be found in a Mafia-owned drag bar in Green-wich Village, but rather in a conference hall at a gathering of women's organizations at the Second Congress. These are differences that matter in this historical game of truth that represents a battle over the nature of lesbian identity.

7. One striking example of this comes from a founder of the Daughters of Bilitis, Phyllis Martin (1970/1971). Martin justifiably rebukes her gay male "brothers" for their sexism and announces her belief that lesbians will be better off working with their heterosexual sisters. In the course of her article, she also dismisses aspects of life prior to the Second Congress—cross-dressers and Halloween Balls—which some butches considered a substantial part of their identity and culture. For an account of one particularly important personage who took offense to this position, see Lou Sullivan's unpublished diaries (Sullivan 1973).

8. For a powerful historical/personal introduction to the social, political and cultural changes of the 1960s, see Cluster (1979) and Nestle (1987).

9. For more on the origins of the Women's Movement, see Jo (Joreen) Freeman (1984). See also Judith Hole and Ellen Levine (1971).

10. See Freeman (1984, 706), Echols, (1989, 65), and Ann Popkin in Cluster (1979, 184).

11. Echols (1989, 344) points to Judith Brown's "Florida Papers" as one excep-tion.

12. For more details on the relationship between class and butch roles, see Madeline Davis and Elizabeth Lapovsky Kennedy (1993). Also, Canadian Line Chamberland (1990, 1991) has done similar work on the French-speaking commu-nities in the north.

13. Other important historical accounts of "mannish" lesbians include Newton (1993), Gayle Rubin (1992), and "She Even Chewed Tobacco" a pictorial account assembled by the San Francisco Gay and Lesbian History Project (1992). Femmes are treated in Biddy Martin's book of essays, *Femininity Played Straight: The Significance of Being Lesbian* (1997) and in essays by Joan Nestle, Amber Hollibaugh, Cherrie Moraga, and Madeline Davis, all in the collection *The Persistent Desire: A Femme-Butch Reader* (1992).

14. See Joan Nestle (1987, 1982) and Carole Vance (1992) especially her essays on the Barnard Sexuality Conference and the fallout that followed. See also Snitow, Stansell, and Thompson (1983). All provide excellent accounts of the destruction done to the unique sexuality of butches and femmes as they came into contact with lesbian-feminism.

15. The Gay and Lesbian History Conference (1994) at the Center for Lesbian and Gay Studies in New York captured this continuing tendency within historical studies perfectly. At a panel on "Third Sex" (which was subtitled "Classic Debates on Gender and the Homosexual Role"), the panel members all emphasized lesbian and gay genders, (e.g. butch and femme) as signifiers of sexual identities. While sexual identities signified by gender presentation continue to receive historical attention,

what is left out of most analyses is the identificatory importance these gender signs have for the bodies that mobilize them. At this historical juncture, gender signs are more than mere cues for sexual likes and dislikes. They are also signifiers of gender identity. This may seem like an obvious point, but in the context of this particular conference, as in many such discussions, it was not adequately addressed.

16. Davis and Kennedy support the claim that even the upwardly mobile crowd in Buffalo was not structured according to butch and femme. For this distinction and its implications see their chapter four. They also claim that black female laborers were butch and femme. If it is possible to substantiate as a fact that feminism ignored black and chicana lesbian cultures, then it may provide an explanation for the fewer number of female-to-male transsexuals in these communities. Of course, alternate explanations to consider are the extent to which class and race issues map onto one another in this scenario, such that class privilege dictates who can afford the costs of medical care over the course of transition.

17. Around this time a common phenomenon at large gatherings of women was the practice of asking women to stand if they ever felt sexual attraction to other women. Large numbers of women often stood. This was followed by breathless waves of experimentation and multiple converts. See for example, the report on a Bay Area conference in Lane (1970, 4–6). Also, see a report on the panel discussion by "C.J." (1970).

18. The headline of the new *Tide* in March 1974.

19. For a feminist discussion that counters Chodorow and other object-relations analyses of female development and tomboyism see PJ McGann, "The Ballfields of our Hearts" (Ph.D. diss., Brandeis University). She problematizes the relationship between tomboy behavior and adult gender/sexual identity, finding that a wide array of adult identities (heterosexual women, lesbians, and transgendered individuals) are correlated with tomboy identities in childhood.

20. For the reasons the FTMs in this study gave, see chapter four.

21. That it is not impossible for gender inverts to identify as lesbian has been pointed out to me by many lesbians, especially by butch women of an older generation who self-define as male. This points to the fact that the lesbian-feminist revolution that defined lesbians as "woman-identified" was not a total revolution, but was certainly the dominant or hegemonic paradigm after 1970.

22. There were occasional references to transsexual couples (a pair made up of an FTM and an MTF) (Bowmen and Engel 1956, Randell 1959).

23. See the Lou Sullivan collection at the Gay and Lesbian Historical Society in San Francisco for the unpublished manuscript of Sullivan's journals that document his protracted battle with sexologists for permission to transition to gay manhood. See also Sullivan (1990).

24. See especially Donna Minkovitz's (1994) article in *The Village Voice*, "Love Hurts." Minkovitz writes, "Brandon Teena was a woman who lived and loved as a man. She was killed for carrying it off." The use of female pronouns and the references to Brandon Teena as butch created an uproar in the FTM community. For an

opposing view from the transsexual community, see *Transsexual News Telegraph*, "FTM Murdered in Nebraska" (1994).

Chapter 3. Betrayed by Bodies

1. See Rubin's article "Of Catamites and Kings" (1992) for her observations on these similarities between FTMs and butch dykes. Esther Newton made similar claims in a personal communication with me.

2. See PJ McGann's doctoral thesis (1994) for a thorough treatment of the tomboy phenomenon. McGann challenges the standard social psychology of women biased toward feminine female development. In addition to her critique of sexological accounts of children categorized as "gender dysphoric," McGann draws on interviews with self-identified (grown-up) tomboys to suggest that tomboy identity was neither trouble-free, nor completely stigmatized as "sissy boys" were.

3. That these FTMs reported a childhood that was mostly unproblematic until puberty contrasts sharply with the accounts of male-to-female transsexuals, many of whom report very early experiences of trauma that they quickly framed as gender-related. The early untroubled FTM youth and the difficulties of specifying and framing their troubles may be due to the fact that the most significant embodiments of a female self (menses and breasts) are not present from birth, while the penis, the male body part that carries the most representational weight, is there from the start of life. See Anne Bolin's (1988) ethnography of a community group of male-to-female transsexual women.

4. I problematize the notion that the human species is dimorphic. It has been estimated by one biologist, Anne Fausto-Sterling (1993), that an underreported four percent of babies are born sexually indeterminate or intersexed. For the most part, these children are altered non-consensually by physicians who believe that no parent will possibly be able to give an intersexed child the love and affection that child needs for emotional development. While the intersexed community has a different (sometimes conflicting) agenda than transsexuals, their marginality and deviance from cultural norms provides some space to work out an affinity. Generally speaking, it is important to stay open to the possibility that there are more than two ways to develop and grow.

5. Lee and Sasser-Coen acknowledge that with puberty comes a raised body-consciousness for all teenagers, especially girls, and that many become disembodied as a means of survival and of resistance to hegemonic female, feminine, and heterosexual imperatives. "While preoccupation with the body at puberty is in part a developmental phenomenon, the fact that girls specifically experience these particular feelings and behaviors in these ways points to the inappropriateness of thinking that cognitive processes occur a priori of history and culture" (98). The denaturalizing of the adolescent body consciousness serves here as a way of claiming that in another context, young women (and young men) might not experience the same heightened

consciousness of their bodies. It also suggests that FTMs' disembodied awareness is not unique to them, although its focus is different.

6. Though Lee and Sasser-Coen did not hold the participants of their study to a psychoanalytic model that frames puberty as either the reorganization or disruption of body image, they do mention this model and criticize it for its anatomical and psychological determinism (32–33). The FTM experience, though it rests on the tension between the body image and the material body, counters the psychoanalytic model of puberty as the disruption or reorganization of one's body image. For the FTMs, body image remains stable while the material body moves away from that image.

Chapter 4. Transsexual Trajectories

1. See Ann Bolin (1994) for a more encompassing discussion of the changes that are unfolding in both the FTM and the MTF communities.

2. Other readers of an earlier draft of this book have felt that FTM claims to empirical differences are not born out upon investigation. These readers, Esther Newton and Gayle Rubin, have both pointed to the many examples of lesbian women who have characteristics that FTMs claim as their own province. This difference of opinion reflects what Eve Sedgwick (1990) has pinpointed as an irreconcilable tension between specificity and universalism that undergirds most, if not all, debates about gender today. I have followed Sedgwick's suggestion to avoid trying to adjudicate between these positions (a strategy doomed to failure by her account, at least for the present), and pursued the alternate agenda of discovering what function these claims to difference serve the FTMs in this study. I will leave it to investigators of lesbian identity to articulate the function of the claims of similarity lesbians make with regard to FTMs.

3. See chapter three for a discussion of the limits of this kind of feminist reappropriation of female bodies, especially for the FTMs in this study.

Chapter 5. Always Already Men

1. In my opinion, this is a partial explanation of why most popular treatments of transsexuals have focused on MTFs. The existence of male-to-female transsexuals is seen as a phenomenon that remains in need of an explanation, whereas FTMs seem to be making reasoned choices in a man's world.

2. Whereas the title of my dissertation on this same group of men was "Transformations: Emergent Female-to-Male Transsexuals," I have changed the title of the book in order to emphasize this point. These men have not transformed who they are. From their perspective, they are merely making it possible for others to see them as they truly are and have always been. They do acknowledge, however, that they have to make themselves over through the transition process. This active process of

"making the man" does not mean that they have changed who they are. They are, as Francis puts it, "becoming more of who they always already were."

3. See especially Joshua Gamson's book on television talk shows, *Freaks Talk Back* (1998).

4. "Expressive gender identities" are contrasted by Judith Butler with "performative genders." (Butler 1990, 278–79) Butler claims that the expressive model of core identity is the more dominant belief system. She suggests that the notion of a core identity ultimately obscures the ways that a core identity is a product, not the source, of gender roles and sexed bodies. Butler sometimes seems to argue that the belief in a core gender identity is an impediment to resignification of gender norms. She seems to be saying that hegemonic or stereotypical gender is maintained by the idea of a core gender identity. However, Butler does not believe that we can voluntaristically shed our gender identities, nor should we refrain from saying "I."

5. These are just a few of the many authors who have criticized transsexuals explicitly for their continued adherence to gender norms, the "natural attitude," and/ or heteronormativity. Others include King 1996, Billings and Urban 1996, Bem 1993, Grosz 1994, Hausman 1995, and Lorber 1994. Though few are as vindictive and hateful as Janice Raymond's manifesto against the so-called "Transsexual Empire," they nevertheless demonstrate the persistent transphobic ideas that fuel the fear and hatred of transsexuals. Transgendered people who make visible their life histories or maintain some visible gender ambiguities are less subject to such criticisms because they appear to undermine the "natural attitude." For an elaboration of my criticisms of some of these authors, see Rubin 1998.

6. Again, this is merely a sampling of some of the most popular and influential writings that attempt to counter the negative ideas cited above. For a fairly comprehensive analysis and criticism of these authors and the valorization of gender ambiguity or gender "crossing" over gender passing, see Elliot and Roen (1998).

7. On the morning of this writing, I read an exchange on an email list about this very subject. The thread of this discussion started in response to a negative movie review in of the highly acclaimed documentary film *You Don't Know Dick: The Hearts and Minds of Transsexual Men*. In an article entitled "Getting to Know Dick: Transsexuals As Guardians Of Gender Status Quo" in a gay publication, transsexual men are accused of replicating stereotypical masculinity (Ledger 1998).

8. Again, see Halberstam (1998) and G. Rubin (1992) for a butch point of view on this distinction.

9. This is a misreading of Butler, who has made a clear distinction between ethnomethodological accounts of gender as dramaturgy and gender as performative. See Butler's exchanges with Lynne Layton (1998).

10. If one needs a theoretical justification for the reinvigoration of culturally hegemonic conventions for unauthorized purposes, one need not look any further than Michel Foucault (one of Butler's many founding fathers), who employs the term "reverse discourse." A reverse discourse, or "counter-hegemonic discourse," does not work outside of the terms of the culturally dominant discourse; it merely revital-

izes and reinvigorates those terms for purposes other than those that were originally intended. As Butler (1990, 1993) states, however, not every reinvocation will be subversive. Reverse discourses are, as often as not, normative reinvestments in hegemonic cultural conventions.

11. Of course, one cannot help but notice that in this set of associations, the men are suggesting that testosterone, which "makes the man," is linked to activity (versus passivity) and activity is linked to maleness.

12. Kessler and McKenna (1978).

13. As I have suggested elsewhere in this book, the interview method I have employed in this section of the book provides intriguing and informative insights about the experiences that these men have had. While this method provides important data, these claims are less easily proven in the strong scientific sense of the word. For example, although I can confirm the effects that testosterone had on their *bodies* (by observing and comparing pictures of them before and after), I cannot validate with complete certainty that their *behavior* was altered by testosterone. That said, I am confident that, no matter the limits on experientially based knowledge, there is something valuable to this form of knowledge. What these men have to say about testosterone is fascinating and will affect the ways we think about bodies and behavior. Though we might not like the news they bring us about the effects of testosterone, I believe we, both men and women, ignore it at our own peril.

15. For example, men with little body hair have been considered effeminate. Based on this difference from the culturally hegemonic belief that men are always hairier than women, these men have suffered social stigma as unmanly and meek. Likewise, Olympic women athletes who have been considered too hairy to be considered womanly have been subject to intense official and media scrutiny in order to prove that they are legitimate female competitors. Of course, even average females have been compelled to alter their appearances (by shaving, waxing, bleaching, etc.) in ways that they might not otherwise if this society was not invested in these culturally dominant ideas about sexual dimorphism.

16. See Olesen and Woods (1986), Gold and Severino (1994), Laws (1985), Figert (1996) on P.M.S. and hormonal determinism. Bird and Rieker (1999), Hunter (1996) Harding (1995), Sherwin (1986) on women's health and hormone replacement therapy, Ricketts (1984) and Ross, Rogers, and McCulloch (1978) on homosexuality and transsexuality.

17. Due to this common correlation, it is a regular practice of endocrinologists who treat FTMs to check testosterone levels. In a conversation with Dr. Stuart Chipkin, the head endocrinologist at the Boston Medical Center who treats many FTMs, he told me that he preferred to step his patients up on gradual dosage while keeping an eye out for violent "secondary effects" of the injections. A study by Dr. Christina Wang at UCLA ("Does Testosterone Equal Aggression? Perhaps Not, Research is Suggesting," *New York Times*, June 20, 1995) argues that friendliness is related to higher testosterone levels. This study of fifty-four hypogonadal men (men with test-

osterone deficiencies) also found that higher levels of testosterone correlated with lessened irritability. The results of Wang's study seem to be confirmed by Shadow's account of his "before" and "after." Shadow believed that he had a core male self that should dictate the type of treatment he receives. Like these hypogonadal men, Shadow felt better physically on testosterone. He also believed that being recognized as himself contributed to his sense of well-being and said that he is now able to stand firmly on the foundations of his identity and stand for whatever he believes.

18. See Kerwin Kay and Jill Nagle's recent book *Male Lust: Power, Pleasure, & Transformation* (2000) for a treatment of the complexities and contradictions of male desire.

19. See Rubin (1998) in the special "Trans" issue of GLQ for a fully developed critique of the claim that transsexuals are merely the dupes of the hegemonic gender order and falsely conscious of their true interests as possible gender outlaws.

20. Among the best of the sociologists working on masculinity and its more oppressive forms, see R.W, Connell (1987, 1995), Michael Kimmel (1987, 1996, 2000), and Harry Brod (1987, 1994).

21. See Rubin 1997, "Reading like a Transsexual Man" in *Men Do Feminism* for a more in depth discussion of the compulsion to be regarded as real men.

22. This is, by now, a standard claim of the object-relations school of feminist psychology (Butler and Layton, Benjamin, Chodorow, etc.). Benjamin defines splitting as "a defense against aggression, an effort to protect the 'good' object by splitting off its 'bad' aspects that have incurred aggression. But in its broader sense, splitting means any breakdown of the whole in which parts of self or other are split off and projected elsewhere. In both uses it indicates a polarization, in which opposites— especially good and bad—can no longer be integrated; in which one side is devalued, the other idealized, and each is projected onto different objects" (Benjamin 1988, 63).

23. Holly Devor (1997) gives an excellent overview of the difficulties that persist past transition in private or semi-private settings.

24. Butler writes that merely coming to terms with the discursivity of the self does not mean that "we" cannot speak from a position of embodied subjectivity. Butler has clarified her position in her later work (1993); the core self is a *fiction*, but absolutely necessary to subjects who hope to speak for gender justice.

References

Abbott, Sidney, and Barbara Love. 1972. *Sappho was a Right-On Woman*. New York: Stein & Day.

Albert, Roberta. 1970. Letter to the editor. *The Ladder*, August/September.

American Heritage Electronic Dictionary. 1993. Wordstar International. Houghten-Miflin Company.

Atkinson, Ti-Grace. 1974. *Amazon Odyssey*. New York: Link Books.

Baer, Beth. 1970. Letter to the editor. *The Ladder*, August/September.

Baer, Tommy. 1970. Letter to the editor. *The Ladder*, August/September.

Benjamin, Harry. 1954. Transsexualism and Transvestism—Symposium. *American Journal of Psycotherapy* 8, April: 219-44.

———. 1966. *The Transsexual Phenomenon*. New York: The Julian Press.

———. 1969. Introduction to *Transsexualism and Sex Reassignment*, eds. Richard Green and John Money. Baltimore: Johns Hopkins Press.

Benjamin, Harry and Charles Ihlenfeld. 1970. The Nature and Treatment of Transsexualism. *Medical Opinion and Review*, 6,11:24-36.

Berger, Peter, and Thomas Luckmann. 1966. *The Social Construction of Reality*. New York: Doubleday.

Bogdan, Robert. 1974. *Being Different: The Autobiography of Jane Fry*. New York: Wiley.

Bolin, Ann. 1988. *In Search of Eve: Transsexual Rites of Passage*. South Hadley: Bergin & Garvey.

———. 1994. Transcending and Transgendering: Male-to-Female Transsexuals, Dichotomy and Diversity. In *Third Sex, Third Gender: Beyond Sexual Dimorphism in Culture and History*, ed. Gil Herdt. New York: Zone Books.

Bowmen, Karl, and Bernice Engle. 1956. Medico-Legal Aspects of Transvestitism. *American Journal of Psychiatry* 113: 583–88.

Brown, Rita Mae. 1976. *A Plain Brown Rapper*. Oakland: Diana Press.

Burana, Lily, Roxxie, and Linnea Due. 1994. *Dagger: On Butch Women.* San Francisco: Cleis Press.

Butler, Judith. 1990a. *Gender Trouble: Feminism and the Subversion of Identity.* New York: Routledge.

———. 1990b. Performative Acts and Gender Constitution: An Essay in Phenomenology and Feminist Theory. In *Performing Feminisms: Feminist Critical Theory and Theatre*, ed. Sue Ellen Case. Baltimore: Johns Hopkins University Press.

———. 1993. *Bodies that Matter: On the Discursive Limits of Sex.* New York: Routledge.

Butler, Judith, Seyla Benhabib, Drucilla Cornell, and Nancy Fraser. 1995. *Feminist Contentions: A Philosophical Exchange.* New York: Routledge.

C.J. [pseud.]. 1970. A letter from "Readers Respond." *The Ladder,* October/November.

Cauldwell, D. 1949. Psychopathia Transsexualis. *Sexology* 16: 274–80.

Chamberland, Line. 1990. Social Class and Integration in the Lesbian Sub-Culture. Paper presented to Learned Societies in British Columbia. May 28.

Chauncey, George. 1989a. From Sexual Inversion to Homosexuality: The Changing Medical Conceptualization of Female "Deviance." In *Passion and Power: Sexuality in History,* eds. Kathy Peiss and Christina Simmons. Philadelphia: Temple University Press.

———. 1989b. Christian Brotherhood or Sexual Perversion? Homosexual Identities and the Construction of Sexual Boundaries in the World War I Era. In *Hidden From History: Reclaiming the Gay and Lesbian Past,* eds. Martin Duberman, Martha Vicinus, and George Chauncey Jr. New York: Penguin Press.

Cluster, Dick. 1979. *They Should have Served that Cup of Coffee.* Boston: South End Press.

Cordova, Jeanne. 1992. Butches, Lies and Feminism. In *The Persistent Desire: A Butch Femme Reader,* ed. Joan Nestle. Boston: Alyson Publications.

D'Emilio, John, and Estelle Freedman. 1988. *Intimate Matters: A History of Sexuality in America.* New York: Harper and Row.

Dally, Ann. 1991. *Women Under the Knife.* London: Hutchinson Radius.

Damon, Gene [Barbara Grier]. 1970. Women's Liberation Catches Up to the Ladder. *The Ladder,* August/September.

Davis, Kathy. 1995. *Reshaping the Female Body: The Dilemma of Cosmetic Surgery.* New York: Routledge.

Davis, Madeline, and Elizabeth Lapovsky Kennedy. 1993. *Boots of Leather, Slippers of Gold: The History of a Lesbian Community.* New York: Routledge.

Derek. 1993. Correspondence to "Male Box." *The FTM Newsletter.* San Francisco: FTM International, July.

Devor, Holly. 1997. *FTM: Female to Male Transsexuals in Society.* Bloomington: Indiana University Press.

Dillon, Michael, M.D. 1946. *Self: A Study in Ethics and Endocrinology.* London: Windmill Press, William Heinemann Medical Books.

Duberman, Martin. 1993. *Stonewall.* New York: Dutton Press.

Echols, Alice. 1989. *Daring to Be Bad: Radical Feminism in America 1967–1975.* Minneapolis: University of Minnesota.

Elliot, Patricia, and Katrina Roen. 1998. Transgenderism and the Question of Embodiment: Promising Queer Politics? *GLQ: A Journal of Lesbian and Gay Studies,* 4, 2:231-62.

Epstein, Steven. 1992. Gay Politics, Ethnic Identity: The Limits of Social Constructionism. In *Forms of Desire: Sexual Orientation and the Social Constructionist Controversy,* ed. Edward Stein. New York: Routledge.

Ericsen, Karl. 1970. The Transsexual Experience. *The Ladder,* April/May.

Faderman, Lillian. 1991. *Odd Girls and Twilight Lovers: A History of Lesbian Life in Twentieth Century America.* New York: Penguin Books.

Fausto-Sterling, Anne. 1993. The Five Sexes: Why Male and Female Are Not Enough. *The Sciences.* March/April, 20–24.

Feinberg, Leslie. 1993a. *Stone Butch Blues: A Novel.* Ithaca: Firebrand Books.

———. 1993b. Politics and Gender: An Interview with Leslie Feinberg. By K. Horowitz. *FTM Newsletter.* San Francisco: FTM International. May, no. 23:1-3.

Forfreedom, Ann. 1973. Lesbos Arise! *The Lesbian Tide.* May/June.

Foucault, Michel. 1980a. *The History of Sexuality, Volume I: An Introduction.* New York: Vintage Books.

———. 1980b. *Power/Knowledge: Selected Interviews and Other Writings, 1972–1977.* Ed. Colin Gordon. New York: Pantheon Books.

———. 1984a. Nietzsche, Genealogy, History. In *The Foucault Reader,* ed. Paul Rabinow. New York: Pantheon Books.

———. 1984b. Truth and Power. In *The Foucault Reader,* ed. Paul Rabinow. New York: Pantheon Books.

Freeman, Jo [Joreen]. 1973. The Tyranny of Structurelessness. In *Radical Feminism,* eds. Anne Koedt, Ellen Levine and Anita Rapone. New York: Quadrangle Books.

———. 1984. Women's Liberation Movement: Its Origins, Structure, Activities and Ideas. In *Women: A Feminist Perspective.* Palo Alto: Mayfield Publishing Company.

"FTM Murdered in Nebraska." 1994. *Transsexual News Telegraph.* Winter, 6.

Fuss, Diana. 1989. *Essentially Speaking: Feminism, Nature and Difference.* New York: Routledge.

G.W. Carnrick Co. 1924. *Organotherapy in General Practice.* Baltimore: The Lord Baltimore Press.

Garber, Marjorie. 1989. Spare Parts: The Surgical Construction of Gender. *Differences* (Fall), 1, 3:137-59.

———. 1992. *Vested Interests: Cross-Dressing and Cultural Anxiety.* New York: Routledge.

Garfinkel, Harold. 1984. *Studies in Ethnomethodology.* Cambridge, England: Polity Press.

Glass, S.J., and Roswell H. Johnson. 1944. Limitations and Complications of Organotherapy in Male Homosexuality. *The Journal of Clinical Endocrinology,* 4:540-44.

Goffman, Erving. 1959. *Asylums: Essays on the Social Situation of Mental Patients and Other Inmates.* Chicago: Aldine Publishing Company.

Goldberger, Rita. 1972. Get it Straight. *The Lesbian Tide,* May.

Green, Richard, and John Money. 1969. *Transsexualism and Sex Reassignment.* Baltimore: Johns Hopkins University Press.

Green, James, ed. 1994–95. *FTM Newsletter.* San Francisco: FTM International. Fall and Winter.

———. 1995. Keynote address presented at the First All-FTM Conference of the Americas. Aug. 18.

Grosz, Elizabeth. 1994a. *Volatile Bodies: Toward a Corporeal Feminism.* Bloomington: Indiana University Press.

———. 1994b. Sexual Difference and the Problem of Essentialism. In *The Essential Difference,* eds. Naomi Schor and Elizabeth Weed. Bloomington: Indiana University Press.

Halberstam, Judith. 1994. F2M: The Making of Female Masculinities. In *The Lesbian Post-Modern,* ed. Laura Doan. Oakland: Columbia University Press.

Hamburger, Christian. 1953. Desire for a Sex Change as Shown by Personal Letters from 465 Men and Women. *Acta Endocrinologica* 14:361-75.

Haraway, Donna. 1991. "Gender" for a Marxist Dictionary: The Sexual Politics of a Word. In *Simians, Cyborgs and Women: The Reinvention of Nature.* New York: Routledge.

Harrower, Henry R. 1922. *Practical Organotherapy: The Internal Secretions in General Practice.* 3rd edition. Glendale, Calif.: The Harrower Laboratory.

Harry Benjamin International Gender Dysphoria Association. 1981. *Standards of Care: The Hormonal and Surgical Sex Reassignment of Gender Dysphoric Persons.* New York.

———. 1990. *Standards of Care: The Hormonal and Surgical Sex Reassignment of Gender Dysphoric Persons.* Revised draft prepared by the founding committee chaired by Dr. Paul A. Walker. Houston.

Hausman, Bernice L. 1995. *Changing Sex: Transsexualism, Technology, and the Idea of Gender.* Durham, N.C.: Duke University Press.

Held, David. 1980. *Introduction to Critical Theory: Horkheimer to Habermas.* Berkeley: University of California Press.

Heller, C.G. and W.O. Maddock. 1947. The Clinical Uses of Testosterone in the Male. *Vitam. Horm.* 5: 393–432.

Hertz, John, Karl-Gunnar Tillinger, and Axel Westman. 1961. Transvestism: Report on Five Hormonally and Surgically Treated Cases. *Acta Psychiatrica Scandinavica,* 37:283-93.

Hole, Judith, and Ellen Levine. 1971. *Rebirth of Feminism.* New York: Quadrangle Books.

Hoopes, John E. 1969. Operative Treatment of the Female Transsexual. In *Transsexualism and Sex Reassignment,* eds. Richard Green and John Money. Baltimore: Johns Hopkins Press.

Irvine, Janice M. 1990. *Disorders of Desire: Sex and Gender in Modern American Sexology.* Philadelphia: Temple University Press.

Journal Entry. 1973. *The Lesbian Tide.* May/June, 36–37.

Kessler, Suzanne, and Wendy McKenna. 1978. *Gender: An Ethnomethodological Approach.* New York: John Wiley and Sons.

Krieger, Susan. 1983. *The Mirror Dance: Identity in a Women's Community.* Philadelphia: Temple University Press.

———. 1991. *Social Science & the Self.* New Brunswick: Rutgers University Press.

Kuhn, Thomas S. 1970. *The Structure of Scientific Revolutions.* Chicago: University of Chicago Press.

Lane, Jess K. 1970. Second Bay Area Women's Coalition Conference. *The Ladder,* April/May.

Laporte, Rita. 1970a. Readers Respond. *The Ladder,* February/March.

———. 1970b. The Undefeatable Force. *The Ladder,* August/September.

———. 1971. The Butch-Femme Question. *The Ladder,* June/July.

Laqueur, Thomas. 1990. *Making Sex: Body and Gender from the Greeks to Freud.* Cambridge: Harvard University Press.

Lee, Janet, and Jennifer Sasser-Coen. 1996. *Blood Stories: Menarche and the Politics of the Female Body in Contemporary U.S. Society.* New York: Routledge.

Lothstein, Leslie. 1983. *Female-to-Male Transsexualism.* New York: Routledge.

Lunden, Blue (Doris). 1980. Old Dykes Tales: Interview with D. Lunden. By Elly Bulkin. *Conditions,* 6:27-44.

Lurie, Louis A. 1944. The Endocrine Factor in Homosexuality: Report of Treatment of 4 Cases with Androgen Hormone. *American Journal of Medical Sciences,* 208:176-86.

Lyle, Dorothy. 1970. Masquerade. *The Ladder,* April/May.

Lynch, Lee. 1985. *The Swashbuckler.* Tallahassee, Fla.: Naiad Press.

Maliniac, Jacques W. 1950. *Breast Deformities and Their Repair.* Quoting William Durston. New York: Grune & Stratton.

Martin, Biddy. 1997. *Femininity Played Straight: The Significance of Being Lesbian.* New York: Routledge.

Martin, Del, and Phyllis Lyon. 1972. *Lesbian/Women.* San Francisco: Glide Publications.

Martin, Phyllis. 1970/1971. Goodbye to All That. *The Ladder,* December/January.

Martino, Mario, with Harriet Martino. 1977. *Emergence: A Transsexual Autobiography.* New York: Crown Publishers.

McCully, Robert S. 1963. An Interpretation of Projective Findings in a Case of Female Transsexualism. *The Journal of Projective Techniques,* 27:436-46.

McGann, P.J. 1994. "The Ballfields of our Hearts." Ph.D. diss., Brandeis University.

Medvei, Victor Cornelius. 1982. *A History of Endocrinology .* Quoting John Hunter. Lancaster, England: MTP Press Limited.

Mercer, Kobena. 1990. Black Hair/Style Politics. In *Out There: Marginalization and Contemporary Cultures.* Cambridge: MIT Press.

Merleau-Ponty, Maurice. 1962. *Phenomenology of Perception.* Trans. Colin Smith. New York: Humanities Press.

Meyer-Bahlburg, Heino F.L. 1977. Sex Hormones and Male Homosexuality in Comparative Perspective. *Archives of Sexual Behavior,* 6, 4:297-325.

———. 1984. "Psychoendocrine Research on Sexual Orientation. Current Status and Future Options." *Progress in Brain Research* 61:375-98.

Mills, C. Wright. 1959. *The Sociological Imagination.* London: Oxford University Press.

Minkovitz, Donna. 1994. Love Hurts. *The Village Voice,* April 19.

Money, John. 1952. "Hermaphroditism: An Inquiry into the Nature of a Human Paradox." Ph.D. diss., Harvard University.

Nestle, Joan. 1987. *A Restricted Country.* Ithaca: Firebrand Books.

———. 1992. *The Persistent Desire: A Butch Femme Reader.* Boston: Alyson Publications.

Newton, Esther. 1972. *Mother Camp : Female Impersonators in America.* Chicago: University of Chicago Press.

———. 1993. The Mythic Mannish Lesbian: Radclyffe Hall and the New Woman. In *Hidden from History: Reclaiming the Gay and Lesbian Past,* eds. Duberman, Martin, Martha Vicinus, and George Chauncey Jr. New York: Penguin Press.

———. 1994. Dick(less) Tracy and the Homecoming Queen: Lesbian Power and Representation in Gay Male Cherry Grove. Paper presented at the Fourth Gay, Lesbian and Bisexual Studies Conference. Iowa City, Iowa. November.

———. 1995. Personal communication with author.

Nietzsche, Friedrich. 1969. *Ecce Homo.* Trans. and ed. Walter Kaufman. New York: Vintage Books.

Oudshoorn, Nelly. 1994. *Beyond the Natural Body: An Archaeology of Sex Hormones.* New York: Routledge.

Ponse, Barbara. 1978. *Identities in the Lesbian World: The Social Construction of Self.* Westport, Conn.: Greenwood Press.

Prosser, Jay. 1995. No Place Like Home: The Transgendered Narrative of Leslie Feinberg's *Stone Butch Blues. Modern Fiction Studies* (Fall/Winter) 41, 3–4:483-514.

Radicalesbians, The [Ellen Bedoz, Rita Mae Brown, Cynthia Funk, Lois Hart, March

Hoffman, and Barbara XX]. 1970. "The Woman-Identified Woman." *The Ladder,* August/September.

Randell, John B. 1959. Transvestitism and Trans-sexualism: A Study of 50 Cases. *British Medical Journal* 2:1448–52.

Raymond, Janice G. 1979. *The Transsexual Empire: The Making of the She-Male.* Boston: Beacon Press.

Redmount, Robert S. 1953. A Case of a Female Transvestite with Marital and Criminal Complications. *The Journal of Clinical and Experimental Psychopathology,* 14, 2:95-111.

Rene. 1973. Letter to the editor. *The Lesbian Tide,* December.

Right-On, Radical Rita [pseud.]. 1973. Radical Politics. *The Lesbian Tide.* April.

Rooney, Ellen. 1994. In a Word. Interview with Ellen Rooney. By Gayatri Spivak. In *The Essential Difference,* eds. Naomi Schor and Elizabeth Weed. Bloomington, Ind.: Indiana University Press.

Rosario, Vernon A. II. 1993. "Sexual Psychopaths: Doctors, Patients and Novelists Narrating the Erotic Imagination in Nineteenth Century France." Ph.D diss., Harvard University.

Rubin, Gayle. 1975. The Traffic in Women: Notes on the Political Economy of Sex. In *Toward an Anthropology of Women,* ed. Rayna Rapp Reiter. New York: Monthly Review Press.

———. 1992. Of Catamites and Kings: Reflections on Butch, Gender, and Boundaries. In *The Persistent Desire: A Butch Femme Reader,* ed. Joan Nestle. Boston: Alyson Publications.

Rubin, Henry S. 1994. Field notes.

———. 1996. Report on the First All-FTM Conference of the Americas: A Vision of Community. *The Journal of Gay, Lesbian, and Bisexual Identities,* 1, 2:171-77.

———. 1998. Trans Studies: Between a Metaphysics of Absence and Presence. In *Reclaiming Gender: Essays on Transsexuality/Transgressing Gender at the Fin De Siecle,* eds. Stephen Whittle and Kate More. London: Cassells Press.

San Francisco Gay and Lesbian History Project. 1992. She Even Chewed Tobacco. In *Hidden From History: Reclaiming the Gay and Lesbian Past,* eds. Martin Duberman, Martha Vicinus, and George Chauncey Jr. New York: Penguin Press.

Sartre, Jean-Paul. 1956. *Being and Nothingness: An Essay on Phenomenological Ontology.* Trans. Hazel E. Barnes. New York: Philosophical Library.

Scott, Joan W. 1988. *Gender and the Politics of History.* New York: Columbia.

———. 1993. The Politics of Experience. In *The Lesbian and Gay Studies Reader,* eds. Henry Abelove, Michele Aina Barale, and David Halperin. New York: Routledge.

Sedgwick, Eve Kosofsky. 1990. *Epistemology of the Closet.* Berkeley: University of California Press.

Sedgwick, Eve Kosofsky, and Adam Frank. 1995. Shame in the Cybernetic Fold: Reading Silvan Tomkins. *Critical Inquiry* (Winter), 21, 2:496-522.

Shelley, Martha. 1970. Confessions of a Pseudo-Male Chauvinist. *The Ladder,* June/July.

Snitow, Ann, Christine Stansell, and Sharon Thompson. 1983. *Powers of Desire: The Politics of Sexuality.* New York: Monthly Review Press.

Springvine, Leslie. 1969/1970. Out From Under the Rocks—with Guns! *The Ladder,* December/January.

Stoller, Robert, M.D. 1975. *Sex and Gender, Volume II: The Transsexual Experiment.* London: Hogarth Press and the Institute of Psychoanalysis.

Stone, Sandy. 1991. The Empire Strikes Back: A Posttranssexual Manifesto. In *Body Guards: The Cultural Politics of Gender Ambiguity,* eds. Julia Epstein and Kristina Straub. New York: Routledge.

Stryker, Susan, 1994a. Transsexual Technologies of the Self: Reading Lou Sullivan's Journals. Paper presented to the Fourth Lesbian, Gay, and Bisexual Studies Conference in Iowa City, Iowa. November.

Sullivan, Louis. 1973. Diary Entry. Lou Sullivan Special Collection. The Gay and Lesbian Historical Society. July 13.

———. 1990a. *Information for the Female to Male Crossdresser and Transsexual.* Seattle: Ingersoll Gender Center.

———. 1990b. *From Female to Male: The Life of Jack B. Garland.* Boston: Alyson Publication, Inc.

Turner, Bryan S. 1992. *Regulating Bodies: Essays in Medical Sociology.* New York: Routledge.

Vance, Carol S. 1992. *Pleasure and Danger: Exploring Female Sexuality.* London: Pandora Press.

Voronoff, Serge. 1928. *The Conquest of Life.* Trans. G. Gibier Rambaud. New York: Brentano's Inc.

Weber, Max. 1946. *From Max Weber: Essays in Sociology.* Trans. and ed. H.H. Gerth and C. Wright Mills. New York: Oxford University Press.

———. 1989. *The Protestant Ethic and the Spirit of Capitalism.* Boston: Unwin Hyman.

Weed, Elizabeth. 1997. *Feminism Meets Queer Theory.* Bloomington: Indiana University Press.

Wolf, Maximillian. 1992. In *Female Misbehavior.* Directed and produced by Monica Treut. New York: First Run Films.

"Women's Liberation is a Lesbian Plot." 1970. *The Rat,* May 8–21.

Worden, F.G., and J.T. Marsh. 1955. *Journal of American Medical Association.* 157.

Wright, Clifford A. 1938. Further Studies of Endocrine Aspects of Homosexuality. *Medical Record* May 18: 449-52.

Interviews

Alex. 1995. Interview by author. Tape recording. Brookline, Mass., June 14.

Brando. 1994. Interview by author. Tape recording. San Francisco, Calif., July 27.

Calvin. [psued.]. 1996. Interview by author. Tape recording. Boston, Mass., Dec. 1.

Dani. 1994. Interview by author. Tape recording. San Francisco, Calif., June 24.

Ed. 1994. Interview by author. Tape recording. San Francisco, Calif., Aug. 18.

Francis. 1994. Interview by author. Tape recording. San Francisco, Calif., July 14.

Gregg. 1996. Interview by author. Tape recording. Cambridge, Mass., Dec. 8.

Jack. 1996. Interview by author. Tape recording. Woonsocket, Rhode Island, Nov. 26.

Jake. 1996. Interview by author. Tape recording. Watertown, Mass., Sept. 21.

James. 1994. Interview by author. Tape recording. San Francisco, Calif., July 17.

John. 1996. Interview by author. Tape recording. Woonsocket, Rhode Island, Sept. 24.

Joshua. [psued.]. 1996. Interview by author. Tape recording. Boston, Mass., Nov. 11.

Julian. 1995. Interview by author. Tape recording. Cambridge, Mass., July 19.

Luke. [psued.]. 1996. Interview by author. Tape recording. Arlington, Mass., Jan. 12.

Malcolm. [psued.]. 1996. Interview by author. Tape recording. Taunton, Mass., Jan. 14.

Mark [psued.]. 1994. Interview by author. Tape recording. San Francisco, Calif., July 18.

Matt. 1994. Interview by author. Tape recording. San Francisco, Calif., Aug. 5.

Matthew. 1996. Interview by author. Tape recording. Edison, New Jersey. Oct. 18.

Michael. 1994. Interview by author. Tape recording. Jamaica Plain, Mass., Oct. 23.

Shadow. 1994. Interview by author. Tape recording. San Francisco, Calif., Aug. 29.

Texas. 1994. Interview by author. Tape recording. San Francisco, Calif., July 15.

Wolfie. 1996. Interview by author. Tape recording. New York, New York, Oct. 19.

Index

Abbott and Love, 69, 70, 74, 188n
abstinence, 85, 132, 133, 137
acquired versus innate, 44, 46, 49, 50
activism, 4, 64, 67, 69, 90, 121, 148, 172
Adam's apple, 168
adolescence. *See* puberty
age, 7, 38, 39, 86, 103, 122, 148, 186n
agency, 64
aggression. *See* violence; testosterone
Agnes, 16
agnosia, 11, 27–29, 106, 109, 133, 136,
    151, 179, 181. *See also* body
    dysphoria; anasognosia
Albert, Roberta, 86, 87
Alex, 123, 124, 137, 139, 154, 171
American Psychological Association, 45
anasognosia, 27
anatomy as destiny, 82, 83, 164, 181,
    192n
androgens, 42, 45, 48
androgyny, 11, 24, 87
athletics. *See* sports
Atkinson, Ti-Grace, 69
authenticity, 14, 15, 124, 175, 176, 181,
    182

Baer, Tommy and Beth, 86
beard, 56, 146, 155
beauty, standards of, 60, 108
Benjamin, Harry, 33, 34, 53, 63, 180
Benjamin, Jessica, 14, 15, 165, 195n

biological determinism, 153, 156–63,
    172, 192n, 194n
birth certificate, 49
bisexuals, 81
blending in, 2, 3, 5, 177
body
    anomalies of, 54, 112, 113
        hidden anomaly of, 50, 51, 55, 61,
            141, 151, 179
    appearing normal, 52, 181
    as diagnostic evidence, 53–57, 84–86,
        93, 100, 134, 141, 178, 179
    as expression of self, 145, 146, 149–
        52, 169, 181, 182
    as point of view, 25
    as source of dis-ease, 103, 122, 141,
        142, 178
    betrayal by, 94, 96, 108–11, 149, 164,
        175
    children's, 96
    cultural significance of, 180, 181, 183
    dysphoria, 93, 98, 100, 141, 146,
        149, 191n
    feminist ideology of reclaiming, 136
    hegemonic beliefs about, 144, 149,
        152, 156, 168, 169, 182
    image, 28, 29, 94, 100, 104–7, 192n
    male, 144, 146, 149, 151, 154, 155
        cultural norms about, 166–69,
            172, 181
        heterogeneity of, 170